CYCLE BREAKER

Maryam distills complex neuroscience concepts into practical strategies that can be implemented immediately (though perfected over years). From effective self-care strategies to fostering curiosity about and empathy with children's inner world, *Cycle Breaker* equips parents with a toolkit that revitalises their connection with their children and enables their emotional well-being.

DR. SAMIYA IQBAL, Paediatric Psychiatrist
and Mom of a 1-Year-Old; Pakistan

Reading the book made me feel understood and heard. The unconditional positive regard in Maryam's words gives me hope for myself, my clients, and our traumagenic society. . . . This book is like a warm, compassionate hug that helps us feel hope for that "parent-shaped hole" in our hearts, as Maryam writes. . . . *Cycle Breaker* is the kind of book that I will read again every time I want to receive this validating, compassionate, wise energy.

AFRA KHURRAAM, Psychotherapist and Mom of
Two (ages 9 and 4); Karachi, Pakistan

Maryam's book is an amazing collection of research, strategies, and verbiage for moving past (un)identified traumas and learning how to build a strong foundation for families! . . . With her extensive expertise, readers are given concrete evidence on how we have the power to create a better future with our own children and for generations to come.

NUSRA ALAM, Educator and Mom of Four (ages 10,
7, 4, and 2); Washington D.C., USA

This book profoundly transformed my philosophy and approach to parenting, emphasizing only love and respect as the foundation for self and family. A blend of science, religion, personal experiences, and the author's insights redefined my understanding of raising children, guiding them toward autonomy and personal growth. It has healed past wounds and inspired a newfound joy in parenthood, making it a must-read for parents looking to break free from inner traumas or family taboos.

DR. SHAWANA FAZAL, University Academic (Assistant Professor, Department of Education) and Mom of Three (ages 13, 6, and 4); Pakistan

This book is not just a guide; it's a lifeline for anyone who has ever grappled with the dilemma of wanting to parent with respect and gentleness but feeling lost on where to start. . . . In a world full of stress and a constant fear of messing up, this book is like a friendly cheerleader, cheering us on to accept our imperfections as chances to grow. . . . This book is not just a book; it's an invitation to embark on a transformative journey towards becoming the parent you aspire to be.

REMI SAINILLABDEEN, Software Engineer and Mom of Two (ages 8 and 4); India

Cycle Breaker offers practical solutions and examines issues from different angles, making it a book that empowers you to start working on your parenting from the first few pages alone. This book will welcome you and show the story of a brave woman and parent and help you think about your own story. It may help you metamorphosize into the best version of yourself.

SANA NAQVI, Mom of Three (ages 6, 8, and 13); Canada

This book is special to me because it not only explains everything with science and research-backed concepts but it also connects them profoundly with our part of the world's problems. Our society's challenges are unique from the western world, and this book has all the ingredients for dealing with them with full, proven strategies. . . . It really is like a perfect recipe for parenting—my very own parenting manual!

KHADIJAH NADEEM, Marketing Consultant, Interior Designer, and Mom of Two (ages 4 and 2); Islamabad, Pakistan

Parenting is an individualistic yet a universal phenomenon, and so are the words of this book. Every second or third story in this book reminded me of something I have faced, and the rest were relatable to people around. Trust me, this book is a must-read. It not only gave me a new perspective on parenting but also compelled me to think about things I had been unconsciously suppressing. . . . I can assure you that even as a professional this book gives insight to the world of little brains that's right in front of your eyes but sometimes way outside your vision.

DR. MADEEHA MUHAMMAD SABIR, PhD, Psychologist
and Mom of Two (ages 2 and 6); Karachi, Pakistan

This book is a must-read for everyone looking for courage to embark on their journey of self-discovery and healing. I am hopeful it will help change the world, one reader at a time!

RABIA JALAL, Engineer and Mom of Two (ages 9 and 4); Texas, USA

A beautiful and fresh mix of science and story and therapy! This book, these words, were like a balm to the spirit, giving me the tools, the hope, and the understanding that I AM in charge of how I respond and I CAN bring a change.

HAFSA KHALID, Mom of Three (ages 10, 7, and 3); Kohat, Pakistan

This book breaks the chain of shame and motivates parents to get up, take the first step, and reparent themselves and their kids. . . . [Maryam] offered me a beacon of hope through the concept of neuroplasticity that it is never too late for any of us. We can break the cycle by healing and loving ourselves and in the process learn to parent with connection, joy, and authenticity.

ABEERA SADI, Teacher and Mom of Two
(ages 12 and 8); Karachi, Pakistan

Somehow, this book has managed to expose more conflict than I could ever admit I carried inside me, and at the same time left me with more grace for those involved in my journey so far and excitement for untangling the conflicts as I continue on. . . . It is a heartfelt conversation with a friend, a friend you find yourself opening up to so easily because their warmth, care, and transparency is genuinely disarming.

FIZA KHAN, Educator and Mom of a 3-Year-Old; Ontario, Canada

Cycle Breaker, true to its name, makes mothers confront their triggers and deal with them, eventually breaking the cycle of mother child discord. It's the first book of gentle parenting which incorporates our Islamic values, something which is very important for me. . . . Calling all mothers! Immediately go to your nearest store and pick up *Cycle Breaker*. Save yourself a whole world of pain and make your journey of motherhood a whole lot smoother.

DR. SAMEEM ASAD ALI, Pediatrician and
Mom of Two (ages 6 and 2); Pakistan

It's as if Maryam held my hand and took me through the process of self-love. She showed me through scientific evidence, her life's experiences, and literary excerpts how essential respectful parenting is to break the patterns of the past. With this book, every parent can learn to develop a long lasting relationship with their child!

TOOBA RAHMAN, Physician and Mom of a 4-Year-Old; USA

"The truth is that love is not just a feeling." This sentence from the book kept me in awe for a while. Which mother doesn't love her children, but we don't usually sign the contract of love. We don't accept the terms of loving our children respectfully, and for sure this book is a great learning opportunity to debunk the greatness of traditional parenting. . . . Maryam has done a great effort of collecting evidences from Islam science and experience to make me relate, reflect, and regulate my thoughts and acts.

RABIA SHEIKH, Quran Teacher and Homeschooling
Mom of Three (ages 7, 5, and 3); Bahrain, UAE

The research behind this book is top-notch, evident in the depth and accuracy of the content. What truly sets it apart is the humane and empathetic approach the writer takes with the reader. It's commendable how the author navigates the complexities of human relationships, helping us realize that vulnerability knows no bounds and that there's no age limit when it comes to learning and repairing our connections with one another. . . . Whether you're a seasoned parent or a parent-to-be, this book has the power to transform the way you perceive and navigate the beautiful journey of parenthood.

> **IRAM BINT SAFIA**, Certified Life Coach, Author of *No One Taught Me This, A Transformational Guide for Parents to Lead a Blissful Life*, and Mom of Three (ages 17, 15, and 13); Delaware, USA

It's not just a parenting book! It's a self-help book; it's a relationship book, the kind that is easy to read and offers practical solutions. I had so many "light bulb" moments not just about myself but others around me. . . . I'm a mother to two under six. This book is a reminder that I am their first relationship, and so I need to be better, do better.

> **RIFFAT**, Internal Auditor and Mom of Two (ages 6 and 3); Melbourne, Australia

This book is a must-read for every parent. I remember a time when I was desperate to get the best parental advice that would actually feel right and work as well. This book is a gem that presents all the information in one place. It's basically we all need to know as a parent.

> **RABIA BATOOL**, Mom of Two (ages 7 and 2); New Zealand

With a focus on personal growth and parenting, *Cycle Breaker* has the potential to be a life-changing read for a diverse readership. It's a testament to Maryam's ability to connect with readers and offer valuable insights for self-improvement.

> **HIRA SAMEER AHMED**, UX Designer and Mom of a 2-Year-Old; Denmark

This book is full of Aha moments that take you on a journey of self discovery with compassion. It leaves you with hope that healing is possible and YOU can break the cycle as a parent!

MUZAFFAR BUKHARI, Educationist/Mental Health
Therapist, Founder of Veritas Learning Circle, and
Father of Three (ages 10, 7, and 6); Karachi, Pakistan

I and my wife attended Maryam's Anokhay Parents course back in 2022. We have experienced it to be a game-changer in our journey as parents. But knowing everything about respectful parenting was one thing, and applying these consistently, especially against our very own nature, was the actual challenge. And in that challenge, we desperately needed a manual—something that we could keep handy and keep referring to whenever we needed. This book by Maryam fills that void for us! It is just like an "ABCs" for Respectful, Healthy, Trauma-informed parenting. And I must say that Maryam has done absolute justice to it. Any reader would easily appreciate not only the flow and content of the book but also the practicality in it. The way Maryam has given practical examples at multiple places to help her readers. The simple yet powerful language she has used throughout the book. The way she has explained the core concepts along with the references to the science and research behind it. Maryam has simply shown the way to do it!

It is a 300-pager book but with well-contained, easily graspable knowledge of a 20,000-page encyclopedia on parenting. A must-read and must-have for every parent—now more than ever!

ZEESHAN NOORDIN DOSSANI, Father of
a 7-Year-Old boy; Karachi, Pakistan

CYCLE BREAKER

CYCLE BREAKER

From Trauma to Triumph:
Learn to Heal Your Past & Parent with Joy

MARYAM MUNIR

Published by

MANDALA
TREE PRESS
mandalatreepress.com

Paperback ISBN: 9781954801738
Hardcover with Dust Jacket ISBN: 9781954801745
Case Laminate ISBN: 9781954801752
eBook ISBN: 9781954801769

FAM034000 FAMILY & RELATIONSHIPS / Parenting / General
SEL031000 SELF-HELP / Personal Growth / General

Cover design and typesetting by Kaitlin Barwick
Edited by Justin Greer and Valene Wood

www.teepep.com

To my children and theirs after them.
To my parents and theirs before them.

CONTENTS

CONTENTS

CONTENTS

CONTENTS

FOREWORD

There is a rapidly growing number of us who now recognize that we no longer wish to follow traditional parenting methods. We know what we don't want to do, but we are often left feeling confused about what the alternative approach is. How are we supposed to raise kind, respectful, resilient children? We don't want to yell, punish, or hurt our children in the name of discipline. We don't want to do a lot of what was done to us. We are done with resorting to tactics like bribery, threats, and punishment. We are individuals in search of answers, determined to break away from the harmful parenting styles many of us experienced growing up. We are committed to raising our children with respect, connection, and love.

Despite all of this, one of the central messages of *Cycle Breaker* isn't to vilify our parents as terrible, flawed people who deserve to be shamed. Instead, it acknowledges that our parents did their best with the tools and knowledge they had. After all, we all do what we know—until we learn differently. In the pages that follow, Maryam eloquently advocates for compassion and understanding while empowering us to discover more effective ways of relating to and raising the small humans we're blessed with.

Times have momentously changed in the last few decades, and we are being called to update our "manual" and evolve ourselves accordingly. We now have access to a wealth of research confirming that conditional, punitive parenting is harmful and toxic. The same body of research also shows the most beneficial, productive way to raise children. Now more than ever, we are being called to change direction toward emotional intelligence, respectful communication, and compassionate discipline.

Cycle Breaker inspires us to see that it's time to stop debating issues that have already been substantiated and shift our attention toward positive solutions. Maryam's work provides a clear roadmap for doing just that. She shares heartfelt stories, science, research, and practical strategies for us to become the change-makers our children so desperately need and deserve.

As you will learn throughout the book, neuroplasticity offers us the ability to rewire our brains, moving away from default settings to forming new, healthier habits. We can harness this potential to overcome our old parenting habits. Know that this is both possible and essential for the well-being of our children.

I urge you to trust that there is no better time to be a parent than right now. By breaking the cycles of generational trauma, you are undoubtedly creating a profound impact on not only your own children's path but quite literally the entire human race. We are all on some level deeply connected.

You've been drawn to read Maryam's work—this signals that you're ready to embrace new paradigms and create your own blueprint for nurturing your children with respect and consciousness. Let her wisdom, compassion, and empathy for both parents and children radiate into your heart and soul as you read. This is truly a book that will leave a lasting impression and inspire positive change like no other.

STEPHANIE PINTO

Award-winning Emotional Intelligence Parent Coach,
Bestselling Author, International Speaker, and
Founder of the Let's Raise Emotionally Intelligent Kids community
www.stephaniepinto.com

About This Book

I want you to remember three things while reading this book:

1. All the stories I share of clients use pseudonyms or altered personal details so the clients' privacy is protected.

2. I fully acknowledge how the beautiful religion of Islam is used in our conservative community to judge, criticize, and generally make people feel like crap about themselves, so I've given a religious content heads-up where I've used religion as a reference. This is to respect anyone recovering from religious trauma and not feeling ready for religious references. However, since we are a deeply religious community and I'm a practicing Muslim, it's important for me to bring it in this book.

3. Some stories and substances in this book will be triggering for many. Please remember to pay attention to any signs of distress in your body and take a break when necessary. (For more on how to know your body is in distress, go to chapter one.)

A Note on Trauma and Decolonizing Trauma Work

If you don't know what "decolonizing trauma work" even means, don't worry. It's also taken me a while to understand what it means to "decolonize" anything.

In very simple terms, we can say that it means to hear and elevate the voices of people of color, regarding a subject, rather than white voices. By doing so, we acknowledge the fact that being a white male gets you the privilege of center stage, whether you deserve it or not. Now, there are plenty of excellent white, male, trauma experts—but the fact that their books are bestsellers and their work is constantly cited isn't necessarily because they're the final word on the subject.

There is no bigger evidence of this than the fact that I, as a brown person, hailing from a part of the world that was once a British colony, had to look hard for books on trauma written by POC (people of color). The books that are front and center, in most bookstores, are all written by white men.

So, yes, in this book, I'm unraveling my own colonized mind and practices and am only scratching the surface of doing the decolonizing work. I've tried to be mindful of bringing more voices in this book from people of color, women, and other marginalized communities that usually don't get cited. However, this effort on my part is far from what it should be and definitely a huge area of work for me.

"There is no difference between children and flowers
except flowers don't ask for ice-cream."

Mustansar Hussain Tarar

INTRODUCTION

My two-year-old son, Eisa, and I both sit huddled on the cold kitchen floor, crying. I can feel my stainless-steel fridge's handle digging into my back as I sob uncontrollably into my hands— my black maternity dress draping around me on the floor in a pool of darkness. Eisa sits on the side of my outstretched leg, also wiping his tearstained face with chubby little hands. His eyes steal a look at me every now and then, caught between betrayal and hope. With all my heart, I want to reach out and bury him in a big embrace, but my puddle of shame stands between us like seven oceans. I feel too disgusted with myself to touch his innocence. He doesn't deserve a mother like me, I think. He deserves someone he is physically and emotionally safe with. I pull the hem of my dress tighter around me as if it will somehow protect us both, me and my son, from the demon that lurks inside me.

Just a few moments ago, everything was alright. He was showing me how to land a plane on his new airport rug. Then I suddenly felt a pang of hunger and came to the kitchen to grab something to snack on from the fridge. Each pregnancy, the hyperemesis gravidarum (HG) hit me worse than the last pregnancy. Every minute of every day felt torturous because any smell could trigger the awful nausea that would then consume me and find me bent over a toilet in a retching, heaving, exhausted mess. I share all this not to present an excuse for my poor behavior that will follow but as a factor in activating the trigger. As I stood before the fridge contemplating what wouldn't make me throw up again but also stop the rumbling in my tummy, I felt a little tug at my black maternity dress.

"Eisa, just wait . . . I'm trying to find something to eat . . ."

That did nothing to stop his tugging, but my ears had already started to ring with the beginnings of anger and the activation of the trigger. I can recall the thoughts that started flooding me in that moment . . .

How dare he pull my dress? Can't he see I'm busy? Doesn't he know how sick I feel?

More tugs. Accompanied by that nails-on-chalkboard sound that toddlers use when they don't feel heard, what adults call whining.

I could sense the ringing in my ears getting louder, as were Eisa's protests to get my attention.

And then it happened. That snap that untethered me from reality and took me hurtling somewhere else . . . and before I knew it, I had kicked my poor sweet boy. It was as if this ugly and dark demon had taken over my body and really truly wanted to hurt this innocent little child. It wasn't me, was it? But it *was* me. It was *my* leg and *my* foot landing into his little body and pushing it away until he hit the kitchen cart behind him. What kind of mother was I? Suddenly, as if the demon left me and I landed back in the present, seeing my son for the first time and not some ghost from the past, I fell to the floor and pulled him closer . . . checking if he was ok and if he'd caught any edges from the cart. No, his pearly white skin was smooth as a baby's, as it should be.

But the edges that had hurt him had all come from me. The expression on his face showed me as much; it was that of betrayal, confusion, and deep, deep hurt.

"How could you, my mother, my caretaker, do this to me?" said his eyes. And the crying. It wasn't the typical crying of a two-year-old, it was the anguished howling of an injured soul. Of all the pain in all the world, the one that comes from the most beloved evokes its own kind of sound, doesn't it? A sound that accurately reflects the sharpness of the edges that caused it. It was then that I let go of him and collapsed back against the fridge. Broken, ugly, and defeated.

I want you to know how hard it's been for me to make this story a part of my book and to, in fact, start the book with it. I've shared this story a hundred times in my workshops, and now I've written it and read it over and over through the edits, and each time it leaves me in choked up tears. But I also know that I'm not the only parent who's been in that space, where the shame of how you've hurt your child lives inside your body even years later. I want you to know I see you and have written this book for you and I can promise you that there's so much hope. No matter where you are in your parenting journey, it's never too late.

I wish I could say that this kind of incident only happened once, but I'd be lying. Perhaps this was one of the more intense incidents, but certainly there were several incidents every now and then where I got too "scary" and acted in a way that later filled me with shame, regret, and confusion. Confusion, because I was never the kind of person who ever believed that parenting should involve hurting children. In fact, this was something that I often wondered as a child. How could parents physically or emotionally harm their children? It made no sense to me then and it made no sense to me that day, sitting and crying on the floor with my sweet baby. Didn't love mean not hurting the people we love? Why then was it considered so normal in our culture to hit children?

I remember asking my dad this question before I had kids and he said, "You'll understand when you have your own kids."

I think he meant I'd understand how, despite your best intentions, sometimes you end up losing it and hurting your children. This is certainly a sentiment I hear often from my clients. Most of my first appointments begin with a very distraught and defeated parent sitting before me, struggling to meet my eyes. When I gently encourage them to share what brings them to see me, I hear some version of the following statements:

"I don't want to hit my kids but it happens . . ."
"I keep losing it with my kids—please help me!"
"I want to stop screaming at my kids!"
"I'm so ashamed of hurting my kids . . . please help me!"
"I'm tired of fighting with my teenager!"
"I just want my kids to listen to me without me screaming at them!"

First of all, I assure all parents that they're not alone. That I understand where they're coming from and how proud I am of them for coming to me and looking for help. The really great news about the new generation of parents is that they're really not wanting to hurt their children in any shape, way, or form. So many of them have been there where my son was on that kitchen floor, and the last thing they want is to repeat that cycle of hurt.

They want to be cycle breakers.

I Don't Want to Hurt My Child, But I Don't Know What to Do

Cycle breakers know firsthand the pain and anguish of being hurt by the two humans you love the most in the world, the ones that were supposed to love you and not hurt you. Now the problem with being a cycle breaker is, you know very well what *not* to do but you have no idea *what* to do. That is, parents know they don't want to punish their children or shame them to get them to listen and make good choices, but they don't know what else to do instead. This creates a very difficult conundrum for them—they find themselves often feeling helpless, frustrated, and confused, and eventually, in desperation, resorting to the very practices they were trying to avoid.

If you're a parent like this, then this book is for you. It's also for you if you're not yet a parent but know that you'd never want to be the kind of parent who uses punitive methods. I totally get where you're coming from, because I was once just like you.

I knew I didn't want to hit my son or shame him, but in the heat of the moment, I didn't know how to get his cooperation and what the heck I was supposed to do. Like in the story I shared, when I didn't want my son pulling my dress and I asked him nicely not to, he still didn't listen. As a result, my stress mounted, pushing my brain to its default. And of course, the default comes from whatever we have experienced. Our brain has no way of knowing an alternate route because none has ever been traversed. The only route it knows is the one that it has witnessed, explicitly or implicitly—that is, even if someone was not beaten as a child but saw their siblings/cousins beaten, that's still the only 'blueprint' the brain has for coping with a non-cooperative child.

So where do we go from here? How do we become cycle breakers and stop parenting from these default settings?

The answer is quite simple, though not easy, as you might imagine: we change the default setting. That is, we teach our brain a new pattern. The really remarkable thing about our brains is that they're what scientists call "plastic" or changeable. At any age or stage, we can build new neural pathways in our brain, and when this path is walked often enough, it becomes the new default.

Now, when my kids don't listen to me immediately, my default setting is to get close, remain safe and say, "It's time to sleep . . . can you put the book away or do you need some help with it?" and that's the kids' cue for "mama means business" and they'll do as I asked. And if they don't, my next default is to gently take the book away and co-regulate the big feelings (you'll learn more about this in chapter two).

In other words, no matter where you are in your parenting journey, this book will teach you specific techniques to respond to daily issues that come up with children so that you can create a new "default setting." My goal is to take you from feeling frustrated, helpless, and lost to feeling confident, calm, and safe for your children. You got this!

Where Do We Begin?

"Love is at the root of everything. All learning, all parenting, all relationships. Love or the lack of it."

—Fred Rogers

Love. We begin with understanding what love truly is so we can learn how to give it.

Have you ever been in a situation where someone claimed to love you but you didn't feel loved? And the more they insisted that they loved you, the more unseen you felt? Or perhaps this has happened to you, that you feel like you love someone and they always have complaints about you. The truth is that love is not what most people think it—it's not just a feeling. It's more like a contract. It has certain conditions, and unless those are met, our soul registers the missing "conditions" and records its protest.

Understanding this simple concept really changed how I love people (and children are people too) and how I receive love. A lot of this clarity came from the most beautiful writing on love by bell hooks (she doesn't capitalize her name) in her remarkable book called *All About Love*. In it, she asserts that it's important that we have a working definition of love so we all know what we deserve to receive and what we need to give. I think this is a revolutionary idea. I hate that children are caused so much harm in the name of love. Here are some English statements and their Urdu equivalents we've all heard growing up:

"Parents only hit their children out of love." *(Walidaan ke maar, maar nahi hoti)*

"Spare the rod and spoil the child." *(Bachon ka maar na paray tou wo bigar jatay hain)*

"When I hit you, it hurts me more than it hurts you." *(Ap ko maar kai mujhay ap sai zaida takleef hoti hai.)*

"It's for your own good." *(Bachon ke bhalayee kai liyay pitai zaroori hai)*

"A quick one on the butt is going to fix him right up." *(Aik thappar lagao, bilkul seedha ho jaye gai)*

"I was spanked and I turned out fine." *(Hum nai bhe bohot maraain khayee hain issi liyay aj kisi laeq banay hain)*

I hope that reading these statements in black and white exposes their absurdity to you. How far would a society have to stray from the meaning of love to convolute physical assault with love? Instead, what if everyone knew *exactly* what love is, so we have intense clarity about whether what we're giving or receiving is love or not?

Hooks writes:

> To truly love we must learn to mix various ingredients—care, affection, recognition, respect, commitment, and trust, as well as honest and open communication.[1]

This is a hefty definition, isn't it? Don't worry, we'll be breaking down all these ingredients into actionable items in this book. If you're wondering now what we should call what we've been doing so far, hooks suggests that we should label our efforts correctly by calling them "cathexis." When I first read this word, I immediately looked it up and was blown away by what it means! Here's the Merriam-Webster dictionary definition of it.

> Investment of mental or emotional energy in a person, object, or idea.[2]

In other words, someone can spend half their lives investing mental and emotional energy into someone and that is still not necessarily love. That's where this book comes in—the sole purpose of which is to help you understand exactly how to give love, to yourself and your children, so that it's received as love, in all its gloriousness. You will learn how to practically implement the above ingredients of love, for yourself and your children, and of course all other people in your life.

Why Self-Love Though?

Meet Jamila, who loves her cat. Jamila adores her cat, Mano, to the moon and back. She does everything for her cat, from spoiling her with expensive cat food, cat toys, and even cat clothes to spending thousands of rupees on her medical bills. Now surely, Mano has a cushiony lifestyle that many would envy and yet, Mano is not exactly able to return the love Jamila gives her. At best Mano purrs when Jamila enters the room and settles in her lap. No matter how hard Mano tries, she's really not capable of reciprocating Jamila's level of love.

In other words, how much love we can give someone depends on our capacity to experience the emotion of love and all its ingredients. The love, then, has to already exist inside us for us to be able to give it to others. Our capacity for loving others can't exceed our capacity for loving ourselves. Like the cat, we also can't receive that which is unfamiliar to us. If we don't learn how to love ourselves, we won't be able to accept our children's love. We will find a hundred pieces of evidence that so-and-so doesn't love us when in fact, it is self-love that we're lacking—an inability to hold love within ourselves, for ourselves.

> ### Religious Content
> A sweet friend of mine recently said to me, "Maryam, Allah must really love you because so many people love you." I thanked her and asked her why she thinks Allah also doesn't love her. "I'm not doing amazing things like you are," she said. I understand where she's coming from. I don't know how this happened, but somehow, we've also made Allah's love conditional.

We would not even need the concept of self-love if we believed beyond a shadow of doubt what our Creator tells us over and over in the Quran that His love and mercy for us is unconditional. For as long as we're on this Earth and working towards pleasing Him, we are recipients of His love. In one of my favorite books on the topic called *The Secrets of Divine Love*, author A. Helwa says,

> The Quran makes more sense if we approach it as an algebraic equation with a given x, before we jump to interpreting or solving for y. The Quran begins all of its chapters, aside from one, with the given x = *Bismillahi Ar Rahman Ar-Rahim*, which translates to "In the name God, the Lord of Mercy the Bestower of Mercy." Only once the Quran declares x = God Is Unconditionally Merciful does it then tell us, with that in mind, to go and solve for all our y's—or, better said, *whys*.[3]

But . . . What IS Up with Kids These Days?

The number one comment I get from parents is, "*We* weren't like this!" Right. We weren't. That's because we were raised with a very different premise than the children today are being raised with. In the past, children received some very clear messages from an early age. The biggest message that shaped their "good behavior" (or compliance) was that any expression of opinions or feelings is "disrespectful" and "bad."

Almost any violation of that basic rule resulted in some kind of harsh discipline or at least shaming language, like, "Stop being a bad girl and stay quiet!", "You're a naughty boy for not listening!", "Good kids always listen to their elders!", or "Why are you crying? There's nothing to cry about!".

When this happens, a child's brain goes into the "freeze" mode and acts like a robot because it has learned that blind compliance will keep it safe from hurt. For children, it's evolutionarily not safe to believe that their parent could be flawed. All their brain knows is that in order to survive, it has to suppress certain kinds of responses. As a result, we see a very compliant child and praise them, which only reinforces that belief they've started to develop, "As long as I stay quiet and do as I'm told, 'the ones who control the world and my well-being' will be pleased with me and help me survive this dangerous world."

Most parents I speak to from our generation, seem to think we just happened to be "good kids." By the time a child is four years old, the neural pathways that dictate how to behave to avoid shame and judgment and gain the caretakers' pleasure have already developed. But, as an adult, we don't even have any explicit memories of how we got to be this way! Unfortunately, the "good kids" (including myself) also became people pleasers as adults with little to no concept of speaking for ourselves and taking care of ourselves.

Those with a less gentle disposition tried to fight back and got labeled "the bad kids." They were the ones perpetually stuck in the brain's other defense response, "fight or flight." These kids get labeled as aggressive, rebellious, and noncompliant. They develop other coping skills to survive—like developing an impenetrable armor that protects them from the pain of rejection by their caretakers, but as adults, also stands in the way of developing any meaningful relationships. You will learn more about these defense mechanisms (fight, flight, or freeze) of our nervous system in the next chapter but for now, it's important to know that most extreme behaviors, whether excessive compliance or excessive aggression, are functions of the child's upbringing and not any inherent qualities.

This is not to blame our parents' generation; in fact, understanding generational trauma helps us empathize with our parents and give them grace (though this might come after a process—more on this later). We acknowledge that they did the best they could, with what they knew. A quick look at the history of parenting is a stark reminder of how children have been viewed and parented for eons.

Parenting through the Centuries

Only a few decades ago, Dr. John Watson (1878–1958), renowned psychologist of his time, said this:

> Never hug and kiss [your children]. Never let them sit on your lap. If you must, kiss them once on the forehead when they say good night.[4]

That was the kind of rhetoric that parenting *today* has evolved from. It was legitimately believed that any expression of love "spoils" children. We've all heard our parents' and grandparents' well-meant instructions on not to do this or that, lest we spoil our children. To this day, despite all my work, parents' biggest concern after learning about Respectful Parenting (the abbreviation RP will be used from here on out) is if this "method" will "spoil" their child. In other words, they're asking if treating children with respect will be the ruin of them. Recall those harsh phrases from a few pages ago that are a common part of childrearing.

So, clearly, this was a huge problem and still is. The general assumption seems to be that unless children are dealt with harshly at all times, they're headed straight towards ruin. So much so that in the past, parents were afraid to show their children any physical affection at all. I'm forty years old and still regularly see clients around my own age who recall never experiencing physical affection from their parents. Some even remember being scared to hug their parents as children.

Now we know, thanks to science, that not only is physical affection important for children of all ages but the lack of it can seriously affect healthy brain development. For example, orphaned infants exposed to the bleakest of conditions in eastern European institutions exhibited impaired growth and cognitive development, as well as an elevated incidence of serious infections and attachment disorders. The following image shared by trauma researcher Dr. Bruce Perry demonstrates the dire effects of physical and emotional neglect faced by orphans in Romanian orphanages.[5]

3-Year-Old Children

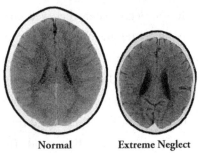

Normal   **Extreme Neglect**

We can also thank Harry Harlow for finally debunking the myths around expressing affection. In 1963, he did some experiments in his lab with baby monkeys to test the need for physical affection.

He made two "moms" for these monkeys. One "wire-mom" (left) who only provided food and drink to the baby monkeys. The other "towel-mom" that only provided warmth and safety. The prevailing theory was that kids only need food and basic caretaking from their mothers.

So, what do you think happened?

The monkeys mostly spent time with "towel-mom," seeking love and warmth. They only went to "wire-mom" when they needed to eat. Harlow also placed a dog toy in their cage to scare them and they'd run to . . . you guessed it, "towel-mom."[6]

Can you imagine that someone had to do scientific experiments to show that children need physical expressions of love? Fortunately, things have

14

improved since then, but plenty of damaging remnant beliefs from centuries and centuries of barely acceptable treatment of children still remain common.

If your mind is still clinging to the belief that corporal punishment "works," you're not alone in this confusion. As I mentioned before, we have been meticulously conditioned to believe in this myth. Fortunately, it's one of the most researched topics by psychologists and we have a lot of solid numbers on the outcomes of harsh punishment.

A Note on Research

First of all, you may be thinking . . . *I picked up a book on parenting, why am I having to learn about research?* Mainly because the book you picked up is written by me and I adore research! But also, it's a really effective way to stop arguing about things that have been proven already and move on to solutions. Also, as a parent yourself, reflect on how many times someone tried to give you parenting advice as if it were a fact and how you were made to feel poorly because, "How come you weren't already doing that?!" By using research-based parenting practices, you can be confident that your choices will lead to raising children who are kind, confident, and resilient.

Solid, peer-reviewed research and evidence-based practices are our friends. They're what separate facts from fiction and what I call RAWR (Random Aunty Random Wisdom). I want to replace the unnecessary RAWR with MEOW (Maryam's Evidence-based Outstanding Wisdom). I hope that won you over on the merits of research and perhaps, even, my humor.

To be fair, all research is not created equal. Every single doctoral student on planet Earth has to write a detailed research-based dissertation. All of these are available online for public consumption. Since online articles are all the rage, they also quote a lot of research that is, upon further inspection, flimsy at best. That means, the research wasn't repeated enough times to ensure it has the same result every time or the sample size used was not big enough or the results found weren't as significant as the article indicated. It could be one of those problems or all of them.

So how do we sift through all the research to include research that is truly impactful and reliable? At least for this book, I've mostly used what are called "meta studies"—studies *about* studies. So, since there are *so* many studies that have measured the effects of spankings, they now have lots of *meta* studies which combine the observations and results of these studies.

For example, one psychologist decided to look at a hundred studies that examined the correlation between parental abuse (I'm calling it abuse) and children's mental health or success in life, and then she analyzed the results of all of them in one study. In the following section I'm going to share the results of this meta study.

Do Punishments Work?

Yes. Very much so. Unfortunately, they also "work" to accomplish things that no loving parent would ever intend. Here, I'm going to share the results of a major meta study with you. That is, this meta study summarizes the findings of the hundreds of studies that have been done to analyze the short-term and long-term results of physical punishment by parents. According to these studies, the use of physical punishment was associated with all of the following:

1. More immediate compliance
2. Lower levels of moral internalization
3. Lower quality of the parent–child relationship
4. Antisocial behavior in childhood and adulthood
5. Lower levels of mental well-being
6. Higher risk of being a victim of physical abuse, and risk of abusing one's own child or spouse as an adult
7. Lowered self-esteem in children

As you can see, we're getting the compliance we seek and we're also getting a whole lot more. If you're still not convinced because you see yourself as a loving parent who would never intend to cause the aforementioned harm, I want to draw your attention to another grave reality of this meta study.

It only considered the studies that strictly view the hitting/beating/spanking as "discipline." We are not talking about abusive or deranged parents here—we're talking about loving parents whose intention is to discipline. In fact, these studies define hitting kids as "the use of physical force with the intention of causing a child to experience pain but not injury for the purposes of correction or control of the child's behavior."

And if you want to hear it directly from the horse's mouth, so to speak, here are the final remarks of the meta-study authors:

> The meta-analyses presented here found no evidence that spanking is associated with improved child behavior and rather found spanking to be associated with increased risk of 13 detrimental outcomes. These analyses did not find any support for the arguments that spanking is only associated with detrimental outcomes when it is combined with abusive methods.[7]

Rewards, Time-Outs, and Logical Consequences: Conditional Parenting Unwrapped

The good news is that most parents I work with are vehemently opposed to parenting how they were parented. Even if they think their own upbringing wasn't "that bad," they still don't need convincing about the harmful effects of physical punishment or shaming. In fact, they are armed and ready to parent with love and respect. It makes a lot of sense that methods like rewards, time-outs, and "consequences" seem a far cry from what we learned above about parenting methods. If you're a parent who's been using these methods, please don't feel bad. I'm so impressed that you knew you had to move away from the harsh methods of previous generations.

Unfortunately, parents like you and me, who were looking for gentler ways of parenting, got lured by the very upbeat-sounding words like "positive and negative reinforcements," "rewards," "consequences," etc. No doubt all these words sound so "civilized." The idea behind them also seems very logical at first. These ideas suggest that if we offer children praise and rewards for every behavior we like or desire and an unpleasant "consequence" for whatever we don't like, then we'll be cementing those "good" behaviors and eradicating the "bad" ones.

When I first read books about some of these methods, I remember feeling like a very evolved parent. There is no yelling, screaming, or hitting involved. You just calmly enforce the positive or negative consequences. Wonderful! For a while I did use these methods, but right away I knew something was not right because I felt incredibly disconnected from my son while implementing these methods. I'm so glad I listened to my instincts and continued my search for the kind of parenting methods that felt right to me.

Eventually I came across RP and slowly realized that rewards, praise, time-outs, and taking away privileges are simply another harmful version of the historically harsh parenting I was trying to get away from.

This bit of news was particularly shocking to me. You see, many qualified professionals also employ these techniques. This is because they belong to a very legitimate branch of Psychology called "Behaviorism." The brainchild of our "friend" from the previous section, Dr. John Watson (yes, the same one who suggested we never kiss children), this theory was built on B. F. Skinner's theories of operant conditioning. The idea is that we can simply condition children's behaviors according to our will by using positive reinforcers like sticker charts, candy, or praise as rewards and negative reinforcement by withdrawing privileges or other items of interest for the child.

What's wrong with a bit of reinforcement, you ask?

A lot, it turns out.

First of all, the theory of behaviorism was developed from experiments done on animals. These techniques, do in fact, work really well on training animals. Children though, are people. Let's investigate what happens when these ideas are applied to parenting.

REWARDS AND PRAISE—"THE POISONED APPLES"

So, what *is* wrong with praise and rewards? Aren't they the very epitome of positive? And, therefore, a part of positive parenting? Occasional praise on its own is fine, of course. Acknowledging our child's efforts or thanking them are also great options that should be part of any beautiful relationship.

However, in behaviorism-based child rearing, we use praise and rewards as tools for conditioning/molding behavior. We believe that if we say enough "Wow, good job!", "You're so brave!", "You are a good girl/boy," we will be reinforcing the behaviors we want to see in our children—but human children are complex creatures. Let's look at what's wrong with these strategies.

1. REWARDS DESTROY INTRINSIC MOTIVATION.

In his book, *Punished by Rewards: The Trouble with Gold Stars, Incentive Plans, A's, Praise, and Other Bribes*, Alfie Kohn says,

> Few readers will be shocked by the news that extrinsic motivators are a poor substitute for genuine interest in what one is doing. What is likely to be far more surprising and disturbing is the further point that rewards, like punishments, actually undermine the intrinsic motivation that promotes optimal performance.[8]

In other words, rewarding every desirable behavior removes any natural desire a child has to make good choices in life. It also makes the dangerous assumption that children are inherently not motivated to do well. This is one major "lens shift" I'd like you to have: *Children absolutely will make good choices, whenever it is possible for them to do so.* They're already on the *fitrah* ("natural path of goodness"), as we say in Islam.

This approach also creates a logistical nightmare for parents who often ask me, "My child is refusing to even eat unless I give them something in return—what do I do now?" or "I've run out of things to offer my child in return for listening to me, what do I do now?" Yes, I hear you. Parenting should never have been about gimmicks and circus tricks.

2. REWARDS LOWER CREATIVITY AND IMAGINATION.

To be fair, rewards do have a purpose. For example, in my workshops I ask participants if they'd be motivated to work hard on a project if their boss promised them a bonus (reward), and almost everyone replies, "Yes." Then I ask them if they'd be motivated to remember their friend's birthday if she said she will only visit them (reward) if they remembered her birthday, and the answer is almost unanimously, "Heck no!" So how come the reward works in the first example but not in the second?

Because, in the first instance, a short-term task needs to be accomplished . . . the goal is narrow and focused. We work hard for a short period, not for the sake of working hard but for the sake of the promised bonus. You see, rewards narrow our vision and limit our thinking to simply winning the reward. As a result, they inhibit creativity and innovation: crucial skills for children's optimal brain development. This has been demonstrated in several repeated studies.

Rewards teach children how to get the reward and not much else. If the idea of letting go of rewards as a parenting tool is scary for you, I totally understand. There is a whole chapter on boundaries and exactly how to invite cooperation from your children. Bonus—you will not be spending lots of money on trinkets and candy.

3. REWARDS MAKE CHILDREN FEEL CONDITIONALLY LOVED.

In the example above, of the friend who asks you to remember her birthday for the purpose of getting rewarded with her visit, what do you think makes almost all the participants not interested in the reward? How come it's ok when the boss offers a reward and not ok when a friend offers it? If you're thinking, well that's because the latter is a close relationship and the reward seems to cheapen it, then you're right.

When a child is constantly praised for "desirable" behaviors, he starts to see that as a form of love and acceptance. After all, his actions are not separate from himself. He then starts associating his parents' love with his "good" actions. This kind of manipulative praise can give rise to so many problematic tendencies in children: people pleasing, perfectionism, anxiety, low self-esteem, lack of empathy, and fear of failure are a few.

In RP, we neither praise the wins nor withdraw affection or acknowledgement when our child makes a mistake. Instead, we accept that making mistakes is not only human, it is an essential part of growth mindset. Imagine never doing something new for fear of failure.

For example, let's say your five-year-old broke her brand-new toy and hid it so you won't be upset with her. When you find the broken toy and ask her what happened, she says she has no idea. At this time, you can either say, "Tell me the truth and I'll buy you another truck," which is conditional parenting and takes away intrinsic motivation to do the right thing, or you could also say, "I understand why you felt the need to hide it. You thought I'm going to be upset with you. The thing is that we all break things sometimes and feel bad about it. Next time when you feel bad about something, can you come and tell me, and together we can find a solution?"

You might brainstorm ideas on how to keep her more fragile toys safe. The important thing is, you used a "fail" to give loving support, and in the process, you built resilience and problem-solving skills while highlighting the importance of honesty and seeking help (without ever going into lecture mode).

Ultimately, kids' confidence grows when they screw up and we give support and provide opportunities to try again. Their self-worth grows when they see that our acceptance of them isn't dependent on their achievements or 'perfect' behavior. When kids, or even adults, are embraced fully for their human selves, they are freed up to be their best selves.

TIME-OUTS AND LOGICAL CONSEQUENCES

Parents are told to use "logical consequences" instead of punishment. The term "consequences" sounds less offensive and more intellectual, but it is punishment with a fancier name. The purpose and concept behind both are the same—to find ways in which a child feels some kind of pain and, supposedly, this pain will make them decide to make better choices. I remember when Eisa, then five years old, first heard the word consequences in a parenting paradigm and asked me what it meant. When I explained it to him, he said, "Mama, why would anyone learn through getting hurt?" Exactly.

Dr. Shefali Tsabury, clinical psychologist and author of *The Conscious Parent*, describes this as a "prisoner-warden" approach to parenting. The "warden" is always watching the "prisoner's" actions, which are either "good" or "bad." The "warden" then dishes out either a punishment or reward or negative and positive reinforcements. Sadly, the prisoner becomes dependent on the warden to regulate their behavior.[9] This analogy also reminds me of those old-fashioned toys that you could wind up with a key and they'd go from point A to B as long as the key was wound. Without anyone to wind the key, the toy was lifeless.

When I once asked a parent why he uses time-outs (a form of negative reinforcement), he said, "So the child has an opportunity to reflect on their actions, and realize that what they did was wrong, and next time they need to make a better choice."

I then asked him if this approach has worked for him and he said, "Yes, I mean sometimes he comes out and apologizes or at least seems calmer."

"You misunderstood me," I told him. "I meant, is that also what works for you when you make a mistake? Like, say, at work, you screw up and your boss sends you to your office to think about what you've done and let him know when you're ready to make amends . . . ?"

The parent was caught off guard. "No, of course not. That's . . . insulting."

Right. Suffice to say, that father wanted to know alternative ways to inspire his sweet boy to learn without using shame and abandonment as a tool. It's also worth noting here that children's brains don't have the cognitive abilities required for critical thinking and self-analysis.

Sadia, another client, had a different reply to my question. "It's just that he needs to calm down before we can problem-solve. I only send him to time-out to calm himself down."

I asked her if it also works for her. "When you're really struggling with something . . . say you're really mad at your child because you found out they watched TV behind your back even though you had decided on no electronics, and now you're really mad . . . what do you do?"

She looked a bit sheepish and said, "I guess I'm not very nice to them when I'm having big feelings."

"Right. So, when you're upset, you're not able to model walking away and calming down before problem-solving . . ."

"No, I'm not . . . I guess that's not a fair expectation, but you agree that it's healthy . . ."

"Yes, it's one way to emotionally regulate ourselves . . . to walk away from a volatile situation until we're calmer. The key is that we *choose* to walk away . . . what does it feel like when someone else sends us away to calm down? What message does that send us? Has that ever happened to you?"

"Yes . . . my husband does that whenever I cry. In fact, he walks away and says he will talk to me when I'm calmer."

"And what do you wish, in that moment, that he did?"

"That he stayed . . . and accepted me with my uncomfortable emotions . . . and helped me . . ."

"Helped you co-regulate?"

"What is that?"

"Help you regulate your big emotions by offering a hug or seeing things from your perspective . . . would that help?"

"Oh my gosh . . . yes! That would be amazing!"

And that, friends, is the key to everything. (More on co-regulation in chapter two.)

So, what *does* work, then?

Respectful Parenting and Reparenting: Breaking the Generational Trauma Cycles

Turns out becoming the kind of parent I was wanting to be, someone who never hits or yells, doesn't use gimmicky methods, and still gets cooperation from her kids, involved basically unlearning and relearning everything I had ever known about myself and my children. That day when Eisa and I sat on the kitchen floor crying was the day I had decided to head to the library to find an answer to my "problem." I had thought I was looking for parenting strategies so I could avoid hurting my son, but I ended up, to sound cliché, finding myself.

Unless we're willing to do the arduous and soul-wrenching work of going back in time to uncover our own wounds as children, we will always keep sliding back to the harmful conditioning of treating children as another species, somehow less worthy of respect and dignity than their adult counterparts. This is also why each chapter of this book begins with *you*—of learning how you can mix the different ingredients of love to give yourself the love you deserve and always deserved. Then, I follow it up with suggestions and ideas on how to show that same love to your children.

Respectful Parenting means to accept that children are a marginalized faction of society and to take into consideration their thoughts, feelings, and perspectives just as we would an adult's. To be able to do this, we must unpack our own trauma from having been a child in this world and not getting many of these same rights. Only by processing our own experience and programming can we help create a better childhood for our children.

If this book is part of your continuing journey to become a respectful person, then I want to congratulate you on your commitment to this treacherous but rewarding journey and I hope this book will take your RP practices to the next level.

If this book is your first foray into RP, then I welcome you with so much joy and so much gentleness because you've undertaken the most courageous journey of your life. One that will transform your and your children's lives and their children's after them. Your future generations will look back at you with awe and respect and say, he/she's the one, the one who was brave enough to be a cycle breaker!

Religious Content

"I served the Prophet [peace be upon him] for ten years," said young Anas ibn Malik, "He never once told me 'uff'. When I did something, he never told me, 'Why did you do that?' And 'why didn't you do this?' when I didn't do it."[10]

The Heirloom

Once upon a time, in a land far, far away, there lived a family of koalas. In this family, on one extra bright morning, Gudda was born. Gudda loved his round furry ears, his big round belly, and his cute spoon-shaped nose. He also loved his parents' furry ears and round tummies and the fact that they could climb trees and hide in the big branches. Gudda loved being a koala. He would go around saying, "I love being a koala!"

But he noticed that no one else was saying it. In fact, they'd say, "Kangaroos are so much better. They can jump so high and their ears are pointy."

But Gudda didn't get it. He loved being a koala.

When he was a little older, his parents gathered him one day in the dark part of their den and told him it was time for him to have "the glasses."

"What are these glasses?" he asked.

"We all wear them, as you can see," said his dad.

"Yes, but what will they do? I can see just fine."

"They will make you see even better," said his mother.

Gudda wanted to see better. He loved his family and wanted to be just like them. He was excited to wear his glasses.

As soon as he put them on, everything closer up looked much bigger! But another strange thing happened.

His furry ears *felt* big and cumbersome. His round tummy made him look ugly and his nose was *so* dirty.

"I don't want to wear them!" he said.

"You must!" said the elders of the family, "It's important to see clearly and besides, you won't be amongst us if you don't wear them!"

Now, as much as Gudda hated the new glasses, he didn't want to lose his family. So, he kept the glasses on.

Life wasn't quite so fun and bright anymore when you had cumbersome big ears and an ugly nose and you didn't like being yourself. Gudda could see now why everyone wanted to be a kangaroo. They're nimble and have pointy ears and can jump so high. He would very much like to be able to move faster, but his ears seemed to weigh him down.

Once he was ready to leave the den, Gudda had been practicing how to jump like a kangaroo. He was sure once he was out in the world, his jumping would be perfect. But boy, was he wrong! Very, very wrong. When he entered the world, he realized that most koalas were already better jumpers than him. Many of them had also clipped their ears so they were pointy, like a kangaroo's.

He had never felt more alone in his life. But he had to go on. He had to gather the eucalyptus, bring it home, and help the elders prepare food. So, he did all that, day in and day out.

But life is ever so hard when you're not who you want to be. When your ears are big and ugly and your fur is dirty and you can't jump and don't have a pocket.

One day, Gudda was especially sad so instead of working, he snuck away to the pond where he used to play when he was little. But even that made him sad because he could see his reflection in the pond and he wasn't a kangaroo. He was about to turn away when he slipped and fell into the pond. Thankfully, he knew how to swim, and he quickly got himself back on dry land, but something was wrong. It took him a moment to realize that his glasses had come off in the pond.

"I'm sure they're just floating somewhere here . . ." he thought, scanning the surface of the pond. But as he leaned in to look for his glasses, he almost jumped back because he thought there was another beautiful creature in the pond staring back at him. It took him a few moments to realize that it was, in fact, his own mirror image.

"I'm so beautiful! I don't need to look like a kangaroo!" he thought. "It's those awful glasses that make me look and feel so ugly! I'm no longer going to wear them!"

He felt afraid as he said those words to himself. He realized how disappointed his parents would be in him and how alone he might be after that because every last koala in the community did wear them. But he wagged his tail and felt the lightness. He looked again in the pond and saw his beautiful round ears and dark furry skin. He didn't understand why no one else wanted to take the glasses off.

Just then, he heard a rustling from behind him.

"Who's there?" he called out. And a creature appeared from behind the bushes. Gudda realized it was also a koala but she had no glasses on.

"You . . . don't have your glasses on . . ." he said, a bit confused.

"Neither do you," she said with a smile. "Hi . . . I'm Guriya. It's nice, isn't it?"

"Hi Guriya . . . Yes! It is! Why doesn't everyone else do it too? Why do we have to carry these glasses?"

Guriya came closer and they both sat down on the dewy log next to the pond. "Are you sure you want to know the answer?"

"Yes, please! I'm so tired of these glasses!"

"Well, a long, long time ago, before our parents' parents and their parents before them, there used to be lots and lots of dinosaurs here and they'd prey on our ancestors and hunt them and kill them. The only koalas they wouldn't touch were the ones who had these glasses on, so even though it was painful to wear those glasses and they made us feel ugly and tired and sad, it was better than being killed and eaten by a dinosaur."

"But dinosaurs don't exist anymore!"

"Yes, and most koalas who are alive today don't even know what dinosaurs are! But they've seen their parents and their parents before them wearing these glasses and they think they keep them safe, so they keep wearing them, even though it makes them hate themselves."

"But . . . can't they just take them off like you and I did? And know that there's no danger and to see how amazing we are?"

"Well, to be fair, there are still those pesky kangaroos that can trample us. That's also why they wish they were kangaroos instead. Kangaroos don't have to be afraid."

"But neither do we! And we don't need glasses to protect ourselves either . . . Just some common sense!"

"Yes, you're right. But it's scary to do something no one else is doing. It's easier to just keep wearing the glasses."

"But they make life so hard!"

"Yes, I know . . . taking them off makes life hard too, because now everyone thinks I'm crazy and no one wants to have anything to do with me."

"I do. I'd love to be your friend. We can, together, not wear our glasses."

"Really? But your own family and even some friends are not going to accept you."

Gudda looked down at the pond and a tear welled up in his eye, "Yes, I guess they won't because they'd be scared . . . But maybe, with time, they'll see that we don't need to live in constant fear. That life is beautiful, and we are beautiful, and we don't even need to be kangaroos. That koalas are awesome too."

Guriya smiled at him. She'd already been down this path and knew the heartache Gudda would see, but she also knew of the joy he'd see, and she knew that nothing was quite so difficult if you had a friend who had seen their own beauty reflected in the pond.

NOTES

1. bell hooks, *All About Love: New Visions* (HarperCollins, 2000).
2. *Merriam-Webster.com Dictionary*, s.v. "cathexis," accessed June 30, 2023, https://www.merriam-webster.com/dictionary/cathexis.
3. A. Helwa, *Secrets of Divine Love: A Spiritual Journey Into the Heart of Islam* (Naulit Publishing House, 2019).
4. J. B. Watson, *Psychological Care of Infant and Child* (New York: W. W. Norton & Company, 1928).

5. B.D. Perry, "Childhood experience and the expression of genetic potential: What childhood neglect tells us about nature and nurture," *Brain & Mind*, 3(1) (2002): 79–100, https://doi.org/10.1023/A:1016557824657.
6. Marga Vicedo, "The evolution of Harry Harlow: From the nature to the nurture of love," *History of Psychiatry*, 21 (2010): 190–205. http://dx/doi.org/10.1177/0957154X10370909.
7. E.T. Gershoff and A. Grogan-Kaylor, "Spanking and Child Outcomes: Old Controversies and New Meta-Analyses," *Journal of Family Psychology, 30*(4) (2016): 453–469. http://dx.doi.org/10.1037/fam0000191.
8. Alfie Kohn, *Punished by Rewards: The Trouble with Gold Stars, Incentive Plans, A's, Praise, and Bribes* (Houghton Mifflin Company, 1993).
9. Shefali Tsabary, *The Conscious Parent: Transforming Ourselves, Empowering Our Children* (Namaste Pub., 2010).
10. Hesham Al-Awadi, *Children Around the Prophet: How Muhammad raised the Young Companions* (CreateSpace Independent Publishing Platform, 23 Mar. 2018).

CHAPTER 1

TRAUMA IS A SCARY WORD

> "Trauma is not a flaw or a weakness. It is a highly effective tool of safety and survival. Trauma is also not an event. Trauma is the body's protective response to an event—or a series of events—that it perceives as potentially dangerous."
>
> —Resmaa Menakem, *My Grandmother's Hands*[1]

What Is Trauma and Why Is It a Cycle Instead of a Bus?

In Pakistan, we refer to a bicycle as "cycle." The word "bus" in Urdu, among other meanings, also means "to stop." So, my double innuendo wordplay here is to ask how come trauma is something that doesn't just stop with one generation but continues through one generation to the next? And why is the answer to this question so relevant to our healing? All shall be revealed in this chapter, but let's start at the start.

What Exactly Is Trauma?

When I pose this question in my workshops, the majority of answers are some versions of the following:

Trauma is a big and scary event that disrupts our life and makes it difficult to go on.

This is not wrong, but it's also not the only definition of trauma. In fact, it's what we call "big T" trauma. Some examples include loss of a parent, an accident resulting in serious medical injuries, severe damage to property, sexual assault, a major incident of physical assault, being robbed, etc.

But the kind of trauma that ravages many people's lives is more insidious. It is not as loud, big, or prominent as we'd expect "trauma" to be and so it slips from our radar of perception, undetected. We aren't aware of it and, therefore, don't understand all the implications of it—thus drowning ourselves in shame and remorse over our failure to thrive.

This kind of trauma is called "small t" trauma and is prevalent in all our lives. If you've picked up this book, you can be certain you have unresolved trauma. It's really that simple. Some examples of small t trauma are: emotional neglect, frequent verbal and physical abuse, poverty, racial microaggressions, domestic violence, etc.

Many people find it surprising that emotional neglect and other examples stated above really qualify as trauma.

You see, the most remarkable thing on the planet is the survival instinct. Our bodies are meant to live, and any threat to this results in the body fighting back with all its might to survive. When there is an injury to the body, the blood strives to clot to plug the bleed. When there is injury to one of the vital organs, like the brain, the body goes into a coma to lighten its load. When there is an infection, our body heats up in an effort to kill the infection-causing germs. And in extreme cases like starvation, our body uses itself for fuel and energy: it starts burning the excess reserves of energy stored in our bodies and methodically starts shutting down the organs that perform non-essential functions like reproduction in an effort to preserve energy. Thus our bodies have built-in systems that go into activation automatically when the body is at threat. However, as we very well know, not all trauma is physical.

WHEN THE THREAT TO THE BODY IS NOT PHYSICAL

What if all the body is physically nourished but emotionally deprived and even threatened? It makes sense that our remarkable body has a full-blown system to also self-protect when faced with this kind of starvation. And much like the systems that work to keep the body alive when there's a physical threat, this system also works in the background, without our awareness and permission. It's called our Autonomic Nervous System (ANS).

Just like the body's ability to activate the survival instincts when faced with starvation, ANS does the exact same thing when we are faced with emotional starvation. It creates various survival techniques meant to help a human child survive childhood when we are at our most vulnerable. This perpetual state of being in childhood survival mode is called trauma.

GENERATIONAL TRAUMA

"History matters, and an awareness of it puts our lives into a context. A disdain for history sets us adrift, and makes us victims of ignorance and denial. History lives in and through our bodies right now, and in every moment."

—Resmaa Menakem, *My Grandmother's Hands*

Imagine someone growing up in a state of perpetual hyper-vigilance. Every move you make, every person you meet, every thought you have, is forever altered. You have on what we call "a trauma lens." It's like the glasses the koalas wore in the story in the beginning of this book. You see the world as a dangerous and unsafe place where people are ill-intentioned. Where every other incident is evidence of your own helplessness and unworthiness.

Can you imagine how it affects your children? Even your own children saying "no" to you is perceived as a threat. You respond to them accordingly. Your autonomic memory is vivid where "no" signals danger and the person saying it is "unsafe." In other words, the traumatized parent is unknowingly teaching their child the same lessons by foregoing their role of the caretaker and taking on the role of the unsafe adult, in turn, making the world seem dangerous and scary to their own child.

EPIGENETICS AND THE LEGACY OF TRAUMA

Epigenetics is an evolving field of genetics in which we're learning how trauma transforms our very DNA. This is a significant finding for those of us that reside in BIPOC (Black, Indigenous, and People of Color) bodies. For example, the principles of epigenetics have found that trauma experienced by one generation lives on in the next two generations at least. Its remnants live even longer, of course, depending on how much healing has occurred in the progressive generations. This means that the trauma my grandparents experienced as pre-partition Muslims living in the subcontinent of India is still carried within my parents and me. In his heart-wrenching book *Midnight's Furies: The Deadly Legacy of India's Partition*, Nisid Hajari recounts one of the many bloody incidents of trains traveling between the newly appointed Pakistan and India:

> On 22 September, after a refugee train coming the other way arrived in Amritsar with dead and wounded, the Akali fighters went berserk. A mob estimated at ten thousand people swarmed a Pakistan-bound train full of Meo refugees, firing automatic rifles, tossing bombs and slashing away with swords. Only 200 horribly wounded passengers survived.[2]

I remember my *dadi amma* (grandmother) telling me gruesome stories of such trains arriving in Pakistan filled with bloodied corpses and decapitated immigrants. I remember her shuddering as she recalled seeing these images on her neighbors' grainy black-and-white television. I remember sensing her fear and pain of the trauma of belonging to a land that was first colonized by the British and then ripped haphazardly into two and then three parts (India, Pakistan, and Bangladesh).

It doesn't matter which side of the border you were on; we all remember hearing some version of these stories as children. We also vividly remember growing up in the cesspool of anguish and hate that comes from being part of such a history. I remember, as a little girl, not being able to understand why or how the popular cricketer Muhammed Azharuddin was a Muslim but played for India.

"But how can he play for the bad guys, Papa?" I'd ask my father, and he'd try to explain the gray complexities of being a Muslim Indian to me. Complexities that were far beyond the reach of a nine-year-old child.

Part of my healing, of course, has been to unpack this hatred that was passed down to me as a young Pakistani kid—to learn to differentiate between the actions of a government and its people. Because that's what trauma does—it makes the truth blurry and inseparable from lies. It makes you mistrustful of whole nations instead of putting responsibility where it belongs.

It feels important to say here that what I've shared is barely the tip of the iceberg when it comes to the trauma of partition. In her book *The Long Partition and the Making of Modern South Asia*, Vazira Fazila-Yacoobali Zamindar writes about the nightmarish logistics of millions of displaced refugees in Pakistan and India. The partition itself was just the beginning of the traumatic events that would unfold over the following decades. I highly recommend her book if you want to learn more about the microaggressions and small t traumas faced by the people of both countries, and eventually the people of Bangladesh as well (originally East Pakistan).

She did a great job of digging up actual documents— newspapers, property deeds, passports, etc.—from that time period and using them to highlight the logistical nightmares that were the outcomes of the partition. One newspaper excerpt she shares shows the agony of families torn apart during the partition:

> Now to bring your families across, long procedures are required. Those who have their family in India, those people who wish to call their relatives from India, will have to use complicated methods. In the past, a Pakistani citizen could get a permanent permit and call the relatives; now, a member of a family has to go

in India to Pakistan's diplomatic office and make an application to become a Pakistani.

Then, it will be sent to Karachi for clearance from the Pakistani government. Once approved, this applicant will get an emergency certificate, and so, instead of a passport, they can show this emergency certificate and enter Pakistan. For this process to be completed, it will take approximately two months. With this situation, thousands of government employees and *muhajirs* will be harassed.[3]

This history of partition is something we read in history books growing up, and you'd think we'd be immune to it by now. I can't speak for the experience of my other countrymen, but for me, any image or excerpt of this brutal chapter of history invokes an immediate bodily response. My throat tightens, tears well up in my eyes, it becomes hard to breathe, and my chest tightens with what feels like an unbearable pain that will never subside. It doesn't matter how many times I pass a picture of Muhammed Ali Jinnah and Fatimah Jinnah, my heart swells with love and gratitude for the work they did. I'm sure my Indian and Bangladeshi brothers and sisters have similar reactions to memories of their brave founders. May all their souls rest in peace. Ameen.

THE TRAUMA OF RESIDING IN A NON-WHITE BODY IN THIS WORLD

"Your husband is letting you study?" asked my blonde-haired, blue-eyed classmate in his Baltimore drawl. I remember a shift in my body at his words. An unpleasant one that I couldn't quite name at the time.

"Yes," I answered simply, deeply aware of the unsaid implications of his question.

"Oh, that's good," he said, breaking into a "relieved" smile.

"My husband isn't like that," I said defensively, answering the implied questions.

"But he makes you wear that thing . . ." he asked, his eyes gesturing towards my hijab.

"No, he doesn't. In fact, he wanted me not to wear it when I came to America but I wanted to," I offer helpfully. I don't want him to think less of me and judge me or my husband. But he seems uninterested in my explanations, already turning away to face the front of the classroom. I also turn back in my seat, feeling discomfort I couldn't understand at the time.

Microaggressions, we call them now.

Carrying the weight of walking the earth as "less than" and carrying the burden of proving myself to be an open-minded, intelligent, and independent woman. Different races and genders of those races carry different weights. Mine, as a modestly clad Muslim woman, is to prove that I'm not oppressed by the inches of my covered skin. Another one is to prove that as a mother of three sons, I'm not raising "terrorists" (a term used exclusively in the U.S. for criminals of Muslim descent). Once when I was out walking outside with Eisa, a couple of white young men passed by and "accidentally on purpose" called my son Osama. I don't think I have to explain that one. Thank goodness, Eisa was too little to be aware of this microaggression.

People who deny the existence of racism or minimize the cumulative effect of microaggressions argue that bad stuff happens to everyone. People are mean to white people too. People are mean to fat people too. When we talk about our

experiences of being discriminated against based on our skin color, they think we're saying, "Bad things happen to me because I'm not white."

And what we're really saying is, "Everything bad that happens to you, also happens to BIPOC people, and *more* bad things to us because of our skin color."

Imagine life being a video game where every player has to deal with the same challenges to get to the next level, except having colored skin makes every level twice as difficult. This is an oversimplification of the problem but hopefully clarifies that we are not saying white people don't have pain.

These are all experiences and reflections that come from living in a Caucasian-majority country for almost twenty years. I haven't even touched upon the generational trauma we carry in our bones from being a colonized nation, but a really helpful way of envisioning what that might have felt like, in some ways, is to turn to Indigenous and Black people for their experiences of living in white-majority countries. Natalie Y. Gutierrez, author of *The Pain We Carry: Healing from Complex PTSD for People of Color,* writes:

> As a Black, Indigenous, and Person of Color, you might find yourself struggling with accumulated trauma or prolonged exposure to traumatic experiences, including facing racial trauma, microaggressions, and marginalization, regularly. Here are some ways you might experience this struggle:
>
> - You might waver between depression and anxiety.
> - You might experience despair, maybe even sometimes wanting to die.

- Your heart might race when you're stopped by the police.
- You might experience intrusive thoughts and memories of times when you were discriminated against, called racial slurs or other oppressive slurs, or abused in any way.
- You might have mastered the survival technique of numbing out, or dissociating, to avoid feeling your feelings.
- You might feel like an imposter no matter how accomplished you are, and feel a constant sense of otherness.

This is CPTSD. You might already know this on a soul level. Let this serve as more confirmation and validation of what your heart already knows and might've just not had the words to describe.[4]

If you hail from the Indian subcontinent, this is the kind of daily experience your ancestors might have had living under British rule. Think of the movie *Lagaan* with Amir Khan in it.[5] His character, Bhuvan, is an impoverished farmer, but even the Indian prince, Rajah Puran Singh, experiences humiliation and oppression at the hands of the colonizers. If you're thinking, that was just a movie, pick up the newspaper and read how invading armies treat the locals. The terror caused by Captain Russell in *Lagaan* will seem like child's play. Literally.

That fear, terror, and oppression our ancestors experienced still lives inside our DNA, as the science of epigenetics explains.

Have you ever seen those funny TikToks that compare white parenting to brown parenting and everyone gets a big laugh at the brown mom whipping out her chappal where the white mom is rational and disciplined? Have you ever wondered why that is? One race is not created superior to another race, and it's also impossible that all members of one race decide to be violent towards their kids. I hope that understanding generational trauma and epigenetics has lent itself to a better understanding of these discrepancies.

Resmaa Menakem says in his book *My Grandmother's Hands: Racialized Trauma and the Pathway to Mending Our Hearts and Bodies* that trauma responses can add up to look like a person's character and this "character" can then be passed on to the next generation as "hereditary traits."[6] No wonder so many of my clients tell me that they're so concerned that their child has "inherited" their grandfather's "legendary rage." I'm glad to tell them that they can be the cycle breaker who offers healing to their child and breaks the "hereditary curse."

If you're wondering at this point if there's anyone who doesn't have trauma, as you might be realizing, the answer is no. We all have healing to do on one level or another. However, every level of trauma piles on more layers of pain and dysfunction. This ACE Pyramid[7] below from the famous ACEs study shows how the various kinds of traumas can stack up.

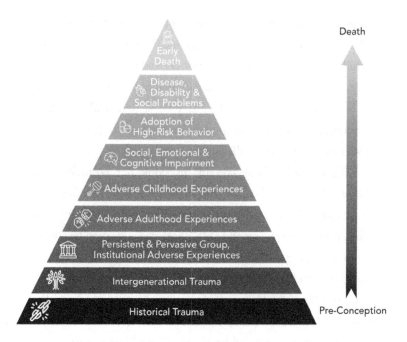

The good news is, as cycle breakers, we can work on healing them all. The bad news is, we will have to accept that what has transpired in generations will also take at least a couple of generations to heal. The days you stumble and fall and make mistakes, remind yourself of where you're standing on this pyramid. What you're doing is back-breaking, soul-crushing, and heart-wrenching work, fraught with many mistakes, missteps, and even regressions. Ultimately though, you will succeed in undoing what no one else in your line of ancestry has been able to do. There's nothing to say to that except congratulations!

The Science of Trauma

As you learned in the introduction and subsequent sections, trauma has a very physical manifestation and the ability to change our brain's physiology. Our brain is the "hub" of all nervous system activity, and unfortunately, trauma skews that entire circuitry so that we're no longer functioning the way we're supposed to. The biological changes caused by trauma wreak havoc on an individual's ability to interact safely with the world. The good news is that the resilience of the human nervous system allows us to recover and heal it so we can have a new chance at life.

POLYVAGAL THEORY:
OUR BODY'S DANGER AND SAFETY PROTOCOL

Dr. Stephen Porges's Polyvagal Theory (PVT) has revolutionized the world of trauma and recovery by helping us understand how our nervous system responds to cues of safety and danger in our environment. I had the pleasure of getting to learn the theory from Dr. Porges himself when I had the chance to attend his master class on it in his hometown of Jacksonville, Florida. Hearing the theory straight from him was a whole different experience. He has a warm and engaging presence and the ability to explain things with clarity and brevity. The following is a basic definition of PVT that I've formed from his work:

> Polyvagal Theory postulates that the largest nerve in our body, called the vagus nerve, has the ability to switch between "safety" and "danger" states, depending on what the vagus is sensing. These states, in laymen terms, are fight, flight, and shut down for

when danger is detected, and social engagement when safety is detected.

To understand and appreciate his theory, we first have to have some basic knowledge of our nervous system and how it works under "normal" circumstances. I will then explain what he discovered and how it has improved our understanding of trauma and recovery.

OUR SECRET SUPERHERO: THE NERVOUS SYSTEM

Our nervous system is actually the Central Nervous System (CNS) and includes our brain, brain stem, and all the nerves in our body that work together to:

- Coordinate all activities of the body
- Respond to internal/external changes

The component of the CNS that we're concerned with here is called the autonomic nervous system (ANS), and in this book, whenever you see this acronym, I want you to say it like it's your friend's name, pronounced affectionately as *Aans*. This is because ANS is our superhero and protective friend who protects us without us even knowing (and thus it's our "secret superhero"). It's made up of two further pathways called the sympathetic nervous system (SNS) and the parasympathetic nervous system (PSNS).

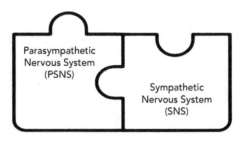

These two fit together conceptually like puzzle pieces because they do a complementary job. PSNS comprises the rest and digest functions of ANS, and SNS activates the fight and flight functions of the ANS.

So far, so good. We've known about these aspects of the ANS forever, but what Dr. Porges discovered (accidentally, as he shares in his book) was that the PSNS has an additional "pathway" that gets activated when fight or flight are deemed unhelpful by ANS.[8] That means that our body doesn't just have the fight or flight defense mechanism, it also has the "shut down" mechanism, which causes us to dissociate completely from reality when ANS senses the demands on us to be overwhelming and/or scary. Have you ever gone into paralysis when you've had too much to do and no amount of willpower gets you out of the "procrastination mode"? Yup, that's shut down mode for you—and why you weren't just being lazy! But this phenomenon is incredibly important because it answers another million-dollar question: why are some kids so compliant and obedient (like most of our generation)? It's because their nervous system learned the hard way that shutting down and just doing what's asked is the only way to survive.

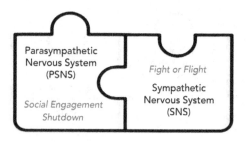

BLIND OBEDIENCE INDICATES
AN UNDER-ATTACK ANS

Have you ever stood before your boss or someone else in authority as they told you everything you did wrong? If you tried to slow down such a moment in your mind's eye, you might realize that the feelings and sensations evoked by such an encounter can be described as downright scary. And they are! When your boss ticks off all the things you did wrong or your mother-in-law judges you without even uttering a word, your ANS gets activated and engages the sympathetic nervous system's "fight or flight" response. As a result, you feel either angry ("fight response") or just want to hide ("flight" response).

In due time though, your trusty superhero friend ANS (more specifically PSNS) steps in, gets your vitals back to normal and you feel better once you move away from the "danger." But what if you have someone in your life who treats you poorly day in and day out, *and* you're dependent on them for your very survival? ANS might decide in that situation that you're helpless, and there's nothing you can do, and shutting down and going in a "play dead" mode is the best line of defense.

This is often what happens to children who live in volatile homes; their ANS decides that going into fight or flight is even more harmful and it's better to "play dead" or be submissive, otherwise known as being compliant or "the good kid." It often breaks my heart when clients tell me that their parents never physically harmed them because they were "good kids" but their other siblings did "get into trouble" because "she was just so difficult." The truth is that most people have no explicit memory of the events that led to their trusty ANS shutting off their fight and flight any time their parent got unsafe. All they know is that they were "good," but what they don't know is that it's enough evidence for ANS when it senses another child being hurt to know that it's also not safe for me to express displeasure or "not listen." A really good example of this is a YouTube video that went viral where a dad is trying to feed his toddler who refuses to eat until the dad picks up a stuffed toy and smacks it hard to show the boy what happens when you make Dad unhappy. What do you think happens next? A very scared little toddler opens his mouth right up when Dad brings the spoon near it. He is now "a good boy."[9]

BUILDING RESILIENCE: THE AUTONOMIC LADDER

The first time I ever came across PVT was in Dr. Delahooke's book, *Beyond Behaviors*. In her book, Dr. Delahooke uses color coding for these various ANS states, and I thought it might be easier here for our purposes to do the same. She calls them green (social engagement), red (fight and flight), and blue (shut down). When we or our children are feeling calm, happy, and ready to engage with the world, we are in the green zone. When ANS is not feeling safe, we can either have an aggressive response (red zone), or just shut down and disengage from the world (blue zone).[10]

Dr. Deb Dana uses the 'autonomic ladder' visual to represent these various ANS states. You can't just switch back and forth from red to green or blue to green—you must climb each rung of the ladder to get back to the green zone. This means that this ascent will be slow and will require some work from us. In the case of children, they actively require the compassionate help of an adult to climb back up to the green zone.[11] This is called co-regulation and will be your key skill as a respectful parent. We will learn more about this in the next chapter.

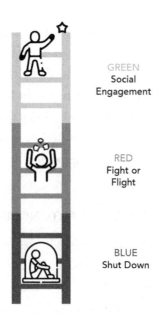

GREEN
Social
Engagement

RED
Fight or
Flight

BLUE
Shut Down

THE "SOUL NERVE"

Manekan calls the vagus "the soul nerve" because, let's face it, it impacts us at the soul level. This is where these three colorful stages in our body exist. They are the soul nerve's three distinct pathways—imagine a highway that forks out. That is, the nerve "forks out" from the brainstem in the three pathways, which are . . . you guessed it! Green, Red, and Blue. Yay, you're getting this!

You can skip this part if you'd rather avoid these terms. I want to be loyal to the science here and provide the information. The green pathway is called Ventral Vagal because ventral means front and this pathway is located in the "front" organs of our body and covers the face, ears, heart, and lungs. The red pathway is the sympathetic part of the nervous system, and the blue pathway is called the Dorsal Vagal Pathway because dorsal means "back" and this is the nerve that reaches our "back organs," namely liver, small and large intestine (stomach), and the bladder. Have you ever noticed that when we're particularly nervous or scared, we end up getting a stomachache? This is exactly why—because ANS is detecting overwhelming "danger" and trying to alert us.

The reason that this is important to know is because we can pay attention to the sensations in our body whenever we're in a defensive state of ANS. When we notice the sensations of our beating heart, ringing ears, and the face warming up, we can identify that we're in the red state of fight and flight. When we have a "bad feeling in the tummy," we can know that something is dangerous enough to our body to want to shut down completely.

Finally, if our ANS is the "superhero," we can say that its superpower is called the Vagal Brake. This is its ability to stay in the green zone even when situations might be causing the body to slide down the ladder into red and blue. How good the brake is, is a great measure of an individual's nervous system's ability to keep the individual feeling safe and engaged.

Trauma can seriously hamper the functionality of the Vagal Brake, where the slightest amount of stress can send someone sliding down the ladder like a slippery slope.

Our goal for recovery and raising resilient children is to enhance the green zone and improve the functionality of our vagal brake. More on this in subsequent chapters.

NEUROCEPTION: YOUR BODY KNOWS THINGS YOU DON'T

Let's talk a little bit more about how exactly our ANS knows that our boss is "not safe" and the stress response must be triggered to protect ourselves. This is what Dr. Porges calls "Neuroception." This is the ANS's ability to detect threat in the environment. It urges the Vagus to activate the Vagal Brake as if it's saying, "Dude! Danger ahead . . . must activate mode shut down or mode fight/flight!" And the Vagus does as Neuroception says.

AUTONOMIC MEMORY: YOUR BODY REMEMBERS WHAT YOU DON'T

Over time, ANS develops its own "memory" of danger and safety based on the cues it gets. For example, think back to that judgmental boss who evokes unsafe feelings every time he comes around. Now he doesn't need to even say anything; your nervous system already knows what will most likely happen next, so it efficiently activates the brain's "stress response system." Your heartrate shoots up when you hear he's on his way and you look for places to hide. This is called the 'autonomic memory'.

In the case of trauma, imagine Neuroception as having bad hearing and poor eyesight—it often detects threat when there isn't any, but the Vagus has no choice but to follow its directions because it has no way of knowing when the Neuroception's information is real and when it's not.

"Trauma can cause us to react to present events in ways that seem wildly inappropriate, overly charged, or otherwise out of proportion. Whenever someone freaks out suddenly or reacts to a small problem as if it were a catastrophe, it's often a trauma response."

—Resmaa Menakem, *My Grandmother's Hands*

In this book, we'll use the term "trauma response" to mean what Menakem has explained here—any response that seems incredibly disproportionate to what has transpired. Someone with a history of trauma (which you know by now is all of us), has faulty neuroception—their ANS can't reliably detect threats and tends to overassess situations as threatening even when they're not and vice versa—lacks the ability to engage the right state and tools to navigate between the states. In cases of intense trauma, some people might be perpetually stuck in either the sympathetic state (always aggressive) or the dorsal vagal state (always shut down).

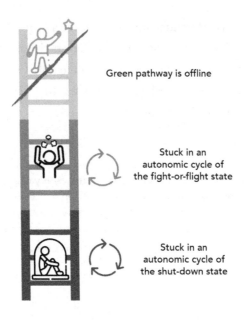

Green pathway is offline

Stuck in an autonomic cycle of the fight-or-flight state

Stuck in an autonomic cycle of the shut-down state

HEALING THE NERVOUS SYSTEM
IS HEALING THE TRAUMA

We've learned how trauma ravages ANS, makes it overly sensitive and unable to stay resilient, often in even very seemingly innocuous situations. We will learn in the following chapters how we can begin to repair our Vagal Brake and increase our window of tolerance, thus building resilience. Window of tolerance means how much we can tolerate before we slide down the autonomic ladder into one of our defense modes (fight, flight, or shut down; that is, the red or blue zones). The purpose of healing is singularly one: build resilience; and it relies on our efforts to heal our ANS.

Resilience means an individual's ability to bounce back from difficult experiences with strength and aplomb. A resilient nervous system has the ability to correctly assess whether there is true danger in the environment or not.

In other words, a resilient parent doesn't easily get triggered by their child because their ANS knows that a child, by definition, is incapable of causing harm.

The more time we can spend in the ventral vagal state, the more we can increase our window of tolerance. This means that recovery is all about relational safety—the more we can feel safe in our relationships, to ourselves and to others, the more we can heal our nervous systems. As explained in the section entitled "Finding Safety and Settlement," we will do this by honoring our needs and we will ensure a healthy nervous system for our children by learning how to meet their needs.

"What Does My Childhood Have to Do with Anything?"

"Twenty years of medical research has shown that childhood adversity literally gets under our skin, changing people in ways that can endure in their bodies for decades. It can tip a child's developmental trajectory and affect physiology. It can trigger chronic inflammation and hormonal changes that can last a lifetime. It can alter the way DNA is read and how cells replicate, and it can dramatically increase the risk for heart disease, stroke, cancer, diabetes—even Alzheimer's."

—Dr. Nadine Burke Harris, *The Deepest Well: Healing the Long-Term Effects of Childhood Adversity*[12]

The above quote by Dr. Harris explains why looking at our childhood is so important. She is the author of the amazing book *The Deepest Well: Healing the Long-Term Effects of*

Childhood Adversity, and her Ted Talk about childhood trauma is one of the most watched Ted Talks of all time. In her book, she explores the relationship between toxic stress (or trauma) experienced by children and the effects of it as they become adults. This is a conversation that makes many people incredibly uncomfortable. It's going to be one of the times when you have to routinely check-in with your body and notice how the discomfort shows up for you.

Again, let's rely on science to answer the powerful question of why our childhood is so relevant even if we've seemingly moved past it.

Children's Brains Are "Blank Sates"

Our brains are made of billions of cells called neurons. The way our brain works is by these neurons 'talking' to each other. Say you want to grab your cup of *chai*, one neuron will "fire," that is, generate an electrical signal that will send a message to another neuron that you're wanting that yummy cup of *chai*, and the next neuron will get your hand to reach out and grab the *chai*. This is an oversimplification of the process but sufficient to explain that the "point" where neurons exchange information is called a synapse.

When children are born, they have trillions of synapses but they're all "empty" because for now, the neurons haven't really communicated much—like "hello, I was just born," says the brain. Imagine when Dubai was first urbanized, it had a ton of brand-new apartment buildings but no tenants—that's kind of how babies' brains are. That's why we call them "blank slates."

As babies grow, more and more of those "apartments" fill up. As they learn to babble and then talk, crawl, and then walk, laugh and explore, hug and be hugged, more and more synapses start being used. People also use the phrase "neural pathways" for synapses and the more a pathway is used, the stronger it gets. Sort of like walking a path in a field of grass—the more often you walk it, the more it becomes "the beaten path," easy to follow and visible in the field. This is why, as you learned in the trauma chapter, our childhoods are so relevant. Scientists have found that the first two months of an infant's life are more impactful than the first twelve years and why not? That's when the very first "foundation" of the brain is being built. Dr. Eliot, author of *What's Going on in There? How the Brain and Mind Develop in the First Five Years of Life*, summarizes this process beautifully:

> A young child's environment directly and permanently influences the structure and eventual function of his or her brain. Everything a child sees, touches, hears, feels, tastes, thinks, and so on translates into electrical activity in just a subset of his or her synapses, tipping the balance for long-term survival in their favor. On the other hand, synapses that are rarely activated— whether because of languages never heard, music never made, sports never played, mountains never seen, love never felt—will wither and die.[13]

That last one is a sobering realization for many. I've had so many parents say to me with a broken heart, "Why can't I truly love my child?" and I gently remind them that it's not their fault. If you never formed the synapses for parental love because your parents struggled to show you love, then you're stuck with the monumental task of building new neural pathways as an adult. This is no easy feat but is far from impossible—it is, in fact, one of the human brain's most remarkable abilities and it's called "neuroplasticity." To develop new pathways, we have to create new experiences, but first let's examine what synapses are formed when a child experiences consistent stress.

TRAUMA AND TOXIC STRESS

Recall again that example of standing before your boss or mother-in-law as they told you everything you did wrong. This time I want you to slow down even more and focus on exactly what the discomfort of those moments feels like in your body:

- Cold sweats
- Heaviness
- Tightness
- Heat
- Tugging
- Pulling
- Closing

Now if I nudged you to think about where you feel all these sensations in your body, I bet you'd be able to name their location as well. This is because all sensations and feelings have a physical manifestation in our body. When we experience discomfort, shame, judgment, or any other difficult feeling, our body gets dumped with stress hormones: adrenaline and cortisol. Your boss, in this situation, would be the "stressor"— the cause of the stress. What if, once he's done talking, he walks

away. Will all your symptoms suddenly disappear? Of course not. In fact, more than likely, you'd continue to feel many of these symptoms along with certain behavior symptoms like overthinking, losing focus on your actual task, lack of appetite, lethargy, etc. Of course, eventually, you'd move around, go outside, talk to a loved one, and all these actions will work to metabolize the stress hormones in your body and you'll be able to move on.

But what if your boss treated you this way every single day? The cortisol would not even have the chance to work itself out of your system; it would keep accumulating and even compounding.

Let's take it a step further. What if, instead of weighing a hundred plus pounds, your body was only 10, 20, or 30 pounds? How would the stress hormones affect you then? Day in and day out, your body being dumped with this toxic stress—that is, cortisol and adrenaline—what would it do?

Evolutionarily speaking, when we were hunters and gatherers, our body's ability to self-regulate with cortisol was brilliant. However, a steady and frequent stream of cortisol triggered by an unsafe environment wreaks havoc on a child's young and vulnerable body. Like Harris tells us in her famous Ted Talk that it's a magnificent thing that our body knows to go into fight and flight when it sees a big, scary bear. We are immediately pumped with the hormones needed to help us flee. "But what if . . . ," Harris pauses dramatically in her talk, ". . . the bear comes home every night?"[14]

In 1995, the U.S. Centers for Disease Control (CDC) and the Kaiser Permanente health care organization in California conducted a groundbreaking study, establishing an astoundingly high correlation of Adverse Childhood Experiences (ACEs) with poor health and behavior outcomes as adults.[15]

In simple words, the study found that the more someone had suffered as a child, the higher their chances of having poor physical health and undesirable behaviors like addiction and academic struggles. Your ACEs score is determined by answering ten questions regarding three major areas of your life as a child:

1. Physical and emotional abuse
2. Physical and emotional neglect
3. Household dysfunction

You can also take the ACEs quiz in appendix A but I'd take the results with a grain of salt, especially if you're just starting on your healing journey. This is because the ten questions are overly simplistic and only cover certain kinds of adverse experiences. Experts agree that this quiz should have at least another ten questions to get an accurate result, but nevertheless, it's a good enough place to start to unpack your own story. More importantly, it highlights the significance of childhood experiences.

IT'S HARD TO SPEAK MY TRUTH

To be born and raised in a Pakistani home is to be taught from a young age that the status of parents is somewhere in the vicinity of the Divine. Children as young as two years are frequently lectured about the respect (read: blind obedience) they owe to their parents.

This is probably not unique to Pakistani culture. As the character Meilin in *Turning Red*, an awesome animated movie about what we carry in our DNA, says in the very beginning of the movie, "We are taught to honor our parents so much so that we sometimes forget to honor ourselves."[16]

As a Muslim and proud Pakistani (and a parent myself who'd love respect from my kids), I don't contest the importance of honoring our parents. I think the issue arises when, as Meilin said, we forget to honor ourselves.

There's a wonderful Montessori school in far-out Manassas, Virginia, called Mountain Montessori, which is run as true to the spirit of its namesake as I have ever seen a school being run. One of its lovely teachers said something to me that immediately stuck out to me and I repeat it often, "Childhood is a time of self-development." She put so succinctly what I had been trying to tell the parents I work with—that childhood is a time of discovering oneself and honoring oneself. This is the foundation of honoring others. *All* others—including parents.

Religious Content

This is in line with the Divine law; we cannot honor others when we deny ourselves the honor given to us by our Creator:

"We have honored the children of Adam; provided them with transport on land and sea; given them for sustenance things good and pure; and conferred on them special favors, above a great part of our creation." (Quran 17:70)

The Arabic word used here for "honor" is *karam*, meaning "something that is precious."

> We have to be able to recognize ourselves as precious and worthy of respect, even when we were children. Even when we acted in "naughty" ways, we were not suddenly bereft of this God-given honor.

It's the right of every child to be spoken to with kindness and respect, even when they do things that are inconvenient for adults. Of course, we know that this is not how children have been raised traditionally.

Their natural stage of "self-discovery" is disrupted when they are continuously, every day, many times, asked to dishonor themselves.

"Of course, you're not too cold."

"She didn't hit you first . . . you always hit first."

"You need to finish your plate . . . there's no way you're full already!"

"You need to study! or else!"

"Studying is more important than playing."

"What is wrong with you? Why are you so sensitive?"

"That's nothing to cry about!"

"Go to your room until you can learn how to behave yourself!"

Now, the problem arises when we try to honor our reality as adults and it clashes with the reality our parents and society have conditioned us with.

Parents can do no wrong.

Parents love you unconditionally.

Parents worked so hard to raise you.

Parents deserve your complete respect.

Etc., etc.

None of these are untrue. Provided that our parents had zero trauma of their own. But we all know that's not true.

BUT MY CHILDHOOD WAS AWESOME

My childhood was, by many accounts, absolutely lovely—that's why it took me so long to realize why existing in my body was so painful. When my brilliant book coach, Azul, encouraged me to be honest in my book, I knew right away that I'd have to tell this story. It weighed on my heart because I too felt that I'd be betraying my parents who had done so much for me and whom I dearly love. But I can't write a book about authenticity and not tell my own story.

Then I found bell hooks's account of her own childhood trauma and it took my breath away. It was like she was writing my story in the words that I wanted and couldn't find. I'm so grateful to her for writing these words,

> I was my father's first daughter. At the moment of my birth, I was looked upon with loving kindness, cherished and made to feel wanted on this earth and in my home. To this day I cannot remember when that feeling of being loved left me. I just know that one day I was no longer precious.[17]

Exactly like hooks, I too was my parents' first child and the first grandchild in my paternal home. I was born after three years of my parent's marriage and my much-awaited birth was celebrated with aplomb and *mithai* boxes. Strangely enough, I have strong implicit memories of feeling this joy in my body. I even have some oddly vivid explicit memories of evoking love and laughter in my parents. I recall them asking me to pretend to be angry and when I happily complied by folding my hands in little fists and making grrr noises, they'd dissolve into fits of laughter. I don't know what's worse—to remember once being the center of your parents' unconditional love and then losing it or to never have experienced it at all. What I do know is that it's a pain that sits inside your body like a dull ache for the rest of your life. Every new rejection and dismissal adding another layer of pain to the ever-deepening wound.

Of course, my healing journey has allowed me to start filling up that wound. I've been through a rollercoaster of emotions through this journey that has traversed anger, grief, mourning, and finally a semblance of acceptance. I'm able to see that if my parents had had the right tools and skills, they'd have continued to pour into me with all the ingredients of love. Definitely they provided me some of those ingredients that they *were* able to, with excellence and responsibility. As hooks says,

> I am grateful to have been raised in a family that was caring, and strongly believe that had my parents been loved well by *their* parents they would have given that love to their children. They gave what they had been given—care.[18]

Isn't that the course of nature? Parents are meant to love their offspring in all the glory of that word, but when that's not the case, it's obvious that something terrible has happened to derail the course of nature. The trauma-informed approach is to make space for this derailment. It doesn't mean that we dismiss our own experiences, but in due time, we're able to make peace with the relationship we have with our parents. We can even learn to carry their story with compassion and empathy.

My father was sent away to a military boarding school at the age of twelve. He was the eldest amongst four sons and two daughters, and his father had a humble job as a clerk at a government office. He instinctively knew from a young age that his family had put a lot of expectations on him. He would be an *afsar* (officer) one day. A man of the uniform. He would serve his country and save his family from the throes of poverty. When my grandfather passed away, my youngest uncle was only a teenager. My dad took the responsibility of his siblings and mother, becoming "man of the house" at the tender age of twenty. He did excellently manage to do everything that was asked of him and more but he never did get to be a child.

My mom was the second youngest of eight siblings. She was a carefree, bubbly, and vibrant young girl when she got married to a man who rarely smiled and expected her to act like a seasoned lady of the home and the eldest *bhabhi* (sister-in-law). All her strengths appeared to be a nuisance to her husband. She got along beautifully with his family—my aunts and uncles adored her and she, in return, adored them. All of this meant little to my father, who always seemed unhappy with her desire for socialization, *gup shup*, and trying to enjoy her life. Everything she loved, he found it frivolous and *"waqt ka ziya"* (wastage of time).

By the time I came along, some of my mom's spark had probably already gone out. She also conceived my brother right after giving birth to me and suddenly found herself stuck at an isolating military base with two babies, a demanding husband, and the support of her own family, many miles away.

I was a feisty kid. My parents tell me my daughter is just like me: strong-willed, loud, rambunctious, and from what I can see, creative, imaginative, and full of love. If I was anything like my daughter, I can imagine that I must have made my mom afraid. She was already paying the price for being a woman who had wanted to take up space in this world. The last thing she'd want is for me to suffer the same fate. She had learned the pain of constantly being asked by society to water herself down, but she also didn't know how to metabolize that pain, and so she expelled much of it at me.

As I explained in the brain science section earlier, a human baby has trillions of synapses. She won't need them all, so the extra ones get pruned. Whatever is not used is done away with. In the first five years of life our brains develop the most and lay the groundwork for all future development. Our experiences shape what synapses are kept and what are done away with. When our big feelings and expressions of authenticity are met with harsh judgment and dismissal, we start to lose the ability to assert ourselves, take up space, be courageous, and believe in ourselves.

It's ironic that people tell children, over and over, that parents are perfect because children already believe that. They only blame themselves. When other grownups reinforce this reality upon them, it becomes a path carved in stone from which a return would be an impossible and herculean task that will span decades. In his brilliant book *Mindsight*, Dr. Siegel explains why this blind trust of the parent at the cost of mistrust of the self is so innate for children:

> From the point of view of survival, "I am bad" is a safer perspective than "My parents are unreliable and may abandon me any time." It's better for the child to feel defective than to realize that his attachment figures are dangerous, undependable, or untrustworthy.

The mental mechanism of shame at least preserves for him the illusion of safety and security that is at the core of sanity.[19]

I've learned from my work that despite all these explanations, many people still struggle to be able to look at their childhood rationally without experiencing extreme resistance—probably because their shame in regards to their parents is intense or perhaps the pain that this shame hides is even more intense. This resistance shows up as some version of the following statement:

But I only have nice memories from my childhood and I know my parents really were kind. My "real" trauma is from my in-laws/spouse/boss/others in current life.

This is also something I hear at least a couple of times in each of my Anokhay Mentors (AM) courses. AM is our twelve-week trauma-informed program focused on healing and self-development. Every batch we do have participants who resist the idea that their childhood is relevant to their current issues. However, by the end of the program almost all the participants ultimately find something in their childhood that explains their current behavior patterns with their children or other people around them.

This "blockage" of these explicit memories might be due to several reasons. Explicit memories start to develop around age four and beyond and are the memories we can access and recall in the form of "pictures," but our brain has an amazing ability to "hide" some of these harmful memories from us. I'm going to say this often in this book: our brain's main function is to keep us alive. The cognitive abilities our brain has are only accessible once the organism is feeling safe, and so it makes sense to bury or not store memories that are particularly painful. My guess is that if you have harmful behavior patterns as an adult and can find no evidence in your childhood, then it's best to not even try and access those memories. They're hidden for a reason.

Sometimes though, as you start to become stronger through the process of healing, your brain might start to "release" more of the memories—not as concrete film reels, but more as sensations, flashbacks, or even "thoughts." This is because a lot of our childhood memories are actually stored as implicit memories. These are not "picture memories" and are instead stored as sensations and feelings. Recall how sometimes a smell triggers a whole memory for us. We're not even always sure what the memory is, or we have only a vague recollection of it, but the sense of smell being triggered is much stronger.

These memories create "procedural memory"—as in, what procedure must be followed when this memory is triggered. For example, many of us have procedural memory when it comes to dealing with young kids based on how we were dealt with as children. We don't even think twice about hitting them or screaming at them when we're stressed/triggered. In order for us to heal, we will have to become aware of being triggered and work on our reactions so that we can build a new "procedural memory" or new neural pathways.

Finally, there's a third explanation for why we might struggle to remember how or why our childhood is relevant. Our brains don't really develop explicit memory until age four or five[20] and by then, a lot of synaptic pruning has already happened. This means our brain has already built the highways it needed to navigate different situations in life.

For example, a woman allows her mother-in-law to boss her around because she only has one way to exist in a relationship: try and make the person in authority happy at my own cost. It stands to reason why repeatedly allowing someone to treat you poorly will result in a very unhappy life. But where was this pattern learned? What prevents this woman from walking away every time her mother-in-law or spouse get abusive? My clients are often shocked when I tell them they're allowed to walk away from anyone who is being unkind. "But won't that be disrespect?" The irony breaks my heart. In other words, they learned early on that it is ok to allow others to disrespect them at the cost of their own dignity and peace if they want to be accepted.

The truth is that if the same woman was raised with real love, she would have zero tolerance for being treated poorly. She would not allow herself to be treated this way. She would hold up her hand and say, "It's not ok to speak to me like that" and if this behavior was repeated, she would walk away from the situation. Her secure attachment to her parents would have taught her that she doesn't need to lose her dignity in order to be accepted, and those same parents are still a source of support and unconditional love. People whose parents were genuinely warm, authoritative, and kind are secure about themselves, resilient when life demands difficult decisions, and kind to themselves, too.

I hope that it's making sense to you why our childhood experiences are so relevant to our current lives. The following quote by Dr. Siegel, in *The Whole-Brain Child*,[21] beautifully summarizes all the concepts I've discussed in this section and why understanding our childhood is central to our healing and cycle-breaker parenting:

> By integrating your implicit and explicit memories and
> by shining the light of awareness on difficult moments

from your past, you can gain insight into how your past is impacting your relationship with your children. You can remain watchful for how your issues are affecting your own mood, as well as, how your kids feel. When you feel incompetent, frustrated, or overly reactive, you can look at what's behind those feelings and explore whether they are connected to something in your past. Then you can bring your former experiences into the present and weave them into the larger story of your life. When you do that, you can be free to be the kind of parent you want to be. You can make sense of your own life, which will help your kids do the same with theirs.

Landmines Everywhere

"Your triggers are pathways to your wounds.
The stimulus is only a door."

—Sanhita Baruah

WHAT ARE TRIGGERS?

Triggers are "buttons" connected to the past. "Pressing" them activates your "trauma story" or "trauma response" that, in turn, incites a reaction from us that seems totally disproportionate for that situation. We already briefly covered this concept in Science of Trauma section but it bears a more detailed discussion.

Imagine that you text your friend and she doesn't write back right away. Her failure to immediately reply triggers your trauma story of being rejected in the past by other friends, perhaps being excluded by your siblings, and so ANS attaches a meaning to that: "See? She doesn't want to be your friend . . . probably because you said xyz." You subconsciously accept this story and start "stalking" your friend online while minutely examining everything you might have said to her in the last 24 hours. You see that she updated her Facebook status. This provides "evidence" for your trauma story: "So she's definitely got her phone on her but won't reply to me . . ."

Now you're starting to experience some big feelings: rejection, disappointment, and perhaps even some humiliation. You had texted her so excitedly. You had wanted to spend more time with her, and she's completely ignoring your message.

Do you see what's happening? This was a small incident: a friend has not responded to a text. In reality, there could be a vast number of reasons why she didn't (yes, even while updating her Facebook status). Has there been a time when you delayed responding to her? Probably yes. And yet, that stimulus of not receiving an immediate answer has triggered a chain reaction of sending you spiraling down a dark path where you've made a horrible and unforgivable mistake, and now your friend doesn't love you.

As far as ANS is concerned:

Not receiving immediate reply = I have done something horrible = My friend now hates me

Some people can also have a similar but opposite equation:

Not receiving immediate reply = Who does she think she is? = I now hate her (who needs her anyway?)

Whoa!

Do you see how that worked?

Now, my guess is, if this is you, you most probably had a caretaker/parent who punished you through silent treatment. As a child, you weren't really sure what you had done wrong. All you knew was that your parent was ignoring you. You're left scrambling trying to figure out what you did wrong. Either you tried to make it up to them by being "extra good" and it worked, so you learned that all you have to do to be worthy of love is to accept that you've done something terribly wrong and now you must make up for it. Or, even doing this didn't get you the 'love' back so now you have no option but to pretend you don't care and that you can survive without love and connection. Your best friend then, when faced with hurt or disappointment in a relationship, is the wall that you can build to protect yourself.

Eckhart Tolle gives one of the best descriptions of a trigger I've ever read even though he doesn't actually use the word. He uses the phrase "pain body," which is as good a descriptor as any:

> [E]very emotional pain that you experience leaves behind a residue of pain that lives on in you. It merges with the pain from the past, which was already there, and becomes lodged in your mind and body. This, of course, includes the pain you suffered as a child, caused by the unconsciousness of the world into which you were born.
>
> This accumulated pain is a negative energy field that occupies your body and mind. If you look on it as an invisible entity in its own right, you are getting quite close to the truth. It's the emotional pain-body.[22]

He further goes on to explain how this "pain body" isn't necessarily 'activated' all the time. In other words, most people aren't operating from their triggers all the time. Go back to the autonomic ladder in the previous section (The Science of Trauma). I explained how most of us go up and down the ladder several times throughout the day and this is totally normal. What indicates intense unresolved trauma is when some people are operating from their pain body or triggers a vast majority of the time. That is, they're perpetually stuck in one area of the ladder (either the red or blue zone). It's almost as if they have no green zone to begin with.

Like Tolle says, for such people, "even a thought or an innocent remark made by someone close to you" can trigger the pain body. Maybe you know someone like this or perhaps you're thinking you are like this. For such people, life is one long series of painful incidents. Your niece not calling you makes you think she hates you. Your brother buying his wife a present makes you feel like he doesn't care about you. Your friend going out with another friend makes you believe she's just stringing you along. Your teen son using your tools without your permission is violating you. Your daughter not making her bed is disrespecting you. Anything and everything is a trigger.

Can you see how so many of the above triggers are rampant in Pakistani culture? How trauma shows up in everyday lives for our people, ravages their lives, and creates unnecessary misunderstandings and heartaches?

Healing ourselves and our communities is tantamount to bringing change in our beloved nation. Good news is, no matter how frequently we get triggered, we can always heal the pain body. We can create our green zone out of thin air.

It's a tall order with a nation like ours, wrought with multi-tiered traumas, but in my work, I daily see my amazing clients accomplish this monumental task.

IDENTIFYING WHEN YOU'RE BEING TRIGGERED

From the above examples, you can see that getting triggered doesn't necessarily result in anger (which is how most people view the idea of being triggered). Any big feelings that don't seem to make sense can be the outcome of a trigger. You might find yourself saying things like,

"I don't know what happened . . . all of a sudden I was screaming at my son!"

"I don't understand why I'm overreacting!"

"I know I shouldn't be sad, but I can't stop crying!"

"Before I knew what I'd done, I'd hit my spouse/child etc." (This kind of hitting is unintentional and comes from someone who doesn't believe in violence as a legitimate mode of communication with anyone.)

Whenever you detect big feelings that don't seem to make sense to you, it's helpful to look for the trauma story and get curious about what's happening for you. Notice, without judgment, any big feelings that come up: anger, shame, sudden tears, etc. and continue to process them using the worksheet in appendix B.

MANAGING THE TRIGGERS

Let's do a walkthrough of an example that I think many of you might be able to relate to.

My eldest was about four years old, and I had been asking him to come to the bathroom before he had an accident. At first, he was ignoring me because he was playing with his little car garage toy, but when my voice got louder, he looked up and said, "No!" This instantly made my voice escalate to a scary level and I said, "Stop disrespecting me! How dare you!" and I felt this red-hot ball of anger in my chest. I immediately wanted to hit him and maybe I even would have if he hadn't suddenly said, "What is disrespectful? What does that mean?"

This clearly innocent remark from him immediately dissolved my pain body and I realized he had no intention to "disrespect" me. He was merely playing and when I kept commanding him to do something, he slid down the ladder and said no in the dysregulated state of the red zone. That, in fact, my own dysregulation had caused him to be dysregulated.

This is a crucial point—lots of parents believe (myself included before I embarked on this journey) that what triggers them is their child's refusal to listen to them. I want to show you that this is not the case by filling out the triggers worksheet. Imagine if I had this tool at that time, I'd have taken a break from the situation and stepped away to evaluate my trigger.

What exactly am I feeling right now?

I'm feeling disrespected

What is the story I'm telling myself right now?

How dare my son disrespect me. Do I not have any authority here? Does he take me for a fool?

What's the trauma story here?

I felt out of control, like I had no autonomy. If I had responded this way to my parents, I'd already be getting smacked. I give him so much freedom and he's still not respecting me.

You might need to pause here and practice some self-compassion before you'll be able to do the next steps. Self-compassion helps us move up the ladder into the green zone so we can think more clearly.

What are the facts of the situation?

I asked my son to go to the bathroom while he was playing and I didn't offer him a choice or any help. I just kept getting louder, which dysregulated him.

Does my story have evidence in the present?

It's not that he's not respecting me . . . he didn't even know what "disrespectful" means.

If not, what's a healthier way of looking at this situation that allows me to stay in control?

He got dysregulated and confused by my anger. If I had stayed calm, slowed down a bit to respect his play, he would've just cooperated with me.

At the time, I didn't know any of this, but I did some of this work mentally each time I was triggered. It was very hard to practice self-compassion because I always felt so ashamed of my unkind behavior. I'd sworn that I'd be a gentle and kind parent and yet these moments kept happening. Over time though, I'm happy to report that my triggers did keep decreasing and their intensity has lessened enormously. Now I almost never get into that blinding kind of rage episode I shared at the beginning. That doesn't mean I'm a perfect parent, but it means that I do a vast majority of my parenting from the green zone, and when I do slip down the ladder, I can quickly climb back up. And of course, I apologize to my kids on the way up.

Now, you might have some difficulty even filling out this worksheet in the beginning of your journey. This is because the conditioning of so many years and the dissociation from painful childhood experiences can make it difficult for us to even know what our trauma story is, or how we're feeling and what we're thinking. I'd say just fill out the worksheet to the best of your ability and keep adding to it as you go further in your healing journey. The next chapter will also teach you how to reconnect with your story and your feelings. At the end of the day, we all need more practice. We're cycle breakers, none of us are very good when we start out because we have zero practice but with time, we will strengthen those new synapses until they become our new normal.

Finding Safety and Settlement

Moving to America was not anything that it was supposed to be. I had never wanted to move in the first place, which is a strange thing for a Pakistani to say anyhow. Most Pakistanis would never pass up the opportunity to move to America. America is the ultimate dream for many Pakistanis, and I'm not even talking about the ones who have financial struggles. America is the "Final Frontier," as my American cousin jokingly put it when she tried to help me find the right words for how so many Pakistanis seem to view it. I'm sure there are many people who immigrate there and find it to be everything they dreamt of. Unfortunately, this was not the case for me, and this was something I had always known.

I had requested my parents to only look into prospective proposals of men who were residing in Pakistan. My dad was very understanding of this and he reiterated to my mom that he had raised me to only focus on my career and not be chained to housework, which is inevitable if you move to a country where there is no house help. However, my mom, no doubt, had her own reasons for pushing me to accept this latest proposal. She would get so disappointed in me every time I turned down a proposal that eventually I said yes out of guilt. Don't get me wrong, I have no regrets and I'd marry my husband all over again, but it was a difficult transition for me.

Everyone told me I was so lucky to be moving to the United States of America. I wanted to believe that. I really did. I felt the weight of living everyone's dream and it really was, *the* dream. I was supposed to be happy. It was all happening. I was getting married. I had found my knight in shining armor. Someone had come to save me.

I was saved. To the land of opportunity, no less. It was going to be amazing.

And for a while, it was. I mean, it was amazing to just be "free" at first. For the first time in my twenty-two years of life, I didn't have parents to answer to. For a Pakistani girl, this in itself is a dream come true. If you're a Pakistani woman reading this, you know exactly what I mean. How often are we told that we must wait for marriage to dye our hair, do our makeup, travel, go out with friends, etc.

So yes, the dream had arrived. The knight, the America, the freedom! It was all here.

So much so that the dingy, mice-infested apartment my husband moved me into seemed like a palace. It was in the "open basement" of the building located in a struggling part of town. The kind of town where apparently mice were part of the living conditions since our apartment office lady sternly rejected all our pleas to call exterminators.

"You're the only ones who complain," she'd say.

I didn't know enough at the time to know that that didn't mean others didn't have a mice problem, just that they were too used to them to complain.

My favorite thing about the apartment was the glass sliding door that looked on to the usually mowed grass outside. My husband had shown it to me on his webcam via MSN Messenger once before we were married and I had imagined it extending into beautiful green pastures that went on for miles. I imagined myself frolicking there, carefree and happy.

In reality, it was a few feet of grass that quickly turned into a grassy hill that dissolved into the scraggy woods from where you could see the CVS Pharmacy that I sometimes walked to for urgent shopping needs. It wasn't quite the green pastures I'd imagined, but the dream was still alive.

I could have all the canned drinks I ever wanted without my mom harping on about how much they cost. I didn't have to eat *salan roti* ever again without my dad lecturing me about the merits of Pakistani food. I could chat on Messenger all day to my friends who were considerably jealous of my move to America. After all, they didn't know about the mice. Or the somewhat dangerous neighborhood I lived in. Or the old, saved-from-the-dumpster furniture my husband had "decorated" our first-ever apartment with. (To give him credit, he wanted me to have a say in the purchase of the new furniture.)

All the same, I was happy to make my friends jealous. All they saw was that I had moved to America. What a dream come true! Also, I had such a "nice husband" who didn't shove me in the kitchen the first day of our marriage and didn't ask me to cook him and his brother a piping hot meal. My husband also didn't forbid me to chat with friends. I had made it! The dream had come alive! I was giddy with happiness. Who said marriage was hard? Everything was perfect!

Looking back now, I can see why it was such a shock to my nervous system when the dream started falling apart. The intense confusion, hurt, and shock I experienced back then, that seemed like such an overreaction to everyone around me, makes perfect sense in retrospect.

The dream first began to fall apart when I started to feel unsafe in my own home. When my brother-in-law who lived with us in our small two-bedroom apartment started getting upset with me for minor slights. His trauma lens seemed to interpret a lot of my seemingly harmless actions as threats to his safety. Not opening the windows when cooking and letting the smell out meant I was "destroying his sleep." When he got lost in the New York City subway after I gave him directions meant I purposefully misguided him. Walking ahead with my husband in Six Flags Theme Park to wait in line for a ride meant that I was "stealing his brother away." And all these messages his trauma lens conveyed to him were delivered to me with scathing anger, often in front of other people. My sincerest hope is that my brother-in-law has since been able to get help but at that time, his actions caused me and my marriage incredible damage.

At first, his attacks caused me to slide down into the blue zone because his intense fight response scared me and I would completely shut down. Eventually though I started going into my own fight response but with my husband. He'd so far been a quiet bystander, but he now started to speak and tell me that I needed to stay quiet and not have "such big reactions." His adherence to his family's strict code of loyalty hit me like a ton of bricks. I felt the harsh sting of betrayal and rejection, no doubt hitting where my original childhood wounds were.

I get it now. I get that families have different conflict styles. I get that some families value silence and peace over everything else. I also get how the grown children of such families have a lot of inert anger that comes gushing out at bystanders. My husband tried to teach me the same code of conduct. He'd respond to my anguished cries of help calmly: "If you just stay quiet and let him have his way, things will be ok." He responded to my crisis the only way he'd been taught: by minimizing, discounting, and pushing hard to pretend nothing happened.

Since then, he's been able to realize this, and we are repairing our relationship, and he's on his own healing journey, but at that time, my own faulty neuroception perceived his lack of action and requests to ignore his brother's behavior as a direct attack on me and I felt all the sharp edges of this abandonment. My trauma lens said to me, "You aren't worthy of defending. You aren't good enough."

Of course, this aligned well with the rhetoric I heard from all around me. A husband who isn't physically and verbally abusive automatically means you've hit the jackpot. Everybody you ever meet is going to remind you how lucky you are. I remember feeling utterly confused. Everyone around me kept telling me how lucky I was and yet I didn't feel lucky at all. I felt utterly alone and heartbroken. Even when I approached extended family members, they told me I was overreacting and that I was "too aggressive" and I should learn how to live with my brother-in-law peacefully by just ignoring his outbursts.

One night after my brother-in-law had screamed at me and my husband had stood quietly by, I couldn't bear the pain of it and left the apartment to find my breath. I remember standing outside under a star-filled sky and realizing that I really was absolutely alone. I remember thinking that if I somehow suddenly didn't exist, that no one would really care. How had my mom talked me into this marriage? Why did I fall for her emotional pleas to agree to this relationship? Is this what marriage meant? Allowing people to treat you horribly and "practicing patience"?

I also remember thinking that perhaps everyone was right and I really was ungrateful and "over-sensitive." What they didn't know and what I didn't know was that my reaction wasn't just to these events (which in retrospect were definitely not minute). My broken heart was a response to the dream falling apart. My reaction was to the stark juxtaposition of the dreams I had been raised with about marriage, womanhood, and America that were now shattering one by one like the four-by-four tiles being stripped from the floor I was standing on.

The feeling that I recall so vividly, even now, wasn't just the betrayal you'd feel at a husband's refusal to defend you or stand by you, or a brother-in-law you had thought was like a friend berating you in public places, or the relatives you'd thought were on your side but who ended up demonizing you instead. No, it wasn't any of those feelings. The feeling was that of teetering at the brink of an edge that gave way to a bottomless pit—a chasm of lost hopes and dreams from where there was no return.

Some fifteen plus years later, when I recalled all of this to Bill, my first ever male therapist, he nodded gravely and said, "So the trauma had begun again. The unpredictability, the poor treatment by people who were supposed to take care of you. You were essentially being retraumatized."

He was referring, of course, to my childhood. To my dad's PTSD and my mom's learned helplessness and their combined traumas that had left me feeling emotionally neglected with debilitating trauma I had been unpacking for a couple years already by the time I saw him. I thought I had known for a while and accepted how my childhood and subsequent life had been. I thought I had worked through a lot of the stuff and made peace with it. But my body had never experienced the kind of safety a skilled therapist provides.

Bill's words of affirmation released a deluge of tears and sobs that wracked my whole body—the kind that are indicative of your nervous system finally feeling safe enough to release the pain it had been holding on to. The kind of release that only comes from another human understanding us and giving words to our pain. This is what we call "feeling safe in our body" when we are no longer afraid to express what is arising from within. What had damaged me the most, you see, wasn't what had happened. It never is. What had cut so deeply was that I had been alone in it. For the twenty-two years that I was in my parents' home and then for the seventeen that I had been in America, I carried my pain alone. And that is the biggest trauma of all—feeling alone in our pain.

LESSONS FROM MY TRAUMA STORY

My life in America taught me three profound lessons of healing:

1. There are no knights in shining armors coming to save us. The only person who can save us, is us. Me, myself, and I.

2. There is no saving yourself without "a mirror"—the support of someone who has been brave enough to honor their own reality and will now help you see yourself the way you deserve.

3. Recovery means finding safety in our previously hurting bodies. We can't read about recovery or talk about it—we have to experience safety through new interactions.

ME, MYSELF, AND I

Recovery involves, in very simple words, filling that "parent-shaped" hole left in your heart, mind, and soul. We do that by "reparenting" ourselves while we parent our children! Reparenting means to see and acknowledge our "inner child"—that little us who's nervous system we're carrying around. That's why, for us to heal our nervous system, we have to learn how to meet the needs of our inner child. Let's discuss what this really means and what it looks like, practically speaking.

We come into this world with some needs apart from our physiological needs. This reproduction of Maslow's Hierarchy of Needs[23] gives you an idea of what I mean. At the very bottom are our physiological needs, followed by our need for safety, love and belonging, self-esteem, and self-actualization.

In my courses, I use a slight variation of this hierarchy of needs. I assume that anyone showing up in my courses or reading my book is in no danger of depriving their child of physiological needs. And as we've already ascertained, "love" is an oversimplified word, so I expand it to include "connection." I also think all of these needs allow us to start feeling safe in our bodies, so I don't limit the safety to one rung of the hierarchy and instead replace it with "boundaries," which specifically serve to protect us in relationships. Finally, I use the word "autonomy" for "esteem" and also include "validation" in our emotional needs. As you can see from my story, when people in my life failed to validate my experiences, I felt abandoned and alone.

Here is our substitute hierarchy of needs model that this book will follow.

As you can see, up top both pyramids is self-actualization because this is our goal. It's where we become a "secure adult" (more on this in chapter 2). Here are some attributes of having a secure attachment:

AS CHILDREN

- Separates from parent
- Seeks comfort from parents when frightened
- Greets return of parents with positive emotions
- Prefers parents to strangers

AS ADULTS

- Have trusting, lasting relationships
- Tend to have good self-esteem
- Share feelings with partners and friends
- Seek out social support[24]

FINDING SAFETY IN OUR BODIES

Of all the terms used to describe healing, my favorite is what author Resmaa Menakem uses. He calls it, "learning to settle in our bodies." Other experts also use the words, "feeling safe in our bodies." Throughout this book, we will learn different ways to settle our nervous systems and use our vagal brake to move between the various nervous system states. But, before we begin, I want to share a story of one of my most resilient clients with you.

When I first met Sadiya, she just wanted to know how to discipline her "out-of-control" five-year-old. According to her, he was extremely aggressive, explosive, and non-compliant. He routinely beat up his two-year-old brother and even his mother. Sadiya was so beside herself with stress and worry that she'd text me quite often in between our consults. She was also carrying around a lot of shame about hitting her son. She admitted that she had no idea what came over her and she often found herself senselessly beating him. My heart went out to her and I could tell right away that she herself doesn't feel safe in this world. Her own nervous system is "faulty" because of her lived experiences. She can't and won't become a safe person for her sweet boy until she can learn to feel safe within herself. I gently started investigating her story and encouraging her to tell her story. At first, she was hesitant but once she found me an empathetic listener, it all came pouring out.

Her late father had been incredibly abusive. If I had to guess, I'd say he definitely had a severe case of PTSD. He was in the military and had served in the Pakistan–India war. He had come back from war with his nervous system permanently stuck in the sympathetic state. He had explosive rage episodes where he physically and verbally assaulted his wife and two children (Sadiya being the younger one). Even in his calmest moments, his faulty neuroception made the world a scary place and he treated his innocent children as war enemies. I remember Sadiya once told me that she was even afraid to go in the kitchen and drink water when he was around. It wasn't so much that he'd attack her every time but that she didn't know what he'd do or when. He would also financially abuse them by refusing to pay their school tuitions because, again, he had no way of feeling safe with any human and perceived his own family as predators out to get him. She remembers drowning in shame at school because everyone seemed to notice that her clothes and shoes didn't match the house she lived in. Her mother would sew clothes to make ends meet for her children while her father showered money on relatives to create an impression of his generosity.

It was no wonder, then, that when she grew up and got married, any untoward sight or sound from her son also sent her nervous system into fight and flight. Her nervous system had no way to distinguish an innocent child's big feelings from a grown man's rage episodes and so it responded exactly in the same way . . . by sending her whole body into the survival mode that would serve her best—fight—and she'd end up hitting him.

"Trauma comes back not as a memory,
but as a reaction."

—Bessel Van Der Kolk, *The Body Keeps The Score*[25]

All of this was about three years ago. Sadiya is doing astonishingly well now. With just some support from me and a couple of friends, she has healed so much of her nervous system. She no longer gets debilitating panic attacks, she speaks confidently in public instead of cowering with fear like she used to in the past, and she has learned to take care of her needs by allowing herself to rest when she needs to and not be on the constant move (flight) to appease her survival mode. Most importantly though, her relationship with her now almost eight-year-old is a stark difference from what it was when I first met her. He no longer hits his brother and often demonstrates kindness. He's more vocal about his emotional experiences rather than being reactive. He doesn't push away his mom's hugs and kisses. He's starting to make friends and be more of the kid he always would've been if his mother hadn't been stuck in survival.

I have many, many clients like Sadiya. In fact, it's getting to know clients like Sadiya that made me even more interested in learning about trauma and studying it formally. I realized that Parent Coaching must have a trauma-informed approach. Healing is not just a top-down approach; that is, learning new ideas and knowledge is only one part of the equation. The bottom-up approach of honoring what's happening in the nervous system and learning to settle in our bodies is essential to true and long-lasting healing. Working with the Pakistani and South Asian community, I could bet, every time, that behind every child who's being beaten up in the name of discipline is a parent or two parents who were once that child too. Unless I address their trauma, hear their story, and help them reparent themselves, those beatings will never stop. Like we say in Anokhay Mentors, "Healed people heal others," because as you saw in Sadiya's story, once she started feeling safer in her own body, she could be a safe space for her sweet son. Since

Anokhay Mentors is a group coaching program, one of the most beautiful things to witness is that when many safe bodies come together to learn how to settle and heal together, there is simply no match for it.

Shame: The Inevitable Offspring of Trauma

"Shame works like the zoom lens on a camera. When we are feeling shame, the camera is zoomed in tight and all we see is our flawed selves, alone and struggling."

—Brené Brown, *The Gifts of Imperfection*[26]

Understanding exactly what shame is and how it manifests in our life is a non-negotiable part of healing. If you recall Siegel's quote from the previous section, he explained why children internalize the messages of shame and how these painful messages stick with us because they're essential for survival. That is, when children are repeatedly given the message that they're incompetent, "too much," "misbehaved," or just plain old "bad"—they hold on to these beliefs about themselves for the rest of their lives. Brené Brown is a shame researcher whose work has revolutionized our understanding of this difficult emotion. Let's look at her definition of shame,

> I define shame as the intensely painful feeling or experience of believing that we are flawed and therefore unworthy of love and belonging—something we've experienced, done, or failed to do makes us unworthy of connection.[27]

Shame should not be mistaken with guilt. There's an important difference between the two. You see, guilt is a helpful emotion that flashes a light on where we might've gone wrong and what we can do better. Guilt says, "You made a mistake" but shame says, "You *are* a mistake."

SHAME SAYS NO ONE IS GOOD ENOUGH

All my life, I had the perfect vision of the "perfect best friend."

First of all, she'd be someone who fawns over me like I'm her wounded pet any time I was hurting. She'd practically swoop in and rescue me from life's every hurt. In other words, a best friend in shining armor.

My other false assumption was that I'd see her and she'd see me, and we'd talk deep into the night and be besties forever after that. In other words, this connection would happen like a bolt of lightning. Love at first sight sort of thing.

But so far, all my expectations had been shattered by one friend or another. In fact, I would mentally check off friends in my head once I realized they didn't meet my criteria. I'd continue to be friends with some on a certain level but in my head, they had already disappointed me and weren't good enough.

Sahar was my childhood friend. With much aplomb and ceremony, I had awarded her the title of "My Best Friend." I showered upon her praise, gifts, and exclusive honors she had never asked for. It never seemed of relevance to me to find out or be curious about what she needed from me or this friendship. She fit my description of "a best friend" and that's all that seemed relevant. I remember her once gently trying to bring this to my attention by saying, "You give me a lot of importance but I don't really do anything special. You're always giving me gifts and saying nice things about me . . . I don't think I deserve any of them."

I remember being slightly taken aback. I didn't know what to make of her comments. In the back of my mind, I remember feeling like it was a disclaimer of sorts. Like small print at the bottom of a long agreement one must sign before proceeding with a subscription. "We accept no responsibility for the image you have created in your head. We accept no liability at the breakage of this image since we had no part in creating it."

Well, little good did that disclaimer do. In 2007, my husband and I visited Sahar and her husband in Vancouver, Canada. I had excitedly announced to her on the phone that we're coming to stay with them for ten days . . . I had thought it would be an amazing surprise and she'd jump for joy. That's not what happened.

If you remember from the previous chapter on triggers, one ironic and cruel manifestation of trauma is that it makes you almost incapable of considering other people's reality. The only thing that matters is you, yourself, and your reality. The truth of multiple realities is unfathomable to survivors of trauma.

When Sahar, who lived with her husband in a one-bedroom apartment, very understandably asked me how long our stay was going to be, I immediately felt the hot gooey trickle of shame.

"She doesn't really want me to visit."

"She's not happy that I'm coming."

"I shouldn't have planned this trip."

Those old messages of not feeling wanted and loved came flooding back. I tried to curtail my disappointment and told her ten days and she started telling me about the sleeping arrangements. Anyhow, we went to Vancouver and that initial feeling of not being wanted never left me despite Sahar's best efforts at hospitality. When we returned, I decided she wasn't worthy of my friendship and I told her as much. She could've said many things . . . that she had never really invited me in the first place and for an uninvited guest, she did the best she could. But she remained kind and said something that has always stuck in my mind for some reason. She said, "Maybe I couldn't love you the way you wanted . . . but I hope you'll understand one day that it's still the most amount of love I can give . . . for me, it's truly my best."

But her best wasn't good enough for me.

It never is.

No one can ever fill the parents-shaped hole left in our hearts. No one can ever make up for the love deficit left over and accumulated over a lifetime. That's why no one ever seems enough. No amount of love or care or concern ever seems enough and in fact, we mostly punish those who dare to try and fill that hole in any way at all.

It's almost as if our love-hungry heart clings on to those poor souls for dear life. It detects a source of pure, unconditional love, that was the forte of the parents, and demands more. And more. But a friend can't love us like a parent. It's not their job. So, we're setting them up for failure . . . plain and simple.

In this way, we end up sabotaging our most precious relationships and risk losing them forever.

I'm fortunate that Sahar's own parents are the kind who didn't leave that gap, so she was able to never hold my poor behaviors against me. She had been a childhood friend so maybe she saw where I was coming from or maybe she just chose to see the best in me . . . I don't know. Either way, she didn't give up on me or our friendship. She kept reaching out to me and about twelve years later or so, when I had finally started to heal, we were able to reconnect.

I was traveling to California to attend a retreat with Dr. Dan Siegel and Dr. Tina Bryson, authors of some of my favorite parenting books. Sahar warmly invited me to stay with her and I extended my stay in California a couple of days so I could accept her invitation. We had a lovely time together and, on our way back to drop me off at the airport, she was talking about a friend who was struggling with mental health issues and how she tries her best to be there for her, and anticipate moments of self-harm and intervene. Her kindness for this friend warmed my heart and I told her how happy I am for her friend who has someone like Sahar in her corner. Sahar responded to my comment with something I had never expected. She looked away towards the car window and almost said to herself, "But I couldn't do anything for you . . ." Her eyes watered up as she said this.

It broke my heart. Half from the joy of being seen by a loved one but also from the pain I had clearly caused her. Is this what we do? People like me? We make others feel like a failure even if they've tried their best? I fought off the shame that threatened to engulf me and stayed present for the moment.

I held her hand and told her she absolutely did everything she could do, and it wasn't her job to save me. She hadn't failed me, and I was incredibly grateful for all my childhood memories of a friendship like hers: stable, secure, and ever-present. Her home had been my safe haven. The calmness and predictability of her home and friendship had helped create some of my best memories from a childhood otherwise mostly deprived of them.

We've continued to be friends—the kind only old friends can, where you might not talk for months but when you do, it's like there was no gap. I feel lucky that she never gave up on me.

With Kate, I wasn't so lucky.

SHAME SAYS YOU ARE NEVER GOOD ENOUGH

Kate and I became friends on a Facebook group she created for women expecting twins in the fall of 2016. There were other women in the group, too, that I became close to as well, but Kate was different. She had that special ability I mentioned earlier to give the kind of unconditional, genuine love that one craves from one's parents. And sure enough, I repeated my self-sabotage pattern.

I expected more and more from her until I tired her out. The moment of reckoning came when a few of us from the Facebook group went to stay at Kate's place in LA once all our twins were a little older. It was supposed to be the best trip of my life. I was thrilled to finally belong. To be a part of the group where I was valued, loved, and respected. I was the only Muslim and brown woman in this group and yet I'd never felt more comfortable in it—such was the vibe of this group of women who built each other up and were so incredibly supportive.

How then, could I possibly screw this up? There's a cliché line you must've heard on social media memes: if you can't love yourself, you can't love anyone else.

As cliché as it is, it's also the truest thing ever said.

When I arrived in LA, it was my first time meeting these women in person. And it was my first time meeting Kate. When I saw this gorgeous blonde woman and her confidence and how much she was loved by everyone else, my first thought was, "There's no way she can love me. She's going to find out how terrible I am in reality and she'll stop being my friend."

And that's how I sealed my own fate. When wellness gurus encourage us to use positive self-talk . . . they're not lying. How we talk to ourselves becomes our reality. I literally willed this thought into existence and action. From that point onward, I saw everything Kate did or didn't do as evidence that I wasn't good enough for her. I had already presented myself with a hypothesis and now all it needed was proof. Oh, and there's always proof, let me assure you of that. Whenever we go looking for proof that we don't belong, we will always find it.

"Stop walking through the world looking for confirmation that you don't belong. You will always find it because you've made that your mission. Stop scouring people's faces for evidence that you're not enough. You will always find it because you've made that your goal. True belonging and self-worth are not goods; we don't negotiate their value with the world."

—Brené Brown, *Braving the Wilderness*[28]

Our nervous system is our friend and tries to always protect our reality. The problem happens when our trauma stories show up and masquerade as our reality.

I noticed every time Kate didn't talk to me and talked to others.

I noticed when she didn't want to sleep in the same room as me.

Or when she walked with so-and-so and not me.

Or when she didn't worry about what I wanted and gave others what they wanted.

The evidence was stacking up.

I wasn't worthy.

She didn't love me.

Shame had taken over, and like it wants to do, it hid all the signs of belonging I could have embraced. My shame played out my trauma story and only showed me evidence that aligned with that story.

I didn't notice her smiles and hugs.

I didn't notice her text to apologize to me for not being able to spend more exclusive time.

I didn't notice others being more demanding while I tried to disappear in the background.

I didn't notice myself shutting down.

I didn't notice her confusion and hurt at my withdrawn attitude.

I didn't notice her efforts to draw me out.

Or, maybe I did, but I wanted to punish her and used her attention to further withdraw.

It doesn't matter that I was drowning in my own shame of lack of self-worth. And that shame was making me do what it often does: shame and blame others.

When I got back from California, our friendship was never the same again. Kate was brave and honest enough to tell me that she had been surprised by my "real life" self. Instead of listening to her concerns, I had gotten defensive. Over time, we drifted apart—my own trauma story and shame had stood in the way of a beautiful friendship, once again. I had returned Kate's kindness and goodness with complaints, judgments, and criticisms because she had offered safety and love. When unconditional love is such an alien experience, it can engage our defense mechanisms, making us act from a place of fear and uncertainty.

That's the biggest irony of shame. It repeatedly tells us we aren't worthy of love and belonging even when those are the things we desire most in the world. Shame is much like tar. Sticky, thick, and gooey. The more you try to get rid of it, the more it sticks and spreads, leaving a messy trail of darkness wherever it goes.

BUILDING SHAME RESILIENCE

Brown tells us that even though shame is a part of everyone's life, it doesn't have to take over and ruin everything. It's an emotion and like all emotions, we don't demonize the emotion itself and instead try to make sense of it. What is it saying and why? How is it trying to take care of us and why? Once we can answer these questions with non-judgmental curiosity, we can manage our feelings of shame rather than letting them take the reins like I did in the above stories.

STEP 1: SHAME AWARENESS

Learn to recognize the signs of being in a "shame tunnel." The physical sensations can feel like being in the quagmire of quicksand. When I ask my workshop participants what shame feels like, they say some version of, "I want the earth to open up and swallow me!" The behavioral symptoms can be an inward turning in the form of overthinking, withdrawing, tuning out, or self-deprecation. They can also be outward-bound like blaming or shaming others. Parents often report feeling this way when they're driven to shaming their children. When we dig deeper into their feelings, we discover that it was their own shame of not being a "good enough" parent that made them be so unkind to their own child.

STEP 2: HEAR WHAT SHAME IS SAYING

Shame says,

> *There is something inherently wrong with you.*
> *No one wants to be around you.*
> *You're not worthy of love and belonging.*

Why does shame say these things? Because ironically, it's trying to protect us from ostracization. Shame tells us to make ourselves small, like I tried to do when I was in L.A. with my friends. Because, it reasons, if you make yourself small enough, then no one will be able to see you, and if no one can see you, then no one can see your ugliness and try to get rid of you.

Sometimes, shame tells us that if we can be loud and mean and blame others, then we can justify to ourselves why no one loves us, and we can have control over our own exile. In the absence of true connection, control can seem like a suitable replacement. This is also why so many parents end up being so controlling of their children. They have no role model for what true connection with a child looks like and their shame around not being good enough makes them think that controlling their child will surely result in a "good enough" child.

When we are aware of these messages that shame brings, we can acknowledge the arrival of them and use our inherent worth to remember that none of these things are true. That, in fact, we have as much right to be loved as anyone else. That it's ok to make mistakes and screw up. It's also a wonderful thing to model this shame resilience to our children.

STEP 3: EMPATHY KILLS SHAME

The process of healing allows us to dismantle the shame that intertwined itself with our identity. We learn to identify our shame stories and how they've impacted us. Doing so in the presence of an empathetic someone who is willing to say, "It's not just you . . . I've been there too," can remind us that we're not alone and it's very human to act and feel the way we did. This is what we can also do as parents when our kids screw up, share our own story of how we made the same mistake.

I remember one time when my son came home from school and instantly dissolved into tears in my lap.

"I made fun of my friend *accidentally* and my other friend said that's not cool. Now they all hate me and will never want to be my friend."

Ah, the classic shame story.

"Looks like you feel really bad about what you did and it's making you feel like no one will ever want to be your friend again," I offered helpfully.

He nodded.

"I've been there too . . . that exact feeling of *no one will ever want to be my friend again*," I said quietly.

"You *have?*" he said, incredulously. His eyes were wide with wonder, his body visibly flooded with relief. He wasn't alone. He wasn't a screw up.

I nodded and shared my story. We hugged. He decided to apologize to his friends. The world was alright again.

NOTES

1. Resmaa Menakem, *My Grandmother's Hands: Racialized Trauma and the Pathway to Mending Our Hearts and Bodies* (Central Recovery Press, 2017).
2. Nisid Hajari, *Midnight's Furies: The Deadly Legacy of India's Partition* (Houghton Mifflin Harcourt, 2015), 168.
3. Vazira Fazila-Yacoobali Zamindar, *The Long Partition and the Making of Modern South Asia* (Penguin Group, 2007).
4. Natalie Y. Gutierrez, *The Pain We Carry: Healing from Complex PTSD for People of Color* (New Harbinger Publications, Oct. 2022).
5. *Lagaan: Once Upon a Time in India*, directed by Ashutosh Gowariker (India: Aamir Khan Productions, 2001).
6. Resmaa Menakem, *My Grandmother's Hands: Racialized Trauma and the Pathway to Mending Our Hearts and Bodies* (Central Recovery Press, 2017).
7. National Center for Injury Prevention and Control, Division of Violence Prevention, "CDC-Kaiser ACE Study," *Centers for Disease Control and Prevention*, last reviewed 6 Apr. 2021, https://www.cdc.gov/violenceprevention/aces/about.html.
8. Stephern W. Porges, *The Pocket Guide to the Polyvagal Theory: The Transformative Power of Feeling Safe* (W. W. Norton & Company, 2017).
9. K Thug, "Best Thug dad in the (globe emoji)," *YouTube*, Jul 21, 2019, https://www.youtube.com/watch?v=UKAXqMjvj-w
10. Mona Delahooke, *Beyond Behaviors: Using Brain Science and Compassion to Understand and Solve Children's Behavioral Challenges* (PESI Publishing & Media, 2019).
11. Deborah A. Dana, *Polyvagal Theory in Therapy: Engaging the Rhythm of Regulation* (W. W. Norton, 2018).
12. Nadine Burke Harris, *The Deepest Well: Healing the Long-term Effects of Childhood Adversity* (Houghton Mifflin Harcourt, 2018), xv.
13. Lise Eliot, *What's Going on in There? How the Brain and Mind Develop in the First Five Years of Life* (Random House Publishing Group, 2000), 32.
14. Nadine Burke Harris, "How childhood trauma affects health across a lifetime," *YouTube*, Feb 17, 2015, https://www.youtube.com/watch?v=95ovIJ3dsNk&t=4s.
15. Felitti VJ, Anda RF, Nordenberg D, Williamson DF, Spitz AM, Edwards V, Koss MP, Marks JS. "Relationship of childhood abuse and household dysfunction to many of the leading causes of death in adults. The Adverse Childhood Experiences (ACE) Study." *Am J Prev Med*. 1998 May;14(4):245-58. doi: 10.1016/s0749-3797(98)00017-8. PMID: 9635069.
16. *Turning Red,* directed by Domee Shi (United States: Walt Disney Pictures and Pixar Animation Studios, 2022).
17. bell hooks, *All About Love: New Visions* (HarperCollins, 2000).
18. bell hooks, *All About Love: New Visions* (HarperCollins, 2000).
19. Daniel J. Siegel, *Mindsight: The New Science of Personal Transformation* (Random House Publishing Group, 2010), 196.
20. Tania Johnson, *Childhood Brain Development: Interpersonal Neurobiology Made Easy*, https://instituteofchildpsychology.com/product/making-sense-of-child-brain-development/.

21. Daniel J. Siegel, *The Whole-Brain Child: 12 Revolutionary Strategies to Nurture Your Child's Developing Mind* (Random House Publishing Group, 2012), 91.

22. Eckhart Tolle, *The Power of Now: A Guide to Spiritual Enlightenment* (New World Library, 2010), 36.

23. Saul Mcleod, "Maslow's Hierarchy of Needs," *Simply Psychology*, 24 Nov. 2023, https://www.simplypsychology.org/maslow.html.

24. Kendra Cherry, "The Different Types of Attachment Styles," *Verywell Mind*, 26 May 2022, https://www.verywellmind.com/attachment-styles-2795344.

25. Bessel Van Der Kolk, *The Body Keeps the Score: Brain, Mind, and Body in the Healing of Trauma* (Penguin Publishing Group, 2014).

26. Brené Brown, *The Gifts of Imperfection: Let Go of Who You Think You're Supposed to Be and Embrace Who You Are* (Hazelden Publishing, 2010), 68.

27. Brené Brown, *I Thought It Was Just Me: Women Reclaiming Power and Courage in a Culture of Shame* (Gotham, 2007).

28. Brené Brown, *Braving the Wilderness: The Quest for True Belonging and the Courage to Stand* (Random House Publishing Group, 2017).

CHAPTER 2

CONNECTION—THE ESSENCE OF BEING HUMAN

"If all the world hated you and believed you wicked, while your own conscience approved of you and absolved you from guilt, you would not be without friends."

—Charlotte Brontë, *Jane Eyre*

The Story Inside Me

"There is no greater agony than bearing an untold story inside you."

—Maya Angelou

Gulrukh was one of my first in-person clients in my Islamabad office. Like most of my clients, she wanted to see me because of her son. She felt he might be autistic or ADHD (frequent concerns). Except, only 5% of her conversation was about her son. Most of it was about her mother-in-law and husband. They seemed to believe that there was something wrong with the child. And that made Gulrukh feel inadequate and not good enough. She was the reason everything was wrong with her son.

For the next six of her eight sessions, she only spoke about all the ways her husband and mother-in-law had made her feel less than since the day she was married. The food she cooked wasn't good enough. The clothes she ironed weren't smooth enough. Her desire to see her family more than once a month wasn't appropriate enough. So much so, that even her wish to grab a *challi* (corn) on their way home from work was "asking too much" for her husband.

I listened to all her stories. They came fast and furious. The six years she'd been married was rife with stories of their mistreatment, unkindness, and entitlement. I was definitely proud of her for being able to tell her stories, but at the same time, I was curious about her desire to share more and more stories instead of moving on to the natural next state of our storytelling . . . resolution and problem-solving. So, one day, as she finished telling yet another story of her mother-in-law's unkindness, I said to Gulrukh,

"Sounds like she was, once again, accusing you of something you hadn't done and ignoring your actual helpfulness . . ."

"Yes, exactly! Why can't she see that I'm a good person who genuinely wanted to be kind to her but I'm tired now!"

"Do you believe that?" I asked her.

"Believe what?" she asked, a bit confused.

"That you are most definitely a genuinely kind person, but at this time, due to her behaviors, you're unable to practice more kindness?"

She suddenly became quiet. And that look came over her. The look that tells me I've said something that has hit its mark.

"No . . . I don't . . ." she said quietly.

"Ahh . . . that must be hard, Gulrukh. For you to not be able to believe in your own kindness."

Her eyes teared up.

"Do you think I'm a good person? Because I feel like I'm not. Maybe if I was a good person, my husband would like me better and defend me."

There it was. The self-doubt, the pain, the "I'm not good enough" story so many of us tell ourselves.

WHEN WE STRUGGLE TO OWN OUR STORY

The stories of oppression and injustice we speak with our words are only a wounded cry for validation that we are good. We want someone, *anyone* to help us see ourselves as good. Ultimately, though, we have to validate our own story before we can really, truly, get to the bottom of it all. The irony is that when we aren't ready to own our own story, we aren't even interested in the people who are happy to validate our story for us.

As I shared in the last chapter, for years after moving to United States, I struggled to adjust there. As you can see, my story was that the move made me incredibly unhappy and lonely. I felt like a ship lost at sea, wandering aimlessly on moonless nights, looking for a shore and finding none. Technically, this is very black and white. After all, who can know better than myself how I truly felt and how much it impacted me? Unfortunately, this is not how our brains work. We seek connection from those that surround us by sharing our stories— it's a very human need. And most people who surround us have their own stories that often prevent them from honoring ours.

As an outcome, we start doubting our own stories, disconnecting from our own reality as well.

For example, when I moved to the U.S. and was in pain, the first person I turned to for connection was my husband, but like most typically raised Pakistani men, he didn't have the first clue on how to listen to my story or sit with me in my pain. Whenever I shared how difficult things were for me, he panicked and dissolved into his own shame. In retrospect, I can see that he felt like he was a "bad husband" who couldn't "fix" his wife's feelings and the shame made him withdraw and shut down. His sliding down the ladder into the blue zone (shutdown) was perceived by my broken heart as rejection and dismissal. I sank deeper into my own loneliness.

When I shared my story with other family members or friends, many of them also struggled to understand what I was talking about. Perhaps me being so open and honest about how I felt as an immigrant was a hard truth no one wanted to hear or perhaps some people had been able to forget what it was like when they first immigrated. Whatever it was, I felt more and more diminished by my story. It didn't seem like anyone truly cared or understood.

Many years later when I learned how to tell my own story even if it was dismissed or minimized by others, I realized that there was no deficit of people willing to hear my story and accept my reality. But the reason I hadn't believed them was because I didn't truly believe I deserved to *have* a story. My underlying beliefs had gotten in the way of me even noticing the people who were willing to understand me. I thought:

- My feelings aren't valid enough.
- Perhaps I'm ungrateful.

- It's all in my head.
- If I were a good wife, I'd be happy.
- If I were a good Muslim, I'd be grateful.

What had truly stood in the way of me telling my story was my own disconnection to myself. This is why I had been paying attention only to the people who invalidated me and dismissed my story. This is also my clients' favorite question to me when I talk about this concept, "Why do we take those who believe us for granted? Why are we so fixated in trying to convince the ones who, most likely, will never validate our story?"

The answer is simple. We lean towards those whose truth aligns with our own truth and when we're hustling for self-worth, our truth is that our story is not believable. That *we* are not believable. That we are not enough. That *we* are simply not good enough. And so we go ahead and dismiss everyone who wants to believe us and sees us as good enough and we run after those who will, most likely, never be happy with us.

So, it's a catch-22, isn't it? Until we can learn to tell and believe our own story, we can't foster meaningful connections and we will keep running after people who minimize and invalidate us. Thus, our connection to others can only be as deep as our connection to ourselves.

BUT I HAVE THE WORST MEMORY!

Ultimately, telling our story is one of the most powerful ways to regain ownership of our life. This is also the first module of Anokhay Mentors. The participants are intrigued and always ask me what "story" even means. They say things like "I don't even remember my childhood!" "I have the worst memory!" etc.

Let's first examine why so many of us don't have a lot of childhood memories. You might recall from chapter one that our brains have very good reasons for not storing certain memories. When we start our healing journey, we often don't have many concrete memories that can make us feel like some kind of failure. "What's wrong with me! I can't even remember my childhood!" or "All I remember is having a good childhood . . . there's no real story to tell here . . . What am I missing?" Ironically, this very narrative of "something is wrong with me" tells us a story. It tells us that our brain has done a wonderful job of helping us survive by blocking out whatever wasn't helpful. As you continue on your journey and become stronger, you'll unblock some memories. Enough to help you move forward and leave the baggage you've been carrying from your untold story.

HOW DO I TELL MY STORY ANYWAY?

Your story is anything that happened to you at any time. The purpose of "telling your story" is that you take the narrative back in your hands. In simple words, we believe the version we're telling. We believe the feelings, thoughts, and perspectives we have and know that our version of these things is what truly matters in how our life unfolds. Let's divvy it up into three steps:

1. Share and own your feelings
2. Choose your audience
3. Practice your free will
4. Share and own your feelings

Do you feel like your mother-in-law is mean to you even though others insist she's a saint?

Well then, we will go by your experience of her because that's what's relevant to your story. It's possible that she really is a "saint" to the people who are calling her that, but it's also true that she's mean and unkind to you.

Do you feel like being a stay-at-home mom is wonderful and fulfilling even though everyone says women should also have a career?

Well then, you should live according to your experience and enjoy being a stay-at-home mom because that's what's relevant to your life.

Do you feel like having a career and waiting to have children is the right choice for you, and your spouse is on the same page, but everyone is lecturing you that it's a bad choice?

Well then, you should focus on your career and not have kids.

1. CHOOSE YOUR AUDIENCE

So does that mean we shouldn't care about what anyone thinks and just live to please ourselves? No, not at all. As I mentioned in the beginning of this chapter, human connection is vital for our thriving existence. Decide who is worthy of your stories. Think back to the autonomic ladder's green zone. Who are the people whose presence keeps you in the green zone and doesn't threaten to push you down the ladder into red or blue zones? Those are your safe people. Usually, there's no more than two or three people in anyone's life, so don't be discouraged if you realize that most people in your life aren't safe. As you move along in your healing journey, you'll expand your safe circle and shrink your unsafe herd.

2. PRACTICE FREE WILL

Have you ever noticed that when something scary or disturbing happens to little children, they want to talk about it again and again? This is their attempt at telling their story and they do so intuitively because their brain knows that this is how you move through something difficult—by talking about it with a safe person. You'll also notice that once children have done this a few times, they move on.

The purpose of telling our story is to ground ourselves in our reality, to truly connect with our experience, and find out what we were needing. Once we discover what we need, we should then go ahead and give ourselves what we needed so we can move through our story instead of staying stuck in it. When we aren't able to show ourselves mercy by giving ourselves what we need, we can remain caught up in the past and keep collecting many regrets along the way. Every story has a conflict—figure out what yours is and how you can resolve it.

Let's consider the above examples and see how the storytellers might move through their story by identifying the conflict and resolving it using your inner wisdom:

1. Do you feel like your mother-in-law is mean to you even though others insist she's a saint?
    Conflict: I have to accept that I don't have the best relationship with my mother-in-law and in my culture, this is somehow my fault.
    Inner wisdom: It's not really my fault because I tried my best. Time to create some boundaries. (More on the how-to of this in the next chapter.)

2. Do you feel like being a stay-at-home mom is wonderful and fulfilling even though everyone says women should also have a career?

    Conflict: What if everyone is right and I will one day regret killing my career and wasting my education?

    Inner Wisdom: Education is never wasted. I can take small steps that will help me with my career once I'm ready to step into the workforce.

3. Do you feel like having a career and waiting to have children is the right choice for you, and your spouse is on the same page, but everyone is lecturing you that it's a bad choice?

    Conflict: What if everyone is right and I won't be able to have children later?

    Inner Wisdom: There is no science to support the claim that delaying having children results in infertility. If my biological clock is ticking, I can look into embryo freezing. I'm also ok with adopting.

At the end of the day, this is your story, and you get to write how it goes. There are no wrong answers here.

Why On Earth Do I Need to Connect to Myself?

Hadeeqa was one of my gentlest clients. She was the Executive Director of a big finance firm in London, UK. Her job was incredibly stressful and demanding, but I could tell she was really proud of herself for getting as far as she had. That's why I was so surprised when she told me she was leaving her job one day.

"Tell me what's happening," I said, using my typical "let's deep dive" phrase.

"I guess I'm just really angry at my boss which I know I shouldn't be . . ."

"Pause! You 'shouldn't be' feeling an emotion? Is that what I just heard?" I cut her off, wanting to know more about what's causing her to judge her own feelings.

"Well, I mean, he's my boss and he's a nice person . . . but I'm just so mad at how he responds every time I ask for time off . . . which I rarely do. But he makes me feel like I'm doing something wrong when I ask for time off . . . and that makes me angry at him even though he's a nice person . . ."

I hold up my hand to pause her again.

"Hadeeqa, I wanna get to the bottom of whatever you're feeling. I'm worried we never will because you're having trouble allowing for your anger."

"What do you mean? I *am* allowing it, aren't I? I'm here talking about it . . ."

"And for which I'm really glad . . . tell me more about why you're saying over and over that he's a nice person. Do you feel like I'm going to judge him?"

"Well, no. I'm worried you'll judge me because I'm being so mean."

"Tell me what makes you think I will judge you for sharing your concerns about your boss."

"Sharing my concerns? Yeah, I guess that's what I'm doing . . . so you know that I'm not the kind of person who goes around like millennials complaining about their boss?"

"Like millennials?"

"Yeah, don't you know? People say that millennials are really flaky and fragile and can't survive in a work environment.

I'm not like that though. I like my boss but when I asked him for time off because my mom was sick, he denied it and I've never gotten over that. I couldn't take care of my mom because of him . . . she died wishing she could have more time with me and now I never can . . ."

And with that, her voice broke and she started to cry quietly.

I finally understood what was happening.

"So, your anger at your boss . . . is really your grief about your mother's loss . . ."

She nodded, still crying.

"Tell me what your tears are saying," I asked her gently.

"That I miss my mom . . . and wish I'd spent more time with her."

"Ah . . . so some regret is showing up there too," I observed.

She nodded again.

I waited for her to settle down a bit.

Then I said, "Thank you for sharing that, Hadeeqa; that wasn't easy for you."

"No, it wasn't . . . I never really wanted to admit that I regret how I showed up for my mom . . . or didn't show up for her . . . just because of my stupid job."

We went on to talk about how and why it hadn't been as simple as not taking time off from the "stupid job" and how hard she'd worked to even get that job and climb that corporate ladder—and that leaving the job would've also meant losing her salary, which she had used to get the best care for her uninsured mom. We also talked about how she had never found the courage to explain to her boss that her mom had a terminal illness and was on her deathbed and not just sick with a common illness. Over the course of our sessions, she was able to sort through her grief and regret and forgive herself and understand that she really did do her best for her mom. She was able to manage her feelings towards her boss so she didn't have to leave her hard-earned job.

When our sessions ended, she thanked me for helping her shed her baggage, but the truth was that all I did was help her reconnect with herself. Everything she'd needed to move on from the great loss of a parent's death was already inside her, but she wasn't able to connect with it. She kept blocking the feelings of grief and regret that were knocking on her door. Those feelings were hiding behind anger and her worry about "acting like a millennial," and so, instead of allowing for her anger, she kept trying to justify it away.

The problem is, if we don't allow for anger, then how can we manage it?

"What do we do with the mad?" the kids ask Mr. Rogers's character in *A Beautiful Day in the Neighborhood*, and he gives us the solution.

"Anything that's human is mentionable, and anything that is mentionable can be more manageable."[1]

We have to be able to talk about our anger without feeling guilty. Without being able to talk about what we're feeling, there's no way to get through that feeling and on the other side. We can do this by learning how to sit with our feelings.

RAIN: LEARNING THE SKILL OF SITTING WITH FEELINGS

RAIN is an acronym used by Tara Brach for the practice of leaning into our feelings and resolving them. The first order of business, 'R,' stands for *recognizing* the feeling or naming it correctly. I use the Feelings Wheel (Appendix C) with my clients for this since most people (including myself) have a hard time correctly naming what we're feeling. Start with the inner most circle and then move to the outer circle. Pick the feeling word as close to what you can sense as possible.

Next up, 'A,' is for *allow*. How do we not allow feelings? you ask. Usually when people feel an uncomfortable emotion like jealousy, anger, frustration, ingratitude, resentment, or even dislike, they usually try to convince themselves that feeling such an emotion is "bad" and "good people/Muslims" don't feel these emotions just as Hadeeqa felt that she shouldn't feel angry at her boss. They then try to talk themselves out of the feeling.

There's no reason for me to be jealous.

I have so many blessings.

I should be grateful.

What's wrong with me? Why do I get so angry?

Anger is not healthy.

Why am I getting so frustrated?

I need to learn patience.

You see, each feeling is a messenger and tells the story of a need. If we're willing to hear, it gives us vital information about what our body, mind, and soul are in need of.

Next, we have 'I' for *Investigate*. This is getting more curious about the message it brings.

For example, jealousy often says that we are missing something and there are always healthy ways to seek that which we miss or to process that feeling in some other way that's beneficial. Processing a feeling begins with honoring it like a welcome "houseguest," as Rumi says in my favorite poem of his:

The dark thought, the shame, the malice,
meet them at the door laughing,
and invite them in.
Be grateful for whoever comes,
because each has been sent
as a guide from beyond.[2]

So ask your feeling, "And what message do you bring for me today?" Ask it with openness and kindness, and no judgment like how I asked Hadeeqa to get curious about her anger. Then listen to the message and honor it as best as you can.

"Ah so Jealousy, you're saying you too wish you could do everything as well as your SIL (sister-in-law)."

"Yes . . . but am I bad?"

"No, no, Jealousy, you're not bad. You just are. Tell me more about the SIL."

"I'm here to say that everyone says nice things about her and no one appreciates you. After all, you both reside in this home and both do your best and yet everyone seems to like her more . . . why do you think that is?"

"Ahh, because she's good with boundaries. She hasn't allowed people to be mean to her, but I was always trying to be nice . . . I didn't wanna stand up for myself because I wanted to keep peace."

"Looks like keeping peace has cost you your own inner peace."

Here, jealousy has brought us an important message that our needs are not being met and we're feeling violated and disrespected. Now we want to nurture this feeling, figure out what it needs from us. Let the inner dialogue continue:

"Jealousy, how can I nurture you? What are you needing from me?"

"Perhaps it's time to also start setting some boundaries, even if it makes some people unhappy . . . you have to take care of yourself so that I don't come knocking again . . ."

"Yes, I think so . . . but . . ."

"Oh look, here's fear now. I'm gonna take my leave."

Jealousy is replaced by fear.

"Well hello, Fear . . . what message do you bring?"

"I say that you're afraid that people will say you're not as nice as you pretended to be."

"Yes. But I wasn't pretending. I really was nice . . . I just wanted everyone to be happy . . ."

"Right . . . and how did that go?"

"Not too well. Most people still aren't happy with me . . . and now I'm very unhappy too and Jealousy visits more and more."

"Ah yes . . . so shall you and I be friends? Unlike Jealousy, I'm here to stay because you haven't stood up for yourself before so when you do, I'll be with you, but I won't stop you . . . unless you let me."

"So, you'll be my friend? You won't stop me?"

"No, I won't. I'm just a feeling. You can do hard things even when I'm around. I'll go away once you get used to those things."

"I see. Alright, I'm ready to be your friend."

This might seem like a kooky conversation, and over time it may not need to be so detailed. Usually when I do this with my clients, they report feeling an immediate lightness. They're also surprised to find that they'd known the answer all along. The power of connecting with ourselves and tapping into our own inner wisdom is a beautiful gift we give ourselves.

What the Heck Is Connection Anyway?

In my work, I often see people use the word "connection" in an ambiguous way. Parents will often say they have a wonderful "bond" with their children, but they don't understand why their child won't listen to them. People will also say they love their parents and, yes, their connection with their parents is very strong, but when I ask them if they share hard things with their parents, these same people will shake their head no, immediately. That's because if we go back to those ingredients of love, honest and open communication is missing, and without it, the connection often feels like it falls short significantly.

It's important, then, to define exactly what "good connection" means, or what a connection really is, because it's at the core of any relationship. It's what sustains the relationships, and the lack of which erodes the relationship. If we can understand the essence of connection, we can troubleshoot what is missing where, and work on that.

For children, connection is attachment and attachment is essential, especially in those early years because you may recall from the first chapter, all our essential and vital synapses related to relationships are formed when we are children.

DEVELOPING A SOLID CONNECTION
WITH YOUR CHILD

The amazing fact about children is that it's never too late to form new synapses and build connections even where none existed. What's of utmost importance is to always be willing to repair a broken connection. My favorite thing to tell parents is that you don't even need extra time for most of the following strategies, so even the busiest of parents can be hopeful!

In the following section, I share some concrete ways for you to connect or reconnect with your child.

1. CO-REGULATION

Have there been times when you saw your seven-year-old or ten-year-old or seventeen-year-old have really big feelings and you thought, "Aren't they too old for this?" or perhaps your toddler has some really big angry feelings and you think, "Isn't she too young to have such intense anger?" These are common thoughts that many parents have. The good news is that no one is ever too young to be angry or too old to be very upset and cry. In fact, it would be fair to say that emotional regulation is not a developmental milestone like walking or talking. There's no certain age at which children will automatically learn how to regulate their emotions.

The only way a child can learn how to regulate themselves is through co-regulation by their attachment figure (main caregiver). This is also why your own regulation skills are so important and why practicing RAIN (see previous section) and dealing with our own triggers (chapter one) is tantamount to becoming a safe adult your child can learn emotional regulation from. *Co-regulation is simply helping your child slowly ascend the green zone of the autonomic ladder from either the red or blue zones.*

The good news is that most likely, you've already done this many times when your child was an infant. They cried and you calmly picked them up and soothed them. Your body was calm and confident and you managed to transfer your calm to your child. Your regulated nervous system worked to settle your child's. This is co-regulation, but it gets harder when our kids get older because our own stories and triggers keep coming into play. Let's walk through the steps.

Step 1: As soon as you see your child showing big feelings (fight or flight response), check in with yourself. What is happening inside your body? Where are you on the autonomic ladder? Use your knowledge of your nervous system to evaluate what your neuroception is saying. Noticing your own thoughts and feelings can bring you into the present moment so your body sends cues of safety to your child. This is important—nothing you say matters if your nonverbal cues indicate to your child that you're getting triggered or agitated.

Step 2: Once you're certain you're feeling safe yourself, you can then get as close to your child as they will allow. Your nonverbal cues of safety will indicate to your child that you're ready to take care of them. Their nervous system will register that and start to climb up the autonomic ladder from the red zone to the green zone.

Step 3: Now your child should be ready for some verbal cues of safety as well. Saying "yes" is a great way to send signals of safety to your child so you can start there, "Yes, you're so unhappy because we have to leave the park!" Just acknowledging the emotions works to regulate the nervous system. For older children, you can offer something more complex ("Not having a phone must be making you feel really left out"), but be sure to sound authentic.

A lot of times parents say to me, "My child hates it when I offer them empathy during co-regulation!" This is because if you don't actually feel empathy, kids see right through your words. If you're struggling to feel empathy, just try to stay present without saying too much. Later, you can do work on the triggers worksheet and try to figure out why it was difficult for you to feel empathy for your child in that moment. Lots of parents struggle with this because they rarely experienced genuine empathy from their own caretakers for "childish" matters. As much as they want to empathize with their child, a part of them is saying, "Ok, but this really isn't a big deal, because look at everything I had to deal with as a kid!" It's important to honor this part of you and say, "Yes, you're right. It really wasn't fair what happened to you. You, too, deserved genuine empathy and kindness."

Finally, remember that co-regulation takes time and practice. Give your brain time to develop those new synapses to respond to your child's big feelings with compassion and presence. For encouragement, I want to share one of my favorite memories of co-regulating my then four-year-old son. This is one of the twins, so you can imagine that this is six years after the incident with Eisa at the beginning of this book, and by this time, I'd had lots of practice!

I've never been a morning person, except I was determined to have an early-to-bed and early-to-rise schedule for my kids. This often meant that my kids woke up before me and once they did, I was only half asleep with lots of interruptions. One such morning, Yahya woke me up crying about something for the tenth time. I started to feel irritated. This was my first bodily cue that I might start sliding down the ladder. I noticed the thought that had crept up on me: "I've already given him his morning snack so I could sleep more and I've listened to his nine other interruptions . . . what now?" Noticing the bodily sensations as well as the thoughts allowed me to feel a bit calmer because noticing allows us to engage our "Thinking Brain." I managed to groggily but kindly ask Yahya what was up.

"I no find my race car shirt," he said.

I groaned. I was behind on the laundry and had forgotten to put clothes in his drawer. He usually changed in the morning after waking up.

"Oh no! You want to wear that very shirt?" I tried to acknowledge.

"Yes! That's my favorite!" he answered with the I'm-about-to-have-some-big-feelings tone.

Again, I sensed my own body detecting "danger" as his body was starting to slide down the ladder. "It's ok, I'm safe. This is just my little boy needing help," I said to myself and followed him to his room, hoping that that shirt was somewhere in the clean laundry pile.

Unfortunately, I couldn't find it so I told him it was not there and he'd have to find something else.

The words barely left my mouth when he threw himself on the floor in his room and started writhing as if he was in intense pain,

"I NO WANT OTHER SHIRT!!!"

He screamed.

Once again I sensed my own body responding to his stress. My stomach fell as I thought, "Oh no! How long is this going to last?" and once again, I noticed these sensations and feelings of dread. Once again, the noticing brought me back to the present. What does he need from me? I asked myself. Empathy, of course.

"You're upset because you really wanted to wear that race car shirt."

He was screaming so loudly that he could barely hear my words but my gentle and empathetic tone had made a dent and I could sense his stormy feelings tone down just a notch. A very tiny notch, but a notch nevertheless.

"I. WANT. THAT. SHIRT."

He screamed again. I considered saying something but thought better of it and focused instead on my nonverbal cues. I made sure my face was calm and turned towards him. I sat down on the floor so I was not looming over his little body. I knew my eyes reflected the genuine empathy I felt for his struggle, and there we both sat on the floor, much like me and Eisa had six years earlier. Except this time, I had managed to befriend my nervous system and notice its responses without getting carried away by them.

For a while I just sat there. Eventually I tried to reach out and touch him gently but he swatted my hand away and continued to writhe. By now I'd regained complete charge of my nervous system. It was staying in the green zone, fully present with Yahya.

"I'm sorry this is so hard for you, sweetness," I said finally when I sensed he was ready for my words.

He didn't seem to hear me but I could see that the softness of my words had created safety for him.

He was another few notches up the ladder.

I remember thinking, "I'm here right now. With this little boy whose storm needs my calm. This here, is the most important thing I could be doing."

And so I returned to the task at hand and attempted to touch him again . . . this time he let me.

"Can I hug you?" I asked.

"NO!" he said. But a little less firmly that time. A few rungs more to go, I thought.

"I'm sorry I'm so behind on the laundry . . . I will try my best to find that shirt for you later today . . . no job is too big and no mama is too small!" I said the last part in the *Paw Patrol* tone and it made him smile ever so little.

"I wear other shirt," he said then, much more calmly.

"Oh wonderful! Thank you for your patience," I said, genuinely grateful for little big heart.

He got a big smile then on his face and I got rewarded with a hug.

That was co-regulation at work to make a young child feel safe and seen with his mother. Imagine how differently it would have gone if I hadn't worked on my triggers of "How dare he disturb my sleep!" or "How dare he make a deal out of something small—doesn't he know how much I have to do around here?" That's where the real work is for us. No script and no step-by-step process will ever truly work if we haven't had the courage to go back in our past and unpack the pain we carry.

2. MINDFULNESS (SLOWING DOWN)

Just like you don't have to set aside time to co-regulate your children, this is another way you can build connection without necessarily expending any extra time. If you have younger children who need care tasks from you (bathing, diaper changes, getting ready, etc.) then you can use those moments to really slow down and stay present. I remember as a young mom always feeling like I needed to hurriedly do these tasks because then I could move on to "more important" tasks. In my hurry I would get exasperated with my toddlers for "slowing me down." Until I slowly started to realize that I was hurrying even when I had no specific tasks ahead of me. I wasn't even sure why I was in such a hurry. As I mentioned earlier, due to excessive synapses children get overwhelmed easily and their world needs to move slower for them to stay regulated. When we can stay present with their pace, it allows us to truly connect with them and realize that these moments are just as important as any other task that calls our attention.

For older children who no longer need our help with care tasks, we can be present with them during car rides to school or other activities. We can listen to podcasts together and connect over their content. Throughout the day I'll often go to my eleven-year-old and stand and watch whatever he's doing. He'll eventually notice me, smile at me, and share something. These are precious moments of connection that can add to a child's bucket of connection.

3. SIBLING RIVALRY

All siblings fight; it's natural and normal and even healthy because children need to learn conflict resolution. Who better to practice this with than the people who will love you no matter what? Siblings also spend a heck of a lot of time together, and so it makes sense to have more conflict with someone you see every single day for several hours at least. As parents we need to show up mindfully in these situations so we can use them as connecting moments rather than disconnecting ones.

When you're asked to mediate between your children or one child comes up to you complaining about the other, see your role as that of a helper and observer rather than a referee who will decide who's right and who's wrong. When we take sides and act like referees, kids tend to fight more because then it becomes a survival instinct, "Who does Mom/Dad like more?"

As opposed to that, a mediator merely states the problem:

"Sadia wants the remote and Ahmed wants it too . . . hmm . . ."

"There's only one cookie left and you both want it. I wonder what we can do . . ."

When the problem is more complex, stick around and state each child's concerns to the other while being deeply attuned to what each child is trying to say. Sometimes kids will say something unkind and you can rephrase it in a kinder way,

Sadia: "He's stupid because all the shows he watches are stupid!"

You: "Sadia doesn't like any of the shows Ahmed watches."

When mediation isn't working because both the kids are still in the red zone, separate the kids with something neutral: "Woah! Looks like a break is needed here."

Always make sure that you remind yourself that there are no good guys and bad guys here, only kids. If you really feel bad for your "victim" child, the one who always seems to get the short end of the stick, have faith in him/her. They will surprise you as soon as they get the opportunity to step out of the victim's role.

4. ACTIVE LISTENING

For older children, we can also use active listening to deepen our connection. Often our children share something difficult and challenging with us and it's easy to start lecturing or offering quick solutions. Active listening involves setting aside our own needs in that moment and really listening to what their concerns are. This means we respond in the following ways:

1. By simply listening with an open mind and nodding while maintaining eye contact. Just doing this much, you'll notice your child open up more.

2. You can use minimal verbal cues like "Oh, I see," "Hmmm," etc.

3. Ask open-ended questions, "How did that make you feel?" "What do you think you'll do?" "What did it make you decide?"

4. Respond to these questions with more minimal verbal cues and refrain from offering advice or your own strong opinions. If you do have a perspective, you can share it in the form of a "thoughtful question" like, "What do you think might happen if we keep spending time with people who hurt our feelings?" or "Do you think telling that person how their words made you feel is a good idea?"

5. CHILD-LED PLAY

Modern parents catch a lot of flack, but the truth is that our generation of parents as a whole is the first generation that actively engages with and plays with our kids. I really want to take a moment to acknowledge how absolutely wonderful this is because play is therapeutic, healing, and connecting. Sometimes, this loving desire to play with our kids can become more adult-led than necessary which has the opposite effect than what we were intending. That is, if we feel like we need to come up with ideas for what to play or the "right responses," we can easily start to feel burdened. This burdened feeling is sensed by our kids whose "connection bucket" doesn't get refilled as we had hoped. As a result, we feel like we're spending a lot of time with our kids and we (rightfully) feel that children should play by themselves after we've played with them, except the play had no real value for the child. Here are three things we can do to make sure that whenever we play with our children, it fills up their bucket by leaps and bounds:

1. Let them control every aspect of the play including what to play and how to play it. For example: Instead of saying to your teen, "Let's go and play some cricket outside." You can ask them what they'd like to do and proceed to do it enthusiastically. Younger children often ask us to do things, for example, your child says, "Baba, become a bear!" and you say, "How do I become a bear? What should I do? (Hug me like a bear!) Yeah? Hmm . . . I wonder how a bear hugs . . . can you show me?"

2. Consider your role to be that of an avid observer until your child invites you in their play. When you're observing, you can comment on what you see: "You're stacking all those red blocks first," "You really know what to do with that controller!" "You're painting something blue right now."

3. Feel free to decline to play with your child if you're not up for it. No one wants to spend time with someone who doesn't want to spend time with them. See if you can suggest another time when you have more energy.

6. THERAPEUTIC TOUCH

Do you remember the towel-mom experiment in the introduction of this book? Touch is an essential element of a close relationship. Safe and gentle touch initiated with the child's permission is one of the most beautiful ways to connect with your child of any age. This is especially important to remember with older children. My eldest who's almost eleven still loves daily hugs and other forms of touch like massage. Starting and ending your day with mindful hugs can be very regulating for children. Other forms of touch can include letting your kids apply makeup on you or groom you, taking turns giving "spa pedicures" (we use a plain shallow bucket with water and conditioner mixed in), letting your kids climb all over you, using rocking motions to soothe them, touching noses and cheeks, etc.

WHEN CONNECTION SUFFERS

When Covid started and I was stuck at home trying to entertain four young kids while my husband had to work from home, things slowly started to go south. Whenever the stress in our life increases, the new synapses we've formed tend to get bypassed by older, stronger ones. I found myself snapping left and right at my kids, especially Husna. Bedtime became a battlefield. She would absolutely refuse to settle down and insist on jumping all over the room, resisting sleep. Eventually I would get incredibly triggered, slide down the ladder into the red zone of fight or flight, activating *her* fight or flight, and thus wake up her brain even more! This went on for a few nights and I started to feel overwhelmed with sheer exhaustion and the shame of being so mean to my sweet daughter.

Fortunately, our basement renter, Elizabeth also became our friend and babysitter over the years. She and I both say that God sent us each other to make life easier. She would babysit for very reasonable charges as much as her health allowed. One such day, by the time she was done and heading back to the basement, she looked over at me to say goodbye. I was probably so deep into the blue zone that I could barely return her wave. She realized something was not okay and came and sat next to me and asked the question that unraveled me.

"Are you ok, Maryam?" she said.

And I couldn't hold it together anymore and just burst into tears as if a floodgate was opened. She walked right over and put her arm around me. I just sat there and cried.

It felt good.

It felt good not to have her say to me, "Don't cry!" Or "What's wrong?" Or the worst thing, "It's gonna be ok!" (It doesn't matter that it's going to be ok, right now is *not* ok!)

After she let me cry, she asked if she could help. I told her I feel bad asking her for more help because she also has health issues. She shook her head and told me I needed to go out for a walk.

"I got the kids, you go take a walk outside. You need fresh air," she ordered.

And it felt good. So good. For someone to tell me what I need and make me do it. Sometimes we're so horrible at taking care of ourselves. The truth is, I could've had my husband watch the kids while I took a breather outside. I had felt bad for him, too, and didn't want to ask him, but it had already pushed me over the edge. How was that helpful for anyone?

I thanked Elizabeth and threw on my coat and shoes and went outside.

I walked up to my favorite spot and sat down. There was a little hill in my neighborhood overlooking the woods. I loved it because the ground there was always filled with dried pine needles and fallen pinecones and reminded me of Murree (a hill station town in Pakistan). I lived there with my parents when I was little and my dad was posted there (he was in the Air Force). If I closed my eyes and focused on the sounds and smells, it almost felt as if I was back home. The stillness and familiarity of the moment helped my body settle and I could sense my nervous system slowly climbing the ladder into the green zone.

Eventually, I got up and started to walk back, and for the first time in days, realized that spring was here. The cherry blossoms were blooming in all their glory; my neighbor's impeccably pruned hedges that always spurted with a shock of flowers in the spring were almost all pink. I could smell the neighborhood's freshly cut grass and the flurries from the cherry blossoms floated in the air near my face. These sounds and sensations increased the safety I had started to feel in my body and I realized how stuck I had been in the lower rungs of the autonomic ladder—unable to use my vagal brake.

I realized that my connection to myself had been non-existent lately. No wonder my connection to my kids was also suffering. Instead of taking out at least some time for myself, I'd been feeling guilty and not taking care of myself at all . . . not even to just take a walk outside. And what had happened as a result was very, very natural—we can't give love to others when we fail to give it to ourselves.

So, despite feeling bad for Elizabeth and feeling "selfish" as moms often do when we practice self-care, I walked around my neighborhood leisurely. Enjoying the sights and sounds, soaking in the joy of spring, reminding myself I'm worthy. I, too, deserve care. By the time I got back home, only thirty minutes or so later, I felt like a different person. I hugged Elizabeth and thanked her. I hugged my kids and told them we were going to have some fun.

I talked to Husna and asked her how I could help her sleep at night without being so upset. What was making her upset at bedtime every night? She couldn't exactly answer that question, but she did tell me about her nightly vigils of going downstairs and missing her friends.

I realized she needed more love and positive attention, and because she acted "ok" during the day, I never realized nights were hard for her.

"When everyone is asleep, it's quiet, Mama. It helps me imagine my friends," she said.

It broke my heart. She had been missing her school friends since Covid had shut down all the schools. I listened to her story and held space for it. I sensed the snuffed-out candle of our connection starting to light up again. She and I made a plan for her bedtime that would help her feel calmer and more loved (massage, stories, surahs). That night, I followed through, she shared more stories of her friends, and I listened intently and offered her genuine empathy for what was clearly a very difficult time in her life. She then fell asleep within minutes in my arms, with a smile on her sweet face.

NOTES

1. Fred Rogers, as qtd. by Tom Hanks, *A Beautiful Day in the Neighborhood*, Marielle Heller, dir. (Sony Pictures, 2019).
2. Jalaluddin Rumi, "The Guest House," translated by Coleman Barks, *Rumi: Selected Poems* (Penguin Books, 2004).

CHAPTER 3

BOUNDARIES ARE LOVE

"We learn that it is not the rays which bodies
absorb, but those which they reject, that give
them the colours they are known by."

—Thomas Hardy, *Far from the Madding Crowd*

From "Danger" to "Wonder Woman"

I'm on a beautiful beach in Jacksonville, Florida, watching the waves crash, or rather hearing them crash because I've closed my eyes to really take in the joy that the ocean sounds are. I'm soothed and comforted. My nervous system is thanking me. I can just feel my chubby little sorrow cloud drifting away, allowing the sunshine to hit me. The breeze is strong and gentle at the same time. It's got the perfect blend of coolness and warmth. I notice myself smiling every now and then.

What is it about nature that's so healing? I like to think being close to the Creator's creation with gratitude held in our hearts is what causes the healing effect. It's not enough to just be in nature. It's important to let it nurture you and take care of you. I will talk about many things that took me on this journey of becoming more whole, and allowing myself to be in proximity to God's creations is one big factor.

In my darkest days, when I feel like the depression and anxiety are taking over, I notice I can't get out of bed, let alone out of my house. The heaviness in my heart seems to chain me to the indoors as if this bubble around me is the only safe place. Even getting out of bed seems overwhelming. I want you to know, if you ever feel this way, it's not you. It's the mental illness.

A lot of people imagine depression to be an illness where someone is perpetually sitting in a dark room, wallowing in grief. In reality, most people (including myself) have what's called functional depression. The more I manage my illness, the more good days I have. Even though I openly talk about my diagnosis and treatment of this mental illness, most people are still shocked when I tell them I'm living with depression.

"Still?" they ask.

Depression is not like pneumonia—you don't necessarily get cured from it. Perhaps you will, if it were brought on by a specific event in your life, but for most patients of depression, it's a lifelong thing. Notice I don't use the phrase "battling depression" because I refuse to battle with any parts of me. My depression is also part of me. We're friends and we make life work. And it's a very good life.

Susan Cain, author of *Bittersweet*, said on her podcast with Brené Brown, "We are creative beings meant to create art from sorrow."[1]

Don't mistake this idea though—it's not meant to romanticize or glorify pain—this statement is merely a fact. This is what wise people observe over and over, that pain gives birth to the kind of beauty that can't exist otherwise.

And so that's where we are . . . Wonder Woman was born out of Maryam Danger. I don't know that the former could exist without the latter.

But first, let me tell you the story of the Danger Woman. This was my brother's nickname for me for the longest time. He had saved my name in his phone with these words. You might think "ouch," but I didn't because I never believed it. I never saw myself as an unsafe person. When it came to my brothers, my self-image was that I'm full of generosity and kindness and they're cold, distant, dismissive, and even cruel at times to me. Don't mistake me, I loved them dearly and did a lot for them and their wives and children. If you asked them that, they wouldn't deny it.

But.

There were a lot of buts.

I might have done all that and I might have been a good person, but my motivations for all the goodness were wrong. I thought a good person is someone who gives and gives and forgives and then gives some more.

This was a pattern that showed up in all my relationships. I'd do a lot for people and always end up feeling like no one cared. Then I'd try to do more to make them care and I still wouldn't get whatever I wanted. At some point, I'd huff and puff and either walk away from the relationship (in the case of friends) or just resort to silent treatment and passive aggressiveness in the case of family. But with family, it was always short lived, and I'd end up going back to giving. That further reinforced my self-image of being a very forgiving person "who doesn't harbor bad feelings" in her heart.

But all the while, a lot of stuff was definitely festering in my heart because none of my relationships brought me any joy. I found myself posting those lame memes about how no one cares for "good people" and everyone just uses them. From the inside, I was a perpetually victimized soul, a casualty of my own "too good for myself" heart. I'd sigh in self-pity upon reading these memes and complain about my too good heart and how hard it is to be a sensitive person and how one gets used.

Ah, yes! My list of complaints against the world and its inhabitants was never ending.

What I didn't know then and know very, very well now is that a good person is, in fact, not someone who just gives and gives and then forgives. There's a huge piece missing from this definition of a good person. A good person is foremost good to herself. Without that, her goodness looks to others like mine did to my brother, full of "danger." Now what does being good to yourself and others at the same time look like?

- Being kind and also having boundaries.
- Forgiving and also holding people accountable.
- Saying kind words and also not allowing others to say unkind words to us.
- Telling the truth but also honoring our own truth.
- Being generous with our resources but also asking for help.
- Overlooking others' faults but also protecting ourselves from them.
- Giving time to others and also reserving time and rest for ourselves.
- Supporting others in their dreams and also pursuing our own dreams unapologetically.

- Believing others without detailed explanations and also not overexplaining ourselves.

This is called self-love, and there is no love for others without it. This is the secret of finding joy in relationships that is honoring our most intimate relationship: The one we have with ourselves.

When I moved back to Pakistan, I wasn't on talking terms with my brother. I had been deeply hurt by his rejection on my last trip. But when I moved back, I noticed his efforts to patch things up and due to my own healing, I was able to accept his efforts and, ever so gingerly, open up my heart once again.

There's a famous saying that always makes me laugh.

"If you're feeling very enlightened, spend a week with your family."

The first time I read it, it resonated so well for me. I *had* been feeling very enlightened and I thought I'd conquer even my family, but little did I know that your family is the final battleground between you and the demons that haunt you. They've known us too long and we've been around them too long. Our nervous system easily falls into old patterns. Before we know it, all the enlightenment is out the window.

So this time, once again, I was wary. I had to be gentle with myself. I kept that "good person list" in my mind. I knew I had to take care of myself too. I couldn't get overexcited about my brother finally seeming to care about me and throw all self-love rules out the window. Let me give you an example of what this looked like.

Our mom has Alzheimer's and my dad is her main caretaker. Whenever he has to go somewhere, he asks me or my brother if we can keep mom. One afternoon, I got this text from my brother: "Dad left Mom in my tv lounge without even asking me."

Before I knew what I was doing, I had typed up, "Oh no . . . let me come pick her up!"

And then I paused. This was my autopilot response. I just wanted to make my brother happy without even checking in with myself. Not to mention the fact that he hadn't even asked me a question, he had simply shared a thought. It can be argued that this is how he "requested" a lot of things from me in the past. I had gotten him used to me reading his mind so he never even overtly asked for anything. And later, when I'd be resentful and say, "But I did xyz for you!" he could easily say, "I never asked you to."

Now I know what you're thinking. That my brother wrongfully used my generosity of soul. I disagree.

You see, all of us just want our lives to be easier. If there's a person who always seems to be stepping up to relieve our burden, we don't think too much about it. It just becomes the norm. I bet you can think of someone in your own life who's always quick to help you out without you even asking. Perhaps it's your mom even. Do you think you purposefully abuse their kindness? I'm gonna guess your answer is no. You might say something like, "Well, she *likes* to help me."

My brother would say the same and rightfully so. How on Earth is he supposed to know my boundaries when I've never made them known?

Back to that text. I noticed my urgency to come to his rescue and then deleted that message. I realized I had a client coming to see me in thirty minutes so I wouldn't be able to watch mom.

I wrote instead, "Oh no . . . I'm sorry . . . Did you have plans? I have a client I'll be done with at 3 and I can come pick her up then."

As you can see here, I took care of myself and him at the same time.

"Thanks *yar*. Really appreciate it," he wrote back.

And where do you think this repeated act of self-love took me?

He and I were going for *taraweeh* (special prayers in Ramadan) one night and I forgot my phone at home. Without my phone, I wouldn't be able to reach him after the salah. He had to give me his phone since he was with a friend. He showed me how to unlock it. His list of dialed calls showed up.

Missed call from "Wonder Woman" caught my eye.

"Wonder Woman?" I raised my eyebrows.

"It's your number, see?" he said, opening the contact.

And it was, in fact, my number. This affirmation was so unexpected that I spontaneously blurted out if it was in sarcasm.

"What? No! You've changed a lot . . . you really are a Wonder Woman."

And that, coming from a family member, is the best compliment anyone could ever ask for.

But Boundaries Are for White People!

Whenever I first bring up boundaries with my clients or workshop participants, I hear a lot of concern and reservations. The common thread seems to be that boundaries are a "Western" concept. This thought in itself seems intriguing to me since most of the time, we love everything Western!

Movies, clothes, food, education—heck, most of us (as in, Pakistanis) love emigrating there without a second thought, so it's interesting that when it comes to relationships, some of our blind spots in biases seem to come out—but perhaps that's another book for another day. For now, I want to show you that setting boundaries for yourself is an act of love and care for yourself. And if you're religious, I'll also show you that boundaries are in fact, incredibly God-endorsed. That's because we can really only do for others what we can do well for ourselves.

This might come as a surprise to you, but you also deserve good things.

Like space.

And time.

And grace.

And peace.

And rest.

And all these things come from the somewhat unpleasant task of setting boundaries for yourself. This is possibly the hardest yet most crucial kind of self-care you'll ever do. It's hard because everything in our culture goes against this. We associate boundaries with those "cold white people"—surely, any self-respecting "good Pakistani Muslim" will not be caught dead setting boundaries, right?

This is obviously a lie. One sign that it's a lie meant to scare you is that it has an "othering" quality. Whenever we make a group of people, any people, "the bad guys," we're engaging in "othering," the purpose of which is always, always to create fear. But why, you ask, would someone try to create fear in us? Great question. Let's see who benefits when we are afraid to set boundaries.

In the workspace, there is Ahmed and there is Arslan. Ahmed can often be seen working late and after hours. He's also often seen missing lunch because he's so busy on a project. Arslan, though, leaves at exactly 5 p.m., and even if you try to hold him back with something "urgent," he will remind you that working hours are over. Furthermore, he has the audacity to actually take breaks because he mutters something about being hungry exactly around lunch break. Does it really matter, then, if Arslan's work is excellent? Because when the next round of promotions comes, who will get rewarded? Yup, Ahmed.

Now, let's consider Nadia. She is the eldest "bahu" (daughter-in-law) and at any given time, she can be seen slaving away in the kitchen, cooking for the whole family. She really wanted to pursue her medical degree and start her residency program, but she knew that doing so would mean that "the house and children" would be "neglected," even though she had the acute sense that her children were already being neglected. But it was for a "good cause" so it was ok. But what if, one day, she decides that she's going to hire full-time help for the kitchen and only be responsible for her kids. Furthermore, she demands from her husband that he do his share of taking care of their children so she can resume her studies. In other words, all of a sudden she has boundaries.

What will happen then? Like I tell my clients, as soon as you start setting boundaries for yourself, you will become *waisee aurat* ("that kind of woman"), *buri aurat* ("fast" woman), *pathar-dil* ("cold-hearted"), etc. That's the fear doing its part and you can see who benefits from this fear. Like Sarah Marshall says on her fantastic podcast "You're Wrong About,"

Often as a woman, it's when you stop harming yourself that people think something has gone wrong in your life.[2]

If you're a woman who's ever created any kind of boundary for yourself, you know exactly what I'm talking about. In her little gem of a book, *Show Up*, Nai'ma B. Robert writes:

> The truth is, many of us grew up watching our mothers serve everyone but themselves. We watched our mothers sacrifice their dreams and desires for us, for the family, for the marriage. We watched our mothers take on everyone's burdens, everyone's worries, everyone's pain, seemingly without complaint. And we learned the lesson well: to serve is to sacrifice. To be a mother is to be a martyr.[3]

It was the year of Covid (2020) and the year I was supposed to finally go back to the university for my masters. My youngest two had turned four and were going to start at their full-time Islamic school. They were thrilled to be joining *apa* and *bhai* in school and I was thrilled to get back on track for studying for my calling in life. But we all know how all our plans were dashed that year—the kids' school turned online, my husband was forced to work from home, and my day was spent keeping the kids out of his way. I don't think I have to explain to anyone who's lived through "the quarantine" how difficult this period was, so I'll skip ahead to the next year when the quarantine continued. In the February of 2021, after almost a year of being home, I decided to put kids in a "summer camp," which is just a word for a structured play camp sort of thing. The only one I could find that had space was in Alexandria, a city 40 minutes away from Centreville where we lived. I'd drop off the kids at 10 a.m. and pick them up at 3 p.m., and though they always had fun there, they weren't happy about the long car drive.

One day after drop off, I had a call with Bill and he noticed that I was unusually anxious.

"What's up," he asked.

"I don't know . . . I guess I'm feeling a lot of anxiety."

"About anything special?"

"No . . . I mean the kids aren't happy about the long car drive . . ."

"And?"

"I guess I feel bad that they hate the car drive but I take them anyway . . ."

"Ahh, so you have mom guilt!"

"Mom guilt? Well, I know what that is and I teach my clients how there's no point in it because it's just society's way of making us feel bad any time we do anything for ourselves."

"So, you feel like you shouldn't feel 'mom guilt' because you teach about it?"

"Yeah . . . I mean I've already worked through it, haven't I?"

"You mean you've worked through it in the past when you've felt it. It doesn't mean you'll never feel it again."

BAM! There it was. Shame had snuck on me again and I didn't even know. I wasn't even allowing myself to feel the mom guilt. I had guilt about mom guilt. Like guilt exponential.

Bill could see that I was processing this in my mind. He let me be for a while and then he asked me a question that blew my mind. He said:

"How many women do you have in your family who have modeled for you what you're trying to live? A mother breaking generational trauma cycles while going to graduate school

144

while managing a thriving business that serves other women? You're a trailblazer, Maryam."

Ah! To be seen like that. Had he really just described *me*?

"None, I suppose," I said, answering his questions about how many role models I had.

"Exactly," he said, "None. You don't even know what it looks like to be the woman you're working so hard to be. All you've seen is women being martyrs. 'Mom guilt' is in your DNA and it's not going anywhere no matter how many times you work through it."

And there we had it. The legacy of "mom guilt." Something every mother carries in our generation because we will never measure up to the "martyr generation." Never. But we can hope and pray that our daughters will never carry the burdens we carry of our moms' sacrifices. I hope we can show our daughters what it's like to take care of ourselves without ever knowing about the guilt we feel when we do it.

What's the solution to mom guilt then?

Embrace it. Look it in the eye with tenderness and say, "I know what you're trying to do. You're trying to protect me from criticism and judgment. But I'm strong now. I can take care of myself. I can be the woman who doesn't parent from guilt or exist from guilt and whose only identity is being a victim of society. I'm a trailblazer. Yes I am."

Where women have "mom guilt," dads have "provider guilt." Their shame stories revolve around whether they're good enough earners for their families because their entire worth is placed on how much money they make and what luxuries they can provide for their families.

The truth stands that whether you're a man or a woman, someone is being served by your fear of boundary-setting. So, we have a choice, we can keep living our life in fear of that fear or we can recognize that we won't be able to serve anyone unless we're serving ourselves first. After all, if working long hours made Ahmed a better husband, father, and son, we'd have nothing against it, but chances are his family is sick and tired of his obsession with work. Similarly, if slaving away in housework all day made Nadia a better mom, wife, and daughter-in-law, we'd say go for it but, in reality, it's making her an impatient and angry mom, and a resentful wife and daughter-in-law, all ingredients for a miserable life.

Religious Content

If you're still uncertain about whether setting boundaries is only a "Western" concept, let me share one of my most favorite verses about boundary setting from the Quran with you.

"O you who believe! enter not houses other than your own, until you have asked permission and saluted those in them: that is best for you, in order that you may heed (what is seemly). If you find no one in the house, enter not until permission is given to you: if you are asked to go back, go back: that makes for greater purity for yourselves: and Allah knows well all that ye do." (24:27–28)

On the surface, this ayah may seem to be talking about something fairly "small"—Knock before you enter? Go back home if no one answers? Go back if you're told to go back? But can you imagine telling your *aunty* who came from Rawalpindi specially to see you that she should go back because this isn't a good time

---

for you? You know you'll be blacklisted for the rest of your life! But in reality, has there ever been a time when someone called you, came over, or overstayed their welcome and you secretly wished that you could say it's not a good time for you? It would require so much courage for you to say that—and that courage is a big part of being a Muslim. Courage means to remember that if you're doing the right thing (justice to yourself) then you must not fear your aunt's wrath. I shared with you, in the chapter before, how the lack of boundaries made me an unkind person overall.

I hope it's making sense to you that not having any personal boundaries is a cultural thing and not at all a religious teaching. The deep-rooted fear we have of taking care of ourselves comes from shame. Recall from the previous section that shame sends us the message that we're 'bad' and deficit in some strongly inherent way.

When I ask people what messages shame around boundaries sends them, they say:

- You're lazy and that's why you don't want to work overtime.
- You'll be left behind if you don't burn the midnight oil.
- You'll be a bad parent if you say no to playing with your kids.
- You'll be a bad provider for your family if you don't take that extra shift.

- You'll be a heartless daughter-in-law if you refuse to cook for all your in-laws.
- You'll be a 'fast woman' if you travel by yourself.
- You'll be a cruel mother if you also have a career.

All of these make sense because these are all the things we have shame around.

I'm going to divide some big areas of boundaries by common gender roles here.

BOUNDARIES FOR MEN

1. I have advice for you from the shame expert, Dr. Brown. She says, "It takes courage to say yes to rest and play in a culture where exhaustion is seen as a status symbol." How much you earn is not a measure of your worth. You deserve to spend time at home with your loved ones instead of working overtime for that next promotion. Yes, ambition is great, but its greatness is in serving you. When it stops serving you then it has lost its greatness.

2. You will not be a bad son if you decide to move out of your parents' house, like 99% of adult men do in this world. You can continue to take care of your parents and family of origin even when you don't live with them. Chances are, you'll serve them better when you have your own space.

3. You are a wonderful son even when you speak up and take action to protect your wife's rights when they're compromised by your family of origin.

4. If other men make fun of you for being a real man and refusing to laugh at sexist jokes, you can walk away from that gathering.

BOUNDARIES FOR WOMEN

1. You don't have to do housework if you have the choice and means not to.
2. You have the right to focus your best energies on your children rather than serving all your in-laws.
3. You can pursue your studies and career and still be a wonderful mom and wife.
4. You have the right to have your own place if living with your in-laws is not working out.
5. If you're a woman who is now a mother-in-law, you can say no to providing full-time care of your grandkids. It doesn't make you a "bad *dadi/nani*." You deserve rest too.
6. You don't have to entertain your children all the time.
7. Your *ghar-ki-roti* does not have a special ingredient in it that only comes from "*maa*" (mother). It's the twenty-first century, and roti/naan is sold for cheap all over the world.
8. You didn't bring your kids in *jahez* (dowry) so no, your husband is not "babysitting" them while you go out. He's having a wonderful time with his own children, building a bond that his own father didn't. Go out with your friends. Travel. Go shopping. Travel for work. When you get back, everyone will be alive and well . . . remember, men are incredibly strong. In the history of the world, they've been doing much,

much harder things than watching children for a few hours/days.

"But they'll be so upset when I do this!" (*Bara hungama ho ga*). Gentle reminder that there is *hungama* right now, too, but it's within you. I know that you wear the invisible burden of keeping the peace, but silencing yourself in hopes of "keeping the peace" comes at a hefty price.

"Daring to set boundaries is about having the courage to love ourselves even when we risk disappointing others."

—Ichiro Kishimi, *The Courage to Be Disliked*[4]

K. C. Davis is one of my favorite TikTokers. When her first TikTok popped up on my "for you" page, I immediately fell in love with this incredibly authentic, quirky, kind, and funny woman. Now she even has a TED Talk! In one of her TikToks, she is responding to the *most* frequently made criticism of respectful parenting, that it makes children "soft."

K. C. says, "Do you know what the softest thing in the world is? The softest, most pillowy fragile being in existence is a fully grown adult that cannot regulate their behavior in the face of something a literal child has done. Gentle parenting is literally just regulated parenting. It is."[5]

The answer she gave 100% mirrors my experience working in Pakistan. It's the 60/70-something-year-old person who falls apart at the smallest "infraction." They have big feelings that they have no idea what to do with and they simply erupt all over the place, annihilating everything and everyone in the process. Or, there's always the silent treatment and passive aggressiveness.

BOUNDARIES MAKE ME FEEL GUILTY!

I think we can all agree that members of the past generation who complain about gentle parenting were not gentle parented themselves, so it begs the question why are they so "soft"? That's because two things happened:

1. Their cup remained empty from a rough childhood where emotional neglect was a common parenting practice, often compounded by harsh punishments. The message they received was, "You aren't worthy of care."

2. As adults, they continue to honor that lesson and never learned to take care of themselves. Now my heart goes out to that generation because they were trauma surviving. But they've taught us a precious lesson: go ahead and have no boundaries for yourself if you want to be a dandelion at age 70!

When my female clients resolutely tell me, "I will not be the kind of mother-in-law I have!" I tell them those are wonderful intentions—perhaps their mother-in-law once had similar good intentions. But in reality, a good mother-in-law is created thirty years in advance—when she creates space for herself and takes care of herself. So go ahead—give yourself permission to start establishing boundaries for yourself. At first you'll feel so guilty because you've been conditioned to feel guilty when you put yourself first, but over time you'll start to notice that when you are well taken care of, you're able to truly come into your greatness. Learn to tell the difference between real guilt ("I think I made a mistake and this is how I can do better next time") versus "conditioned guilt" ("Whenever I set boundaries for self-protection, I feel like a bad person"). I hope that you are able to see that if we want to be cycle breakers in our older age too, we have to start taking care of ourselves now and learn to sit with the "conditioned guilt" that comes with it at first.

ABC'S OF BOUNDARY SETTING

If you've never consciously set boundaries before, it can feel very daunting. I'll walk you through some basic steps that I teach my "boundaries newbie" clients. I invite you to grab a paper and go through these steps as you read them.

Step 1: Make a short list of situations that have lately been making you angry and/or resentful. Both these emotions are a good sign that your boundaries are being violated.

Example: Every time you have to change your plans because your sister-in-law decides to visit unannounced.

Step 2: Decide what's acceptable in this situation and what's not acceptable and then communicate to the relevant persons (starting with what's acceptable).

Example: You might decide that you don't mind your sister-in-law's visits at all and are happy to see her. Except sometimes she arrives suddenly without consideration for your plans. This is what makes you frustrated, and very rightfully so as well. So you text her and say, "Hey, I love having you and the kids over! It's so much fun when you guys come. I'd really appreciate it if you can let me know a couple of days ahead of your visit so I can make sure I'm home." (Yes, she might be "offended" by this because she's not used to you being honest about your needs, but give her and yourself time, you'll both get used to the new reality.)

Step 3: It's up to you to enforce the boundary, so do what needs to be done to execute the boundary.

Example: If next time she comes unannounced again, don't change your plans and go ahead and leave if you need to.

Step 4 (Optional): Include the language of love whenever possible. Some people have hurt us so much that we might struggle to do this step and that's ok. You can skip this step as long as you need to process your feelings about the hurt.

Example: When you're leaving the house, you can say, "I'm so sorry I have to get going—I wish I knew you were coming because I really don't want to miss out on spending time with you but I'd scheduled something ahead of time. Please make yourself at home!" (I know this might sound really cold and offensive but remember that in the long run, it's meant to preserve the relationship. What will destroy the relationship is *not* executing the boundary you'd tried to set.)

FINAL NOTES ON BOUNDARY SETTING

1. Remember that boundaries are not instructions. When we set a boundary, we are the ones who will ensure it's implemented—we can't expect others to "respect" our boundaries as if they're commands written in

stone. We will put in place whatever physical manifestations are required to make sure the boundary is implemented (like leaving the house when you said you won't be available unannounced or locking your office's door to work so your kids don't demand your attention).

2. We are not responsible for managing other people's feelings if their feelings are an outcome of our boundary setting. It's this simple: if you protecting yourself hurts someone's feelings, they have their own baggage to manage. (Conversely, we should always be respectful when others set boundaries for us.)

3. Parents are also allowed to have boundaries with their kids. Yes, you're allowed to go to the bathroom alone, you're allowed to say no to buying them a phone, and you're definitely allowed to have space for yourself when things get too much. In these situations, step 4 would not be optional. For children, we always make sure the language of love comes through ("I love playing with you, *beti*, and right now I really need to finish my work!").

4. When we first start setting boundaries, it's scary for the people around us. Their nervous system registers it as a threat because in our culture, there are either no boundaries or there are spikey walls. They mistake your boundaries for walls and feel the sharpness of the pointy spikes even when they don't exist. However, over time they do learn that you're still your wonderful and kind self, just with a slight modification that delivers superior results.

Only Set Boundaries for the Kids You Love

When I started this work, I thought my biggest challenge would be to convince parents that spanking, yelling, and punishments are not the best way to parent. Fortunately, most parents I work with don't present me with this challenge at all. In fact, I can easily say that I've never had to argue with a client that hitting and punishments aren't helpful. In fact, my biggest challenge has been to convince parents that boundaries are, in fact, a form of love. You are not causing damage to your child by setting boundaries, but the opposite is certainly true.

It makes sense why people think this, of course.

Can you think of what boundaries looked like for you when you were little? How did your parents enforce them?

Recall an incident from your childhood/teenhood when you did something that made your parents unhappy—how did you know they were not pleased with you?

What did their facial expressions look like? What feelings words can you use to describe how these expressions made you feel? (Use the Feelings Wheel in Appendix C.)

What words did they use to convey their displeasure? What feelings words can you use to describe how these expressions made you feel?

What were the consequences of your actions? (Being hit, lectured, silent treatment, ignoring you, pretending nothing has happened.)

If you're like most people, your answers reflect feelings of fear, shame, and anger (if "boundaries" meant hitting, yelling, or rage by your parents).

If you're like some people, your answers reflect feelings of confusion, shame, and rejection (if "boundaries" meant "polite" lectures, silent treatment, or ignoring).

If you're like very few people, you can't really remember what your parents said or did when you displeased them for two reasons:

1. Recall from chapter one why our brain chooses to block out certain memories. Unfortunately, what this means is that by the time your explicit memories started to form, you'd already been disciplined so harshly that your nervous system went into the blue zone. You became a very passive child. A child in the green zone will do many things in the course of their childhood that will displease their parents because the business of being a child is inherently messy, silly, and filled with mistakes. This is always news to many of my clients who remember always being "good kids." Their main source of perplexity is, if I was such a good kid, why am I not a "good adult"? Where does all my anger come from? Now you know, it comes from your "pain body." And you're in the right place to address that, so pat yourself on the back for picking up this book!

2. The second reason you might not remember your parents expressing their disappointment is because it didn't exist. This means that your parents (like many parents I encounter) strongly felt that if they love you then they can't have any boundaries and any kind of feedback about your behavior will result in "damaging" you, so they never said anything.

Many people convolute RP (Respectful Parenting) with this kind of parenting (which researchers call "permissive parenting"), but its anything but respectful.

In fact, that's one of my most frequently asked questions, some version of, " . . . but I have two cousins, one of them is a loser as an adult even though his parents were so loving and respectful and the other is responsible and nice even though his parents were so harsh."

That's not a comparison of RP with mainstream parenting. It's a comparison of permissive parenting with authoritarian parenting; both are harmful. The problem with permissive parenting is that it can masquerade as RP because the parents are genuinely very loving and expressive about their love and adoration for their child. But they make the mistake that authoritarian parents make: believing that a child who is showing "poor behaviors" is being a bad child. The only difference is that authoritarian parents want to fix the child with shame and punishments and permissive parents are so horrified at the idea that their child could be bad that they'd rather pretend nothing has happened and hope that just rug-sweeping everything will make it go away.

RP is so different from both styles because it dismisses the idea altogether that any child is "bad." We understand that children are always doing the best they can, and when their behaviors are challenging, they need and deserve our help. And sometimes, that help looks like establishing a boundary.

Let me explain an activity we do in my workshops to show you what I mean. I read a version of this activity from Jonice Webb's book *Running on Empty* where she describes the exact same scenario encountered by a child who then comes and shares the scenario with his parent. Each chapter of the book describes a different kind of response by the parent and therefore, a different kind of parent.[6] The scenario described here is taken from her book, but the rest of the role play proceeds naturally, as the volunteers see fit.

The activity has three volunteers, the parent and the child and the child's friend who has come from school with the child. The child "comes home" and says the following to his mother:

Child: "Here's a note from my teacher you have to sign."

Parent: "What does it say?"

Child: "It says that I acted out in class today and kicked a chair but that's not what happened. I mean, yes, I did kick the chair but it's because the teacher said something stupid and I told her it was stupid."

Parent: "Oh . . ."

Child: "Yeah . . . I was balancing my pencil on the tip of my finger and she said that it will poke me in the eye. How is that even possible? I'd have to fall into the pencil headfirst for that to happen and I'm not a baby! So yeah . . . I told her that was stupid."

Parent: "Oh . . . how silly! Anyway, dinner is ready . . . where do you need me to sign?"

I then ask the friend what she thinks and the volunteer playing the friend almost always says, "I thought, Wow, what a nice mom! My mom would've yelled at me and asked me a hundred questions!"

I then ask the child how she felt and the volunteer playing the child almost always says, "I felt like she didn't care. I didn't want to get in trouble, but I did want someone to hear my side of the story. I wouldn't even have minded if my mom said I should go and say sorry to my teacher. Her lack of interest seemed harsher."

We then talk about what most people in the workshop would prefer: a parent who doesn't seem to care or a parent who gives an unpleasant consequence. The overwhelming answer, of course, is always someone who seems to care even if that means unpleasant consequences.

Respectful Boundaries with the Peace of Mind

Let's take a three-pronged approach to respectful boundary setting:

1. Changing our mindset about boundaries
2. Learning new skills for boundary setting
3. The nuances of boundary setting

1. BOUNDARY-SETTING MIND SHIFT

Whatever you do, don't skip this section! Understanding these concepts will make your life 200 times easier! There are many reasons why kids don't listen—that is, obey us blindly. Hopefully you've already started to appreciate that obedience itself has no real value and is just a conditioned expectation of parents from children. A more accurate word to use here is "cooperation." Let's investigate with compassionate curiosity why kids don't always want to cooperate with us.

BRAIN SCIENCE: CHILDREN HAVE DEVELOPING BRAINS

Children's brains are major "construction zones": I promise I won't overwhelm you with complicated neuroscience concepts. I just want you to remember the four main parts of the brain that we are concerned with and as you can see in the picture, I even have nicknames for them so you can understand their basic function.

1. The thinking brain (prefrontal cortex)
2. The limbic system
   a. The feelings brain (amygdala)
   b. The memory brain (hippocampus)
3. The survival brain (brain stem)

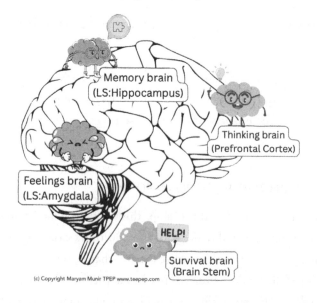

Now the things we expect from our children to do—like see logic and reason, have impulse control over their actions, practice empathy and sharing (emotional intelligence), plan ahead, be organized, etc.—are all part of the Thinking Brain.

The hippocampus, or Memory Brain, is where the explicit memories are stored (recall how they're different from implicit memories) and the learning center is located. This means every time we ask our children to remember to put their clothes in the hamper, or not jump on the sofa, to not touch this or that thing, or to please do their homework, we're expecting them to use this part of the brain.

The amygdala, or Feelings Brain, is self-explanatory, this is where all the feelings originate.

Finally, the brain stem is where our survival instincts of fight, flight, or freeze originate from. You also know from the trauma chapter that this is where our autonomic nervous system originates and connects to all our major organs so it can protect us based on which state is activated (limbs will get a rush of blood if we're in fight or flight, our heart rate will go down if we're in freeze to mimic the life-threatening state).

Now I want you to take a deep breath and carefully look at the table below to see which part of the brain is developed when.

Survival brain (Brain Stem)	Manages your ANS (fight or flight)
	Unconscious responses
	Fully developed at birth
Feelings brain (LS:Amygdala)	Manages feelings
	Feelings of fear trigger the ANS
	Fully developed at birth
Memory brain (LS:Hippocampus)	Manages formation of explicit memories and responsible for learning
	Majorly offline until ages 4–5
	Finishes developing by 7–9 years
Thinking brain (Prefrontal Cortex)	Manages logical thoughts, advanced cognition, impulse control, empathy, planning, EQ
	Comes online by age 4–5
	Finishes developing by 25–30 years

That last row is particularly disappointing for a lot of parents. I usually get gasps of "25??!!" whenever I share this information. In other words, expecting children to do well in regulating their emotions, having patience, understanding logic, making reasonable choices, remembering instructions, and following directions is like expecting a car that's just entered the assembly line to drive and drive well. Let's go a little deeper to find out what being "under construction" really means for a brain.

DEVELOPING BRAINS ARE MOSTLY OPERATING FROM "SURVIVAL BRAIN" OR "FEELINGS BRAIN"

This is the single most helpful concept you might ever learn about your own and your child's brain so feel free to read this several times, until you understand.

You're helping your child with homework, and she makes the same mistake a third time after you've already explained it several times. This time, you lose your cool and angrily remind her what she's doing wrong. She glares back at you, throws her pencil down and says she's done studying. Or she dissolves into loud tears. What just happened for both of you is what Dr. Dan Siege calls "flipping your lid." When we slide down the ladder into the red zone, we've activated our survival brain (fight or flight), the blood rushes away from our thinking brain (the "lid") and to our feeling and survival brain. We also set off our children's feeling and survival brain, thus engaging their defense mechanisms. Whoa . . . what a mess, right?

How do we re-engage the thinking brain? By co-regulating. Here's the most important piece of information: when your child is not in their thinking brain, they're not capable of learning anything. Imagine coming across a snake while you're on a nice walk in the woods, your survival brain needs to kick in and save you. At this time, you can't start reflecting and thinking about the best course of action. Next time, your child is dysregulated and in their defense mode, remember to slow down, self-regulate, and then co-regulate before proceeding.

DEVELOPING BRAINS GET OVERWHELMED AND OVERSTIMULATED EASILY

If you recall from the previous chapter on connection, children's brains have trillions of synapses which means their brain is "open" to taking in a lot of information, and this means they get overstimulated easily. Imagine a toddler whose parents excitedly take them to a loud, colorful, and fun play area. It might be confusing to the parents why the child is now burrowing her head in Dad's chest rather than being excited to try the different games and rides. You might even notice that children tend to go into the "blue state" of nervous system activation, indicating that things are too much for them.

This means that places, scenarios, and people that feel normal and even fun to us are often too much for children and they respond by shutting down instead of saying hi to everyone like we want or interacting with their environment.

DEVELOPING BRAINS HAVE TROUBLE REMEMBERING SEQUENTIAL INSTRUCTIONS

Due to so many synapses and an underdeveloped hippocampus, children aren't able to grasp even simple instructions sometimes and need frequent, gentle reminders. Many parents say that they've reminded their children the same thing many times but as explained earlier, none of these reminders will stick if they weren't done in a gentle and calm tone. If Mom is dysregulated while reminding, she is activating the child's 'survival brain' and learning has stopped.

DEVELOPING BRAINS ARE SLOW . . . MUCH SLOWER THAN WE THINK

We keep saying "developing brains" and now let me explain a part of what that really means. You learned earlier that our brains have billions of neurons. Here's an additional piece of the puzzle; these neurons are either mature or immature. Mature neurons have a fatty insulation called "myelin sheath." This acts exactly like the insulation of a copper wire, preserving the loss of the electric signal and ensuring a speedy transfer. In developing brains, only the survival brain and the feelings brain have these myelinated neurons. Most of the thinking brain has immature neurons, which means that the information transfer is much slower and much of the information is lost while being transferred between neurons.

A fun analogy I give parents is, imagining standing outside in freezing cold weather without your winter coat on and I'm telling you a very interesting (to me) story. How much of it will you retain while you're shivering? Parents will understandably respond to this and say, "But my child is so smart and can totally understand complicated things and ask me complex questions but when it comes to remembering to put their backpack in the closet, they forget every single day!"

Right. Because not *all* the neurons in the PFC are without myelin. Some do have the insulation needed to transfer information fast and efficiently. But if you had the ability to rent a warm fuzzy coat only once a week, would you rather hear *my* stories on those days or do the stuff that *you* need to do for yourself? Yes, childhood is all about egocentrism!

DEVELOPING BRAINS LEARN BY EXPERIENCING

Remember all those synapses that are being formed? The flat's filling up with the "right" tenants? As we learned, that can only happen through experiences. Want to teach your child how to manage their anger? Manage your anger with them. Want to teach your child what empathy is? Be empathetic to them. Want to teach your child how to share? Share with them. We call this skill "modeling," and it's really the only way to teach children anything. You can lecture till you're blue in the face, but they will do what they watch you do. It's really that simple and that scary. Lucky for you, this book is teaching you to become the best version of yourself so you can be the person you'd like your children to become.

MODELING 101

1. Narrate what you're doing, "I'm starting to feel really angry so I'm going to take some space and self-regulate."

2. Be vulnerable, "I don't know what got into me, I said things I shouldn't have said . . . I will apologize to your mom/dad."

3. Be delightful, "Yes I'd absolutely love to share my ice cream with you!"

4. Be gracious, "Yes of course I will help you!" (more on this in the next chapter)

5. Be resilient, "My new job is feeling so difficult and I'm thinking about quitting but I also know that things get easier with time, I think I will keep going."

6. Be grateful, "Thank you so much for putting your dishes away!"

7. Be real, "My workshop didn't go as well as I thought it would but I'm going to work harder next time. I'm feeling sad so I'm just going to sit with my feelings for a bit. I'm sorry if I'm not chattier today." (It's important to be real without dumping our emotions on our kids.)

DEVELOPING BRAINS SHUT DOWN WHEN IN FEAR

"But don't kids need scolding sometimes?" ask a lot of people. Whereas its totally fine to slip up and yell sometimes, "scolding" in and of itself is not an effective parenting tool. As you've learned already, speaking harshly to someone deactivates their thinking brain and makes the brain shut down with fear. If our purpose was to teach, we just killed it.

DEVELOPING BRAINS STRUGGLE WITH TRANSITIONS

One day I met up with an old childhood friend at the mall after a couple of years. While our kids played in the mall's play area, we did what one is wont to do with old friends, we got deep into our conversation.

Our hearts felt full as we caught up on our lives, our minds completely wrapped up in our conversation. At some point, my son came up to me and asked to go to the bathroom. Even though he was right next to me, it was as if I heard him from a distance. At first, I just seemed to ignore him, not purposefully of course, but my brain seemed to be so immersed in my conversation with my friend that I was struggling to detach myself from it.

As my son's protests to go to the bathroom intensified, I expended some herculean effort to detach my brain from our conversation and divert it towards another thought: "He's going to have an accident if you don't get up right this minute, Maryam!" Finally, I excused myself and took my son to the bathroom. Imagine how I did this; I forced my brain to switch its activity from "having fun" to "do something boring" and I did this by using my thinking brain.

I engaged the synapses in my PFC that are responsible for rational thought ("he's going to have an accident") and adaptability ("I was doing something fun but now I must switch to something boring"). In simple words, I used Rational thought and Adaptability. These are advanced functions of the brain (located in the PFC).

I also sensed a feeling of rising irritation as I forced my brain to perform this task of switching activities, but as an adult, I could regulate this feeling without showing my son irritation since that wouldn't be fair.

I hope it's easy to understand why transitions feel so hard to children especially when we ask them to switch from a fun task (watching tv or playing) to a more boring task that they have no personal interest in (studying or cleaning).

DEVELOPING BRAINS HAVE WEAK IMPULSE CONTROL

The fight or flight response is sensitive in children and for good reason. As incredibly vulnerable creatures, their brain needs to be able to act quickly when a perception of danger is received. This is why children seem to have little to no impulse control and seem to act 'without thinking,' like hitting their sibling when their toy is snatched, or banging their door on you when they're not happy with your decision, or not being able to act from logic even when they technically have awareness of something. As they grow, their impulse control improves, and they start to become more logical.

2. LEARNING NEW SKILLS FOR BOUNDARY SETTING

GO FROM "SAYING" TO "DOING"

Look at these two pictures. One is an example of instructions and the other is an example of a boundary. What's the difference? As you might guess from the picture on the right, boundaries have a physical manifestation. Many parents get frustrated because what they're offering are instructions: "Don't touch that!" But what they think they're doing is setting a boundary.

Here's how we know our expectation is not fair: If we're saying the same thing many times and the child is not listening, that means it's an instruction. Now, of course, who doesn't want children who simply follow the instructions—it sure would make our lives easier! The more we practice RP, the more cooperative children will get. In the meantime, we as adults can make a different choice instead of expecting children to make that different choice. 'Doing' boundaries looks like:

Step 1: Offer a simple choice: "Will you go to the bathroom yourself or do you need help?"

Step 2: Provide help if needed: "Looks like you're needing help! No worries, I can help you along!"

Step 3: Co-regulate any resulting feelings.

If it's a teen or preteen, you can playfully drag them to the bathroom. Pretend they're even more heavy than they are. Breathe heavily with exaggeration. Add some humor. Bottom line is, we know kids aren't meaning to "disobey," they just need a little more help sometimes, and if we don't pick fights with them over this small stuff, then they're more likely to cooperate when it really matters.

GO FROM "NO" TO "NOT RIGHT NOW"

Even if you must say no to something, put a time stamp on it. "I'd love to play with you after I'm done with the dishes."

GO FROM "DON'T" TO "DO"

If I ask you *not to* think of a pink elephant, what will you think of? Kids mostly hear the "action" words, so if we say, "Don't scream," they hear "scream". Making our request "positive" or actionable is more helpful.

Example: "You can whisper or talk in this tone." (Instead of "Don't be loud!")

"You can write on the paper." (Instead of "Don't write on the walls.")

GO FROM DISTRACTING TO REDIRECTION

Distracting a child from what they're doing because you don't want them to do it disregards their need for doing that particular thing. Remember, children are always learning and exploring. Their intention for doing something that's undesirable to us is not to thwart us. For instance, children play with shampoo, soap, etc. to meet a sensory need. Toddlers love exploring different textures, so instead of snatching the soap from their hand and distracting them with silly faces, we can acknowledge their need and redirect them,

"Shampoo is for washing hair, let's play with your sensory bin."

"I can't let you use my lipstick but here's your lip balm."

GO FROM SHAMING TO SHARING FEELINGS

When teaching a new skill or habit, instead of shaming the child when they forget what they were supposed to do, we can share your feelings. "I get really frustrated when I see shoes in the hallway." (*"Uff main kitna thak jaati hoon roz zameen sai kapray utha utha kai."*)

GO FROM DISTANCE TO PROXIMITY

Remember my story of delaying listening to my son's call for a bathroom visit when I was chatting with my friend? He really had to yell to get my attention! Parents will often say, "She doesn't do it until I yell," which means "yelling" is an effective task interrupter; it jolts the brain into action and "forces" the transition to happen.

But it's not a very respectful one. So here are some alternative task interrupters:

- Physical touch. Going up to the child and tapping them on the shoulder or holding their hand and saying, "We're leaving the house in 5 minutes . . . can you please put your shoes on?"
- Or a loud but kind "FRIENDLY REMINDER! We leave the house in 5 minutes."
- Or I sometimes speak in a robot voice or a different accent that grabs their attention and makes them laugh and untangle that spaghetti brain.

GO FROM REGRETTING TO PREVENTING:

Instead of being mad and upset that our children didn't do as we expected, we can set them up for success. There is no need to test their immature brain development where their impulse control is weak.

Example: "I told you to turn the iPad off after an hour!"
Preventive: Have an app on the iPad that automatically locks the iPad after an hour (and the children should know about it).

Example 2: "Your stupid rock made me trip! I told you to keep them in your room!"
Preventive: "Sorry love, rocks stay outside only. Yes, I get you really want to bring them inside! You're allowed to be upset about it . . . I'm here for your feelings."

Example 3: "I told you not to hit your cousin!"
Preventive: "I will stay close and help you stay safe."

3. THE NUANCES OF BOUNDARY SETTING

Here are some shocking facts about boundaries that you might not be aware of, and this lack of awareness might be the real cause of your frustration with your children.

THE RIGHT RESPONSE TO AN "AGGRESSIVE CHILD"
IS NOT MORE BOUNDARIES

Our top most frequently asked question in our Facebook group is some version of,

"Why does my child hit everyone!"

"We never hit our children but our son is so aggressive!"

"My daughter bangs her head against the wall!"

"My teen is full of so much anger, should I take him to a psychologist?"

And I think what all these exclamations are expressing is a huge concern and worry that our child will grow up to be an abusive adult. I want you to reframe a child's anger (and even your own) in only one way: it's the red zone on the autonomic ladder. That's all it is every single time—it's the child's brain's healthy response to not feeling safe. By now you know very well how to help your child climb back up the ladder. You also know that co-regulating in this manner over and over will lend itself to excellent emotional regulation for your child as an adult. If you're wondering what to do in the moment to just stop the hitting, you have two options:

1. We know that the red zone indicates a lot of energy in the body from the adrenaline and cortisol that are pumped into the veins for fight and flight. You can help your child channel this energy by giving them a safe alternative. This works well for the twins. When

they get angry, I hold a pillow close to my body and let them kick that. We've also talked about making sure we don't hurt anyone when we're angry but it's ok to safely expel that energy.

2. Sometimes this is not possible because our child's anger triggers our own fight response. In that case, try your best to physically just block the hits if they're directed at you using all your strength. You can hold your child's hand if they're hitting you or someone else and your nonverbal cues will continue to signal safety even while you help your child. Since they're not metabolizing the energy of the red zone, they might take longer to work through their anger. Feel free to take a breather and always let your child know that you're not walking away from them, and you'll be right back after taking some space.

ONLY WE ARE RESPONSIBLE FOR SETTING BOUNDARIES

We can't blame our children for not "respecting the boundary"; that's because we're the ones with true power in this relationship—the onus of responsibility falls on us. For example, if I tell my children not to disturb me while I'm working but then I leave my door unlocked and don't have an arrangement for them to stay safely outside my room with another adult, then I didn't really enforce my boundaries properly. Now, of course, this will happen sometimes that we'll be too tired or not resourceful enough to put the correct reinforcers in place and that's alright. That's when we can have compassion for ourselves and our children—not everything is going to be done the way we wished for. In other words, boundaries are not commands we dish out to our children and expect them to obey. Neither are they random limits placed on children for the sake of "keeping them in line." Boundaries are simply our protective fences meant to help us and our children succeed.

RESPECTFUL BOUNDARY-SETTING HAS THREE C'S

Always remember the three C's of respectful boundary setting; Clear, Confident, and Consistent.

Clear is Kind. This is Dr. Brown's mantra. When we hesitate, act confused, change our minds, and dilly dally with the boundaries, our children don't know what is expected of them. If I don't want my children to interrupt me while I'm working, I will lock the door. Leaving it open is confusing for them and their weak impulse control sets them up for failure.

For example, if you want to start eating healthy, you will stop buying junk food and bringing it to your house. Yes?

You won't tempt yourself with a situation where you know you might fail.

We want to do the same for our kids.

If we don't want them to roam around the whole house and create a big mess that will make us mad, we set up a gated space for them. A physical boundary. When my children were little and we had a tiny house, I got rid of my dining table and made the whole dining area a "Yes Space" (term coined by Janet Lansbury).[7] This space was visible to me from the kitchen and tv lounge where I spent most of the time.

More examples:

- If we don't want them touching something, we keep it out of reach. (And if they still reach it, we laugh at how they're smarter than us and figure out a better hiding place next time).

- If we don't want them to hit their siblings, we provide them separate spaces and we stay close when we know things can get heated.
- If we don't want them to eat more roti than chicken, then we don't serve them roti.
- If we don't want them to put on five outfits in the day, we put a lock on the closet.

Confident is Kind. Fahad was one of the most loving and gentle dads who'd ever come to my office. His kind eyes and the loving way he spoke about his three-year-old made me so happy that a child has him for a father. I was curious to know how he thought I could help him and waited for him to tell me what had brought him in that day.

"I love my son," he began, "but I can't keep taking him to my office anymore. Can you please tell me what I should do?"

I was immediately intrigued. No one had ever asked me that question before.

"Tell me more about why he's been going to the office with you," I asked.

"Because he says so!" he said, simply.

"Oh! Is there no one to leave him home with?" I asked, very confused.

"Oh no . . . his mom is home and a whole bunch of my extended family who all love him but he insists on coming with me."

"Ah . . . I see. You don't like disappointing your son because you love him so much!" I was finally starting to understand what was happening.

175

"Yes . . . I can't see him cry at all. It breaks my heart," he said, and I nodded, understanding his dilemma.

"You feel like if you leave for office and he's still crying, that you're not a good father?"

He was quiet when I said this. I waited for him to speak. I could see that he was wanting to say something that felt difficult to say. After a while, he finally spoke.

"My father worked really hard to raise us. All of us siblings are doctors or engineers." He paused, once again struggling to say what he needed to say. I stayed in the silence with him. Settling down in this space with him. Eventually he spoke again, "But I've never hugged him and he has never hugged me." Then he abruptly stopped talking, as if he'd spoken to much. Just in that moment my heart went out to this gentle man. Not only was he such a loving father but he was a loving son too, struggling to acknowledge his own truth of not feeling connected to his father at the risk of saying something unkind about his beloved father.

"You love and respect your father a lot," I observed. "You have nothing but appreciation for everything he's done for you."

"Yes!" he said enthusiastically, relieved that I hadn't doubted his loyalty to his father. He proceeded to tell me more about the sacrifices his father had made him and his siblings. I listened, nodded, and smiled, validating his father's love for his children. But also waiting for him to say what I know he was trying to say. Finally, it came.

"I don't want to be like that . . . to not hug my kids or show them affection."

"You're afraid that if you leave your son and go to work, that you'll be hurting him . . . like how you felt hurt when your father couldn't connect with you?"

"Ye-es," he said, ever so hesitantly. Every fiber of his being so uncomfortable with what probably felt to him like a betrayal of his beloved father.

My heart went out to this young father who was afraid to set healthy boundaries with his sweet boy because he was worried that he'd be hurting his son, making him feel not heard and seen like he felt as a little boy. He was willing to even take his son to his office, just so his son wouldn't feel that hurt Fahad had felt as a little boy. (Did I have to fight back a tear or two—you bet.)

Cycle-breaker parents are so brave, aren't they? Not only do they make the courageous choices daily, of being different from their own parents, but they also carry the pain of their inner child while also striving to be loyal and respectful to their own parents.

I assured Fahad that he was the farthest thing from being the kind of father who was distant and disconnected from his kids. I taught him about the importance of setting boundaries and how they're a source of safety and comfort for the child. Yes, it's upsetting for children when a parent has to leave, but that upset turns into fear when the parent looks hesitant and confused. They're looking to us for cues of safety and when our own face is signaling "danger" because we're so anxious and stressed, it translates into major dysregulation for the child. Instead, we have to meet their storm with our 'confident captain' persona.

Like Susan Stiffelman says,

When you're the captain of the ship, and your children are stressed, or distressed, or want something, or are unhappy, it's okay with you. You can live through that. You don't need them to like you, or to be cheery and smiling all the time. You, in fact, recognize that for a child to grow up to become a resilient adult, they actually have to live through, discover that they can live through disappointment and upset.[8]

Consistency is Kind. Consistency is not the same as rigidity. I'm not saying that you should decide that your children will never stay up past 8 p.m. and then you must never break that rule. Strict rules and regulations only suit traffic laws or the military. Families are fluid and flexible. The only purpose of consistency is in regards to something that, if not done, will push you over the edge. For example, you don't like your teenager using your car, but when she used it a couple of times, you stayed quiet. Another time you let her know that you're not ready to share your car. Yet, another time you again stayed quiet. She's not understanding whether you are or are not ok with her using your car.

Similarly, your toddler follows you into the bathroom and you let him come because, oh well. The next time he comes again, you feel irritated and ask him to stay outside. Another time you bring him inside. Again, he's not sure if he is or isn't allowed in the bathroom with you.

If something is feeling important to you and you find yourself irritated about it and stay quiet hoping and praying your child will make a different choice next time, most likely you'll end up being unkind about it. This would be a situation in which being consistent will make it clear for your child what's expected from them. If you do make an exception, say so. "I'm usually not ok with you taking my car but I can let you take it today."

BOUNDARIES IN "JOINT FAMILY SYSTEMS" ARE ESSENTIAL

Navigating life in a multi-generational home can be tricky in any case but trying to raise children in a non-traditional way can sometimes feel like a downright battle. The grandparents, aunts, uncles, and neighbors and all other adults who are observing you parent have their own opinions and aren't usually afraid to give them. I don't doubt you for one second when you tell me that you feel judged by them when you don't immediately resort to the Holy Grail of Parenting (scolding, lecturing, punishment, aka *daant, maar, baizti*). I want you to know that this is where your courage comes in. Allowing other people to judge you while you do what's best for your children is an act of profound courage, and I want you to pause here and literally pat yourself on the back for undertaking it.

Do you know what it means to your children and what will happen once they're older and realize what you did for them? That, instead of giving in to societal pressure from other adults, you did right by your children who were voiceless? That, instead of walking in the footsteps of your ancestors, you chose to do the hard work of becoming a cycle-breaker parent? They will be in awe of you and give you the kind of respect you gave them, and people will wonder what on earth you did to command such fierce loyalty from your children.

We spend a lot of time and effort trying to please adults in our life who may or may not appreciate our efforts, but I can promise you that your children will return to you your hard work manifold. Do you know how I know this? I know this because I can't count the number of times my clients have sat before me and lovingly recalled all the sacrifices their parents made for them. Despite those parents being a source of great harm to them, I see my clients over and over choosing to forgive and love their parents for the good they did. And here you are, actively breaking the trauma cycle and choosing your children over societal pressure. Why would you be anything but a super star for your one-day adult children? I hope next time when you feel those eyes boring into you with judgment and when you hear the tsk-tsk of the shaking heads, you can hear your adult children's voices in your head louder than the judgments. That you can hear them say, "Thank you, Mama/Baba, for being brave when it truly mattered."

Alternates to Boundary Setting

As important as it is to set boundaries and be that voice of calm and reason during our children's "storms," it's just as important to realize when it's not a case of coming down with a definitive boundary. Let's explore some scenarios where we don't just need boundaries but something more collaborative.

PROBLEM SOLVING

I first learned about this concept in my Parent Educator certification for a training course for parents of teens from Positive Discipline Association by Jane Nelson and Lynn Lott.[9] These are the main steps of this process:

1. Inform your child of a problem you have with how something is being done (by them) ("I'm feeling worried about . . .").
2. Acknowledge your child's answer by active listening skills ("Yes, I understand . . ." "Wow that does sound

difficult!" etc.) Repeat this step as many times as necessary until you can see that they're ready to hear you out.

3. Once they seem visibly de-escalated, ask them if they'd be willing to work on some solutions.

4. By this time, they should be feeling ready enough to engage (if they're not, work on connection more and let this go for now).

5. If they're ready, let them suggest some solutions without discarding anything they say.

6. Make some suggestions yourself.

7. Once you're both done, go over each solution, eliminating ones that don't work for either of you and pick one that works for you both.

8. Thank your child for walking through this process with you and agree on a day two weeks from that day to check in with how it's going.

9. Vital part of success with this process: for two weeks, make no comments about this process.

Some things to remember:

- This is not going to work if we're still repairing and working on our connection. In fact, the success of this process is a good indicator of where we are with our child.

- This is not going to work if we're not willing to spend enough time on step 2.

- We have to be a little extra mindful when our child is suggesting a solution because some of them will sound ridiculous to us (just as our solutions sound to them) but it's important to listen with a straight face and give them the same importance we want for our own solutions.

- Finally, it's really important to give this process time to succeed. If we start saying "But that's not what we discussed!" or "Remember what we talked about?" it's just not going to work. Space and time are crucial here.

MODELING GRACIOUSNESS

"Modeling graciousness" is one of my favorite things to practice as a parent. I also just really like this phrase, which was made popular in parent coach circles by Robin Eiznig's article entitled exactly that. I'm using an excerpt here from her article to explain this concept and I highly recommend reading the rest of her article.

She intentionally (or so it appears) pours a glass of milk on to the table, where it cascades on to the floor. Having her help clean it up is a logical consequence. You get her a rag, and you ask (or preferably, tell) her to clean up the milk she spilled. She refuses. Or laughs. Or runs off. You go get her and you calmly explain that the milk is on the floor and it has to get cleaned up because if it stays there it will start to smell really bad and it will make the floor slippery and dangerous, and that you'd like her to help clean it up, and that you will help her. You get two cloths, and offer her one, and you ask (tell) her "I need your help to clean up the milk. Here is your cloth and here is my cloth. We'll do it together." Or you get one cloth and a small container of water, and you say "We need to clean up the milk. Would you like to use the cloth to wipe it up or would you like to hold the container while I wipe it up?" *(Pay attention: here's where it gets tricky. don't stop reading now!)* She refuses again. Or laughs again. Or throws the rag. Or runs off again. You're sitting there (undoubtedly frustrated) thinking *"But I asked just the right way! I gave her choices! I offered to help her! She can't just pour milk on the floor and not have any consequence! I have to wait her out or make her come do it—how do I do that? I'm perfectly calm, I'm not getting upset, I'm doing everything the way the books/ experts say to do, and she's still not helping! I have the most out of control kid ever. What now?!?)*

I'll tell you "What now." Model graciousness. Clean it up. Say, with confidence (and feel with confidence, too . . . that matters) that you're happy to help this time and that you're sure she will help next time. Because you *are* sure that she'll help next time (right??) And if it turns out that you're wrong, and she *doesn't* help next time, still have confidence that she will do it the next time (and chalk it up to developmental stage or fatigue or teething or a long day at school or that toy that broke earlier in the day.) Quiet the anxious voices in your head that say *"if I clean it up, she'll never learn responsibility."* Quiet the resentful voices in your head that say *"I'm sick of doing everything for her when she's perfectly capable of doing it herself."* Quiet the punitive voices in your head that say *"she spilled it, she needs to clean it up."* Have trust that she will do it next time. Because one of these times, she will. **She will be like you. Helpful. Generous. Altruistic.**[10]

And there we have it; we have to treat our child the way we'd like them to treat others. Our children have to experience kindness, compassion, helpfulness, generosity of spirit from us in difficult moments to then be able to pass it on to others in their difficult moments. This, this right here, is the hardest bit of parenting you'll ever do. Because it combines all the various elements of respectful parenting into one snowball of difficulty: emotional regulation, facing our triggers, managing our fear and anxieties about the future, building new neural pathways of responding to children with kindness even when they don't do as we asked, and finally, not holding on to resentment or feeling like a victim. If respectful parenting was a four-year degree, we'd put modeling graciousness as the ultimate exam of all you've learned. Therefore, give yourself plenty of time to get here. But once you do get here, you'll see the magic and will never want to go back. (Robin also has a follow-up post on this discussing how, years later, her teen responded to her with graciousness.[11])

SAYING/DOING NOTHING

I give you official permission to often choose this option. Say or do nothing, just as we'd like others to not comment on our mistakes or start immediately looking for "appropriate" ways to respond. When was the last time you screwed up and someone lectured you or at least gave you "the look" and you really benefitted from that? I'm going to guess never. This is a classic case of "but children are not people" manifesting itself once again.

Because this is pretty simple: no kind of people, small or big, want someone on their case at all times.

Your child yelled because they were dysregulated. Let it go.

Your teen banged the door too hard on her way out. Let it go.

Your toddler snatched a toy from the baby and the baby is cool. Let it go.

Here's one of the most profound yet simple lessons I learned about parenting: every waking moment in a child's life is not a learning opportunity. Children deserve to just exist and be left alone just as much as we do.

GIVING SPACE AND TIME

There are many things kids do that are simply a function of their immature brain development or the fact that there's no learning without making lots of mistakes. For example, you signed up your child for soccer practice and they loved it the first time but are refusing to go the next time—let it go. I tell parents not to sign up their child for any structured activity or class until they're at least six years old, and even then, be very, very ready if they loved the idea of it but don't love the actual experience. Most kids aren't actually ready for a structured activity before ages eight to ten.

Similarly, I think of the times I took my kids to what I thought was an exciting place and they refused to partake in it. Sure, I could "hold my boundary" and force them to go in because I've spent the time, energy, and money to bring them and they might even like it after I force them, but, in the process, I've compromised their trust in me. It's ok to gently encourage and slow down, but if they stay firm on not trying out the activity, it's best to back off and try again a few months . . . or years . . . later.

This is especially true for homework and academic woes. Most children need way more time and space to do the things their teachers and parents expect them to do. Their fine motor skills, as well as their brain, just aren't there yet. Slowing down, staying calm, and waiting are often all that's required to raise kids who take charge of their own academics.

SPECIAL TOPIC: SPACE AND TIME IN REGARDS TO RELIGION

One of our most frequently asked questions in our Facebook group is how to "make" children "study the Quran" or sit with their *qaari* to learn their *qaida*.

I have a very lovely part-time helper who helps me take care of the kids and my mom.

The helper (Fauzia *baji*, as the kids call her) is lovely and tells my kids stories about her own kids, especially her two-year-old daughter, Zainab (not her real name).

My six-year-old twins, Yahya and Muhammed, often make drawings for Zainab and send with Fauzia to give her daughter. They didn't meet her for the first six months and only heard stories about her from her mom. Fauzia loves her daughter and talks about her with so much delight and joy. She told the boys fun and interesting stories about Zainab; what she does, what she likes, etc. Fauzia would also tell them that she's told Zainab about them and Zainab thinks they're awesome and how much she'd love to meet them. They loved hearing all these stories and the indirect back and forth with Zainab.

One day Fauzia finally brought Zainab to meet the twins and, as expected, they were absolutely delighted to meet her. It was almost as if they'd been friends with her forever. They willingly and joyfully shared their toys and snacks with her, which we know is not the norm for children their ages.

Obviously, this was all because Fauzia had always spoken so highly of Zainab and more so because she'd told them what Zainab thinks of them and how much she looks forward to meeting them.

Imagine what would've happened if Fauzia had done the opposite. That every time the boys made a mistake, she said,

"Oh, Zainab doesn't like that!!"

"Zainab only likes boys who do xyz."

"Zainab gets angry when you do xyz."

"I'm going to tell Zainab what you did and she'll be very sad."

"You better do xyz or Zainab will be angry at you!"

"I told Zainab what you did and she was so sad and disappointed."

How do you think they'd feel about her then? Would they be excited to meet her one day or be afraid . . . even ashamed and self-conscious?

When children are little, they start asking questions about their Creator. They're curious about Him. Their little brain isn't able to comprehend the complex concept of a Divine Creator but one day it will. Until that day . . . it's crucial how we speak to them about their Creator.

It's important, during this time to focus on our own relationship to Allah and remind them how much He loves them and that His love is unconditional.

Remember that children are already on the fitrah. The love for their Creator already resides in their hearts. The quest for this love also resides in their souls. If we refrain from forcing religion on them, shaming them in regards to it, and instead make it as interesting and fun as possible, they will stay on that path they're already on, the path that leads to the Maker.

NOTES

1. Brené Brown and Susan Cain, "How Sorry and Longing Make Us Whole," *Unlocking Us*, 23 Mar. 2022, podcast, https://brenebrown.com/podcast/how-sorrow-and-longing-make-us-whole-part-1-of-2/.
2. Sarah Marshall, "Karen Carpenter Part 1 with Carolyn Kendrick," *You're Wrong About*, 16 Jan. 2023, podcast, https://www.buzzsprout.com/1112270/12055929-karen-carpenter-part-1-with-carolyn-kendrick.
3. Na'ima B. Robert, *Show Up: A Motivational Message for Muslim Women* (Kube Publishing Limited, 2021).
4. Ichiro Kishimi, *The Courage to Be Disliked: The Japanese Phenomenon That Shows You How to Change Your Life and Achieve Real happiness* (Atria Books, 2018).
5. K. C. Davis (@domesticblisters), "It's not easy. It's hard work and we all make mistakes," *TikTok*, Dec. 14, 2022, https://www.tiktok.com/t/ZT8R1v78b/.
6. Jonice Webb, *Running on Empty: Overcome Your Childhood Emotional Neglect* (Morgan James Publishing, 2012).
7. Janet Lansbury, "YES Spaces—What They Really Are and Why They Matter," *Respectful Parenting: Janet Lansbury Unruffled*, 25 Jun. 2021, podcast, https://www.janetlansbury.com/2021/06/yes-spaces-what-they-really-are-and-why-they-matter/.
8. Susan Stiffelman, in Janet Lansbury, "From Toddler to Teen—How Our Confident Leadership Fosters Resilience (with Susan Stiffelman)," *Respectful Parenting: Janet Lansbury Unruffled*, 12 Jun. 2018, podcast, https://www.janetlansbury.com/2018/06/from-toddler-to-teen-how-our-confident-leadership-fosters-resilience-with-susan-stiffelman/.
9. *PDA: Positive Discipline Association*, https://www.positivediscipline.org/.
10. Robin Einzig, "Modeling Graciousness," *Visible Child*, 2 Sept. 2015, https://visiblechild.com/2015/09/02/model-graciousness/.
11. Robin Einzig, "Modeling Graciousness, Part II: The Long Run," *Visible Kid*, 10 Sept. 2017, https://visiblechild.com/2017/09/10/modeling-graciousness-part-ii-the-long-run/.

CHAPTER 4

VALIDATION—WE ALL NEED A MIRROR

"Grown-ups love figures . . . When you tell them you've made a new friend, they never ask you any questions about essential matters. They never say to you 'What does his voice sound like? What games does he love best? Does he collect butterflies?' Instead, they demand 'How old is he? How much does he weigh? How much money does his father make?' Only from these figures do they think they have learned anything about him."

—Antoine de Saint-Exupéry, *The Little Prince*

Who's Mirroring You?

From the day we're born, we start hearing a story about ourselves.

Who we are.

What we like.

What we don't like.

What are the things we're good at.

What are the things we're not good at.

Parents, grandparents, teachers, and other caretakers all reflect us back to ourselves.

No one is born knowing themselves, and it's through these stories that we get to know ourselves.

The problem arises when the people reflecting *our* story convolute it with their own stories. When they're people who haven't had the privilege or pleasure of knowing themselves and their own stories.

For example, as I shared in the first chapter how my sweet mama would look at my fierce, outgoing nature and it would scare her. Her story, shaped by her upbringing and society, was that women shouldn't have a voice. The more they talk, the more trouble they land themselves in. Women who're fierce and loud are seen as *chalaak* (cunning), manipulative, and "characterless."

She didn't want me to be any of those things, so my outgoing and leadership-qualities personality scared her. She'd often look at me, her small but effervescent eyes seeing much beyond the little girl in front of her, looking at the woman she thought I'd have to be in this world to survive and say, "What will become of you?"

Of course, I, as a child with no critical thinking skills, had no ability to see where she was coming from. All I heard was, "I'm a lost cause."

Pile on top of that, my cultural and societal context of the "chai trolley" system where any woman is "lucky" to be picked to get married. Random strangers come to your house to evaluate you and decide your fate based on your "chai-trolley" etiquette.

These are all the burdens we carry—the weight of the stories from our childhood, reinforced by society and cultural norms. These stories, piling on top of each other like cemented bricks, getting taller and wider with each moment spent in this world surrounded by "false mirrors." This wall stands between our conditioned self and our authentic/true self, creating a painful civil war.

On the one side of the wall is the light of the human our Creator created, our true authentic self created in His light, and on the other side is the mute puppet created by our environment (people, circumstances, culture). The light is always trying to break through the wall and drown out the darkness of the shadows created by the puppet, and this creates a constant inner friction that scrapes the fragments of our being, splintering and wounding us all over.

It looks like me getting married one day, carrying the burden of my stories: "I was a lost cause and here's a man willing to take me on."

The light inside me wanted to disintegrate this burden, it often shone through when the authentic self was being buried even more. It looked like me protesting to my husband that I'm not happy in the U.S. It looked like me pleading with my husband to protect me from his brother's wrath.

If the conditioned-me had won entirely, I'd have stayed quiet.

This is something that happens to all of us. If we quiet our authentic self enough times, its light diminishes to a nondescript amount where it's barely perceptible.

Some of us continue to honor this light by fighting back, as much as we can, and are often labeled "aggressive," like I was, by almost everyone who didn't take the time to understand me.

But the problem is that we don't believe in our own light.

The whole time I protested to my husband about my distress of not adjusting well in the U.S. or of feeling disrespected by his brother, I was operating mostly from my conditioned-self. I was telling the story of my light through the lens of my darkness.

And that's also why neither my husband nor most other people validated me.

I was my own biggest invalidator because I'd grown up not knowing how to honor my light.

So how do we learn then, to honor our light?

How do we learn to break down the wall that stands between our authentic, joyful self and the dark, conditioned self?

By finding a new mirror.

Someone who will reflect our light this time. Someone who will pick up on those shards of light peeking through the wall and reflect them back with heightened intensity.

Have you ever seen light reflected in a mirror?

It's the only thing that isn't a "true mirror image."

Nope.

It's instead, much brighter, often with plays of other dancing colors or halos of more light.

It is, in fact, a much more generous image of the reality.

My mirror was my sweet friend, Bethany. (More about her in the next section.)

She saw my light and multiplied it with her generous interpretations. She is also someone who was lucky enough to know and honor her own light from a young age.

For you, this mirror, a safe, kind, and astute person, can be a therapist. Many people misunderstand the role of therapists and think when they see a therapist, they'll be getting life advice and random deep wisdoms thrown at them. In reality, a good therapist is merely a "true mirror."

For most people though, I encourage them to take a closer look at their own life. You probably have at least one person who always says kind things to you about yourself and most likely you've neglected that person's feedback. I invite you to spend more time with this person and when they offer generous compliments and reflections, resist the urge to dismiss them or water down your own greatness. Instead, bask in the warmth of their reflections and allow yourself to be seen the way you always deserved.

This person and this relationship will be crucial to your healing.

A lot of people complain that they don't have anyone like this in their life, and for such people, I do recommend finding a therapist you feel seen with.

However, I want to remind you that if you're mostly operating from your conditioned-self, then you've unknowingly been dimming your own light, let alone that someone else would have the opportunity to brighten it for you. I recommend taking a pause and shifting your stance and noticing any positive comments you hear from people around you and really taking them seriously and choosing to believe them with all your heart.

I promise you, you'll start seeing a new you.

The Librarian without the Glasses

The doorbell rings and I'm wondering who it could be. In America you don't just show up to people's houses. If your doorbell rings without you knowing exactly who's ringing it, you keep one hand on the door handle and the other on 911. I look through the peephole and it's Bethany. With two bags of Trader Joe's in her hands. What's this lady up to, I think affectionately, opening the door. Her showing up at my door with delicious meals is not an anomaly.

"I'm sorry I have to run off and make another two deliveries but here's your *biryani*. Please put the *raita* in the fridge ASAP or else it might go bad," she says breathlessly.

"Oh, I . . . thank you!" I manage to utter.

And inside I'm wondering why she's bringing me *biryani* once again. I mean, I'm thrilled she's bringing me *biryani*, but I'm also confused. I accept it gratefully and give her a big hug before she rushes off to her next "delivery." That's Bethany for you. Making meals for her friends and delivering them, *raita* and all.

So yes, for a while I did sort of feel like Bethany was helping me out because she likes to give back. This is part of her work as a white person taking ownership of their privilege. I didn't have this language at the time, but I did know about her generosity. The whole community did. She was a much-loved member of the everyone-knows-everyone NOVA Muslim community. I always found it flattering and touching when she showed up at my door, and the only reason I could find for it was that Bethany felt sorry for me and was trying to help. Perhaps if I wasn't so utterly in need of that help, I'd have let my ego reject her help. I didn't have that luxury though.

THE ANGER (PAIN) OF NOT BEING SEEN

After dealing with infertility and finally IVF to have our first child, the last thing we could have ever expected was four children in the span of four years including a set of identical twins. We were ecstatic beyond words. And raising four children, aged four and under, would be difficult anywhere in the world but in America, where I had no immediate family or other support system and no funds to hire help, it was mind-bogglingly, overwhelmingly scary, exhausting, and lonely. When I think of how difficult that time was, my body is flooded with all kinds of emotions.

The loudest of these emotions, at the time of writing this book, is anger. This anger is raw, so real and so fresh that as I write these words and recall that time in my life, my nervous system is kicking into its stress response, sliding down the ladder into the red zone. I can feel my heart rate go up, my cheeks warming up, and my lips settling in an unhappy shape.

This anger that still shows up in my body is irrefutable evidence of how unsafe I felt in those years in America. The lack of safety registered through the judgments and harshness of being repeatedly told by people who were supposed to be our well-wishers that my husband is "so helpful" and therefore I don't need or deserve any other help. The lack of safety that comes from being told over and over that I was "so lucky" that my husband wanted to "help me" after getting home from work. So, the anger is my nervous system bearing witness to the injustice of normalizing suffering for mothers and glorifying fathers for showing up as a father in any capacity. The kind of showing up that actively deducts even more credit from the mother's dwindling credit account.

I often ask the mothers in my workshops how they'd feel if they got the kind of credit their husbands get for changing every diaper. The question makes them laugh at first and then sober up at the implications. Mothers deserve help and appreciation without being penalized and have their worthiness as a mother put on the testing table. This is something Bethany tried to tell me over and over every time she came over "just because." After she showed up at my door for the ump-teenth time, I did ask her why. She lived forty minutes away, had three children of her own, and wasn't exactly swimming in extra time.

"Because you deserve more support, Maryam," she'd say solemnly. Not pityingly but just matter-of-factly.

"But Umar is helpful," I'd offer . . . repeating what had been reflected back to me by those that surrounded me.

She'd shake her head firmly, "You mean your kids' dad? Yeah, no."

"Elizabeth is there . . . in the basement. When things get too hard, I ask her for help," I'd offer again, genuinely confused by Bethany's rhetoric.

"You have four really small children and literally no sup-port, Maryam. You deserve more help." Her words were uttered convincingly and without a shred of pity, and yet I had no idea what she was talking about. Literally no one else in my life seemed to have that view.

Well, not no one. Many strangers did, oddly enough. They'd stop me often when I was out with my kids and ask me if I have help. In a country where no one except very wealthy people can afford paid help, people routinely asked me if I had help because they couldn't fathom that I was a mother of these four young kids without any help.

"My husband is very helpful," I'd say again, repeating the story that had been told to me so many times that it had now become my own.

They'd nod politely, too nice to say that wasn't enough, but their expressions said it all. Expressions much like Bethany's, that confused me because they didn't align with the other expressions I was used to.

My sweet friend Andrea, who's lucky enough to have three sets of doting grandparents (her divorced parents are both remarried) walking distance from her home, also echoed these sentiments.

"Maryam, I don't know how you do it!" she'd say to me often over our long text message chains. "I don't know what I'd have done if I didn't have my family!" I had to admit that I was insanely jealous of her proximity to her family. I also had the pleasure of staying at her mom's house and basically wanted her to adopt me. Having "lost" my own mom to Alzheimer's, my friends' moms are the closest I'll ever get to a mother's care.

WHY SOME VALIDATIONS ARE MORE IMPORTANT THAN OTHERS

You might be wondering by now, if I had so many people validating my difficulties and challenges as a young mother of four kids, winging it on my own with my very helpful husband, why didn't I choose to believe them? Why did I believe the other people who constantly told me that it wasn't so bad and I was lucky and I should be grateful?

Mainly because despite her best efforts, I got to see Bethany once or twice a month, and it's not like she was lecturing me the whole time about how I deserved more help. And who cares what strangers say or a friend who lives ten hours away says. What matters is what the people who are the loudest say, and what people who you interact with more regularly say. No matter how much we heal and grow, we are not islands. We do need and deserve to be surrounded by people who are willing to do the work of knowing us and honoring our truth.

The people who surrounded me and had surrounded me for years were the loudest in telling me their own story and not my own. These were their stories:

- I can't help Maryam and that makes me feel guilty so I will tell her repeatedly that she doesn't actually need help and she's lucky.
- When I was Maryam's age, my life was even harder; at least her husband is helpful.
- Unlike me, Maryam had many years of "freedom" (infertility) so she's obviously very happy now and shouldn't complain.
- My own husband was never as involved as hers so she's definitely lucked out.

Can you see what's common in all these invalidations? They focus on the person having these beliefs and not on my story. To be able to set yourself aside and be willing to really *see* someone, we have to have unshakable self-love. To not conflate our story with someone else's when our own story has clearly nothing to do with someone else's is the purest act of love. The kind Bethany showed me. There are a billion stories she could have told herself to justify why she could neither help me nor was she required to but instead, she chose to see me, understand me, and reflect me back to myself in the most loving of ways so that I saw myself as someone worthy of support.

TO MOMS: YOU DESERVE MORE HELP THAN YOU THINK

The funny thing is that Bethany would always say she doesn't understand why I give her so much credit because she only showed up a couple of times a month and couldn't help me beyond making biryani. The truth is that what helped me the most was not the lovingly cooked food she brought or how often she did or didn't show up at my door—what helped the most, beyond anything else was her validation of my inner world, something I wasn't even really aware of at the time.

I only really realized the power of her validation after moving to Pakistan. Until then I was telling myself the same story everyone else was selling me, remember? Once I moved to Pakistan and could finally hire help and get support from my family, I realized how gaslit I had been. Once the tremendous weight of parenting alone was lifted from my shoulders, I could finally see how much I had been trying to do alone and why I always felt so defeated. If you are an expatriate in a foreign land with no family and support system, I promise you, you're not failing. Society has set you up for hopeless expectations and society has normalized the loneliness and suffering you encounter.

You deserve way more help and support. And yes, it's nice for your kids if they have a father who wants to show up. No one will reap the rewards of his work more than himself when he experiences the kind of love only showing up can awaken in children. But you, as the mother, still deserve more support. You, as the father, also deserve more support. Parents everywhere deserve more support and help. We were never meant to do this alone. I hope that at least the countries who claim to be "developed" can do more to support parents, but until they do, the least we can do is validate each other and appreciate each other.

TO DADS: WHAT WE NEED FROM YOU

First of all, how amazing are cycle-breaker dads who truly are the first generation of dads to do so many firsts like changing diapers, feeding their kids, getting them ready in the mornings, and other mundane tasks that were solely considered the responsibility of mothers. The thing that my husband and so many men like him have had the wokeness to understand and do now is refuse to accept the low bar society has set for men and raise themselves to a higher standard—the one their wife and children deserve. Any time you, as a dad, hear someone telling your wife she's lucky because you, as a father are also showing up, speak up and say, "Actually, all mothers deserve more help and support. My wife does so much and carries the kind of parental mental load that I can't even begin to imagine. Whatever effort I'm putting in, I will also be reaping its benefits." You already know that you acknowledging your wife's efforts is only going to make you win more points, but your wife will feel heard and seen, and people will be more careful before minimizing her efforts. Your validation is important, but even more important is your refusal to accept praise at the cost of your wife.

A HAPPY ENDING

As I shared in the section about shame (chapter 1), I had always envisioned that perfect best friend, and the hopeless romantic that I am, I would often talk about it. Bethany would laugh and say, "You know, one day you will know that I'm that friend. It'll be just like all those cheesy romantic comedies where the librarian takes off her glasses, shakes her hair open, and the leading man finally realizes that it was her all along."

We would both laugh hysterically at this visual as Bethany would pretend to take off her invisible glasses and pull off her scrunchy to shake her own hair. That is how you know you've found "the one"—the best friend you were always looking for, that you can both laugh uncontrollably for hours on seemingly nothing. Laugh so hard that your tummy hurts and tears run down your cheeks. That's the kind of uninhibited laughter only a real best friend can evoke. If you're reading this, Bethany, thank you for loving yourself so fiercely that you taught me how to love myself too.

How to Mirror Your Children

"Children are compelled to give meaning to what is happening to them. When there is no clear explanation, they make one up; the intersection of trauma and the developmentally appropriate egocentrism of childhood often leads a little kid to think, I made it happen."

—Nadine Burke Harris, *The Deepest Well*[1]

Trying to make sense of what is happening to us, no matter how big or small, is perhaps the most human thing to do because it's an organic process of storytelling. As you've already read in the past chapters, telling our stories is how we recover and heal. It makes sense then, that children naturally tend to move towards this therapeutic process. The problem occurs when we are not able to tune into the child's thoughts or feelings about a certain experience. She then has no choice but to make her own story about it, which will most likely place her front and center because of the egocentrism stage unfolding during childhood.

> The stage of childhood called egocentrism, as defined by Jean Piaget, is when children are unable to take the perspective of others.[2]

Here are a few common examples of the stories children make up in the absence of an empathetic adult:

- Ever since the baby arrived, my parents spend a lot of time oohing and aahing over the baby, which means they don't love me anymore.
- When my dad gets angry at me for even making a mistake, it's because I'm a bad kid.
- My parents divorced because of me.

Even when children don't blame themselves, they can be consumed with thoughts and feelings they don't know how to process. This unresolved inner turmoil can result in dysregulation and "poor behaviors."

Here are a few common occurrences that can confuse and overwhelm children:

- Witnessing a scary incident.
- Seeing something disturbing on television
- A parent or other family member expressing big feelings unsafely
- Experiencing a medical procedure

You might be starting to get a sense now why validating such incidents can be hard for parents. Our society doesn't really normalize talking about difficult things. We tend to go the route of distraction or escapism instead.

"Sometimes parents avoid talking about upsetting experiences, thinking that doing so will reinforce their children's pain or make things worse. Actually, telling the story is often exactly what children need, both to make sense of the event and to move on to a place where they can feel better about what happened."

—Daniel J. Siegel, *The Whole-Brain Child*

The process of storytelling is a beautiful demonstration of the brain's plasticity, that is, its ability to change, shift, and create new neural pathways that help us grow. When children can share their story of something unsettling with us, it allows their brain to now "rewrite" the feelings and sensations related to it. What felt scary and overwhelming before can become manageable and safe when shared with a parent who's willing to listen compassionately.

HOLDING SPACE FOR OUR CHILDREN'S STORIES

My three-year-old nephew, Ali, one day witnessed a road accident when he was out with his mom one day. A car hit a motorcycle at high speed, causing the motorcyclist to fall off and get badly injured. He also wasn't wearing a helmet and some bleeding was visible from his forehead. My sister-in-law, Sana, described to Ali that there had been an accident but the injured man would be alright. Ali immediately started repeating what she'd said in his imperfect three-year-old speech.

"Man fall off motorcycle!" he repeated.

"Yes, he was hit and fell off," said Sana, following his lead.

As soon as they got home, he ran up to his dad and told him the same thing. Dad also validated (simply repeating in his own words what Ali was saying). Ali, sensing safety from both his parents, continued to process the incident. He brought his own little motorbike, sat on it, and then pretended to fall off.

"Ali fell off and got hurt . . . blood everywhere!" he exclaimed.

At this point, many parents might have gotten uncomfortable and tried to "correct" him and remind him that he didn't fall off, the man did. But Ali's parents believed in his ability to work through this and instead of correcting him, simply mirrored back what he was saying. This was simply another example of kids his age displaying "egocentrism," something that affected him so much that it almost felt like it had happened to him.

"You feel like it was you who fell off and then there was blood!" repeated my brother.

"Yes! I was hurt!"

"Oh! You were hurt . . . !" echoed my brother.

"You were a bit scared," added Sana. trying to understand what he might have been feeling.

"Yes, Ali scared," he agreed.

When they sent me the video of this conversation with Ali, I commended them on holding space for him and allowing him to tell his story. I encouraged them to repeat the story a couple of times so he can feel heard and seen, allowing him to move through this scary experience. This is one way they could have summarized the incident:

"You saw an accident today that made you feel scared because the man fell off his motorcycle and he was bleeding. It can be scary for anyone to see something like that. Mama and Baba are right here to help you with this. Do you need a hug?"

Sure enough, Sana reported that Ali seemed to have worked through this and stopped bringing it up again and again. She could see the visible signs of him having processed a difficult experience when he happily went back to his play.

Imagine what would've happened if Ali hadn't been allowed to process his feelings. If he'd had no one to mirror his inner world. Or if he'd been distracted from his efforts to talk about what happened. The fear would've not only remained stuck in his body but like all unprocessed feelings, it would have grown. He might've refused to go out or sit in the car. Even if this happened, we'd continue to honor his process and say, "You're still scared because of what happened . . . no worries, Baba can stay home with you while I go out." Or if he must go in the car, we can offer to ride in the back with him and hold his hand. What's important is that he feels he's not alone in his experience.

EXAMPLES OF VALIDATING STATEMENTS

Unfortunately, what usually happens whenever children attempt to instinctively take care of themselves when they're scared or apprehensive, well-meaning adults 'push' them to go ahead and do that thing anyway, distorting the child's view of his own experience. Here are some common examples where adults tend to invalidate children and what we can say instead:

Commonly Uttered Things	How We Respond	How to Validate
"I'm scared!"	"There's nothing to be scared of!"	"You look scared—I can see why that's scary. I will stay close."
You don't love me!	Of course, I love you!	"You're upset with me because I asked you to turn the TV off. That really is upsetting!"

Commonly Uttered Things	How We Respond	How to Validate
You love her more!	I love you both the same.	"You feel like I love her more. I'm so sorry! I want to understand why—what do I do that makes you feel this way?"
I don't have any toys!	Have you seen the number of toys in your room?	"You're feeling bored with all your toys and you're wanting to buy some new toys. We can't do that, but I can find all the pieces for your favorite toy."
My life sucks!	Wow! You're so ungrateful.	"Things are feeling hard for you right now—tell me more."
My friends hate me.	No one hates you sweetie . . . I'll be your friend!	"Oh gosh . . . that's hard!"
I hate homework.	You're just lazy.	"Ugh . . . homework can be such a killjoy!"
I love video games.	Video games are bad for you.	"Video games sure are fun! What's your favorite these days?"
I love money.	Money is just a necessity. Don't be so materialistic.	"You love money . . . I'd love to know why!"
My birthday sucked!	You were having so much fun . . . I saw you.	"Something went wrong on your birthday; let's talk about it."

As you can see, the reason it is hard to validate our kids is because we often disagree with them and don't see things their way. Sometimes, they are maybe even downright wrong. The purpose of validation is to understand someone and make them feel heard and seen.

THINGS TO REMEMBER WHEN VALIDATING

- Validating our children (or anyone) doesn't necessarily mean we agree with them. It just means we're willing to see things their way.
- Being right is overrated. Multiple realities exist. Everyone can have a different experience of the same thing and that's okay.
- Many times, you'll notice that when you validate your children, they'll find their own way out. This is called holding space for them. The space allows for reflection and growth.
- Being right or learning a lesson is not more important than a child learning to trust themselves and know that their thoughts, feelings, and experiences are worthy.
- Being validated by caregivers allows children to also see things from others' perspective. We show them what it looks and sounds like to try and understand others instead of asserting ourselves over others. Narcissism is a function of someone never having been validated and not knowing what it's like when someone puts themselves aside for you.

WE TELL OUR CHILDREN WHO THEY ARE

When children are consistently left alone in their inner world or their experiences are ignored, invalidated, minimized, or simply dismissed, they learn to mistrust themselves and lose faith in themselves and their reality, much like I had. Instead of honoring my own reality of how hard it was living in America and knowing that what I felt and experienced was the only relative truth, I let others dictate to me how I should be feeling. Until I found wonderful friends who were willing to be my true mirrors.

There's a YouTube video on this subject that's the best virtual representation of this concept. It's by this very cool organization called The School of Life. This is my favorite sentence from it:

"Knowing who one is, is really the legacy of having been known properly by someone else at the start."[3]

I hope it makes sense to you now why so many adults don't even know who they are.

Of course, many people think they know themselves when what they know is merely a poor reflection of themselves. The truth is, we're always telling our kids who they are, whether we realize it or not.

"You're so clumsy!"

"You don't like sharing."

"You're so aggressive!"

"You're too much!"

"You're too sensitive!"

And so on and so forth.

The good news is that we can also mirror back to our children all the wonderful things they do, not necessarily as a "positive reinforcement" tactic but as a genuine function of loving and knowing a delightful human.

"I love how funny you are!"

"You were so thoughtful sharing that with your sister!"

"You often come up with cool game ideas!"

"Your gaming skills are next level!"

"That was pretty responsible of you to put your clothes in the hamper."

"You were pretty angry there, but you didn't hit your brother!"

Every child that arrives on this planet is filled with wonder and magic. What an honor it is to be able to reflect this back to them!

NOTES

1. Nadine Burke Harris, *The Deepest Well: Healing the Long-Term Effects of Childhood Adversity* (Houghton Mifflin Harcourt, 2018), 101.
2. See "Piaget's Properational Stage," *Simply Psychology*, https://www.simply-psychology.org/preoperational.html/.
3. The School of Life, "How To Know Yourself," *YouTube*, June 5, 2019, https://www.youtube.com/watch?v=4lTbWQ8zD3w.

CHAPTER 5

BELONGING IS CELEBRATION OF YOU

*"I belong to myself. I'm very proud of that.
I am very concerned about how I look
at Maya. I like Maya very much."*

—Maya Angelou

Were You the "Bad Guy"?

To truly understand what belonging is and how it shapes us, we need to understand how we *lose* our belonging in our families.

The most impactful stories of someone losing belonging in their own family always come from fathers in our Anokhay Parents' course.

I do a poll in the beginning of the week about Belonging and I ask, "What was your role in the family?" and then I give them three options to pick from:

1. I was the good guy
2. I was the bad guy
3. I didn't have a role

A vast majority of people pick from the first two options which tells us something not unsurprising. That most families unknowingly assign roles to children. We'll learn how harmful they can be—but also the good they can do! More on this in the next chapter.

Back to the AP workshops. I usually pick a dad to tell their story of being the "bad guy" because boys are usually more likely to be labeled "the problem child." Statistics also show that more boys are sent for discipline in schools and diagnosed for ADHD.

I distinctly remember Imran's story. He was a younger dad with a kind smile and shy eyes. I remember being so impressed with his commitment to the workshop and showing up every week with his signature smile. When we did this poll, he raised his hand to share his story.

For the first time, I noticed his smile give way to a graver expression. Almost with a look of deep hurt lingering in his eyes, he started his story, "That was me . . . I was the 'bad guy.' Everything I did was wrong or bad. I think somewhere along the way I stopped believing that I could even do anything well."

He paused. Everyone was quiet. Holding space for the little boy he once was—the little boy who could do no right.

"The thing is . . . ," he continued with some difficulty, "I didn't know I was being bad. I don't recall wanting to hurt anyone or anything. In fact, I remember trying really hard to make my parents happy with me. But somehow, whatever I tried seemed to go wrong."

He paused again. A faraway look on his face. His eyes squinting to retrieve a painful memory. After some time, he spoke again,

"I remember one day my dad was complaining about his radio not working. I wanted to fix it for him. I must've been nine or ten. I knew where he kept his tools so I found them and opened up the radio to see what was going on. I'm an engineer now. I think I always had that interest. Even at ten, I remember knowing and understanding the various parts I encountered when I opened the radio. But no one was interested in any of that. My mom saw me 'tinkering' with the radio and immediately called my dad . . . I . . . what happened next was . . . it was hard. I don't think I deserved that."

At this point, he turned his camera off. We all understood. There wasn't much I or anyone could say. He later shared that he had never realized that he was unfairly labeled and that there's no such thing as a "bad kid."

LOOKING FOR BELONGING

Many of the other participants can relate to Imran's story. Every time someone shares a story like this, the chat gets inundated with similar comments,

"I, too, was the 'bad guy' in my family. I always thought something was wrong with me."

"I've always felt broken because I didn't belong in my own family."

"I got so tired of being called 'bad' that I didn't even care anymore about being good."

Where do you go from here? If you're not good enough for the family who was supposed to love and accept you unconditionally then who else ever will? This sense of rejection and loss of belonging in our families is like walking through the earth with several puzzle pieces just missing from the expanse of our existence. The holes left by the missing pieces make us feel inherently broken, damaged, and beyond repair.

Some people respond to these gaping spaces in their soul by becoming louder and meaner so no one dares tell them they don't belong. If only they can control and manipulate others, no one will dare try to get rid of them. If only they can be so powerful that no one can overpower them. This strategy "works" in terms of giving such a person "forced belonging" in the spaces that they occupy, be it home or office or friend circles, because people really are afraid to call them out on their unkindness, but no one can survive such an environment for long, and soon this person finds themselves alone. Perhaps no one asked them to leave, but also, no one stayed.

Others respond to the missing pieces by bending and contorting themselves into painful shapes to fit wherever they are. Contortionists like myself are flexible and easygoing. We just aim to please. We will do and say whatever you want, and we'll hide parts of ourselves that you find inconvenient. We're willing to do whatever it takes to fit in.

The problem though with bending yourself at ungodly angles is that you eventually break. That is, you've betrayed yourself so often and so much that you have nothing but resentment and bitterness left in your heart. You find yourself saying things like,

"I always do so much for people and no one does anything for me!"

"I'm such a giver and everyone else is a taker!"

"This world is a cold and selfish place!"

"Why can't people be kind? I'm so kind!"

And you suddenly go from being a squishy teddy bear to iron man—the armor comes on, nothing gets in, nothing gets out. You're done! Except, you're still lonely and miserable.

Eventually the loneliness and misery of both kinds of people often pushes them into addiction and substance abuse. We now know, through research, that drug use and other addictions are strictly a function of pain and not some moral failing. Or for that matter, moral success because addiction to work and busyness is usually seen as something positive. However, all addictions are unhealthy and a function of dissociation that happens in the blue zone.

FINDING BELONGING

So, what do you do then? As an adult, who has those gaping holes in your soul because you've never belonged anywhere, what do you do?

You show up as yourself, for better or worse, you take off that armor and show up and you let the chips fall where they may. And you keep showing up without betraying yourself even when the stakes get higher, and you remember to stay kind, to yourself and others.

When I started my Facebook group, it didn't occur to me to not be myself. I didn't think anyone would care about my writing. I believed so much in what I was talking about (respectful parenting) that I saw no need or desire to be anything but authentic. You can say that my real belief was in what I was writing about and not who I was, and, in this way, I accidentally discovered the magic of authenticity. I had been practicing RP at the time for several years and had seen the results in my own children and in my own healing, so I believed in it with all my heart.

This allowed me to share my ideas and thoughts about it in an authentic way even when what I was sharing was unconventional and controversial. For example, the idea of validation and how important it is for the parent-child relationship. And it's not like I never got any opposition—I did—and though it made me uncomfortable, I engaged with kindness and an open mind with anyone who was confused and not understanding or agreeing with what I was saying. The result was that the Facebook group became a space where people saw me, really saw me, and loved what they saw.

This was initially shocking to me and also scary. I had just wanted to teach RP. I wasn't interested in becoming popular. In fact, I desperately wanted to remain hidden. My first website had no picture of me and I used the nameless/faceless "we" everywhere instead of the very self-proclaiming "I."

As my work and group became more and more popular, I became more and more uncomfortable. I had never set out to be some kind of an "expert." I had never set out to be an example of the "perfect RP parent." These titles made me superbly uncomfortable, not because I was so modest and humble, but because being put on a pedestal is the scariest thing ever. This was the perfect time for me to hide. I'm not going to lie; I had the temptation many times, and still do sometimes.

VULNERABILITY: THE KEYSTONE OF BELONGING

I distinctively remember, at some point early in my journey, I almost deleted the Facebook group that is now the backbone of our work. And that's because I'd had a shameful moment of pushing my daughter and not even feeling remorse for it until many hours later. I remember sitting there with my mouse hovering over the delete button for a while. Recalling how I'd pushed her and then waiting for the remorse to wash over me, but feeling nothing. It's one thing to screw up, it's another to feel good about it and be so far from feeling bad about it. Well, at the time I didn't know about triggers and I didn't know that the part of me that "felt good" was the little me who felt safe at being able to "protect" myself. (See the first chapter's section on triggers.) So, there I sat, with a hovering mouse in my palm, and shame in my heart and a scary idea hit me:

What if I tell my FB group about what I'd done? Surely, they'll all just leave, won't they?

"What kind of a teacher is this?" they'll say.

"You *hurt* your child?" they'll gasp.

"Who the heck are you to teach us?" they'll say harshly.

"Maybe some of them will understand . . . maybe they'll feel better that you also screw up. Maybe it will give them hope?" a small voice inside me spoke.

As I sat there, weighing my options, something happened that I've since come to anticipate and celebrate. Divine intervention.

I often tell my participants of AM that once you find your path, you also see that all the doors are opening up for you. Not because the universe is conspiring to help you but because this is a path that your Creator has uniquely created for you. These doors exist for you to open them. No one else can open them and no other path will open for you because this is your path.

That day the door that opened was Brené Brown's work on vulnerability. I remember thinking, "So there's a name for what I was about to do? It's called vulnerability? And it exists to douse shame?" And I immediately put it to practice. I wrote a "confessional" of sorts and shared the story of losing my cool and pushing my sweet girl, half certain that everyone would have left the group by morning.

That's obviously not what happened. The following are some of the comments I woke up to.

Thank you so much for sharing this! After a week of being emotionally drained to the point that my four-year-old is asking me mommy smile kidhar hai, you don't know how much this helps in picking myself up again.

This was so relatable! Thank you so much for sharing this!

Thanks for sharing.

It's important to share these moments with the readers. Keep sharing.

Suddenly, I realized, this was bigger than me. My work was bigger than me. And this is not the kind of work that can be done in "ghost mode." I need to show up. People need to see a Pakistani, desi woman breaking the generational trauma cycles and becoming a gentle parent. More importantly, people need to see my mistakes. They will learn more from my mistakes than they could from my perfectly penned posts. And on this perilous journey of being a reluctant leader, vulnerability is the antidote to shame and my new best friend.

BELONGING TO MYSELF

My work has allowed me to make my own island of belonging in this world. My work and writing are the one place in the world that I couldn't *not* be my true self even if I tried. As I just shared, shame did beckon and tempt me to put my armor on, but I didn't accept its invitation this time. I can't say that I knew what I was doing at the time, but I can see how practicing courage and showing all parts of myself have allowed me to find my people. I sometimes joke with my team that we're all "clones" of each other. It makes sense that when we remove our masks and show our true selves, we attract the people who also see themselves in us.

Even though everyone at TPEP has their own unique talents, ideas, and journeys; we all fit together like pieces of a beautifully crafted puzzle. I wouldn't be able to do the work I do or take it as far as it has come if I didn't have this group of amazing women with me on this journey. It is a source of daily wonder and gratitude for me that I belong with this group of women. I've seen us all flourish and grow in the years that we've worked together. Sana and Garima have their own Instagram communities, spreading this amazing work to North America and India. Nabila and Afra, who live in Karachi, are a source of constant support and strength for each other and the Karachi community of our followers. They all also deliver Anokhay Parents and Anokhay Mentors, and it's a joy to see how quickly their workshops fill up and the raving reviews they get afterwards. Even our technical support team members, Saman and Sehrish, are incredibly hardworking and brilliant. Just a bunch of women who support each other and build each other up. No wonder I get so many emails and messages asking me when I'll be taking on more team members (we do have opportunities for volunteering for graduates of our courses). Once upon a time, I used to dream of belonging to such a team. The dream is now a reality, and it all began with learning how to belong to myself.

HOW WE CAN LEARN TO BELONG TO OURSELVES

Here are some takeaways from this chapter:

1. Growing up in a family where we never felt a sense of belonging can make us do weird things to try and "fit in" everywhere. But by doing so, we betray ourselves and eventually this betrayal catches up with us. Inauthenticity shows people that we can't be trusted because we're not even true to ourselves.

2. It can be scary to be ourselves, to say what we believe in even if it's different from what everyone else is saying but silencing our truth won't result in sincere relationships.

3. No matter how strange you think your ideas are, they still deserve to be shared. People who shame you or put you down for your ideas are not your people.

4. When you can find the courage to be yourself, no matter how silly, serious, talkative, or quiet you are, you'll allow other people who are like you to gravitate towards you. These *will* be your people.

I always used to feel that I laugh too loudly and I talk too much, but Bethany tells me that these are her favorite things about me. Now we laugh together so much that our stomachs hurt—and then we laugh more about our stomachs hurting!

"You only are free when you realize you belong no place—you belong every place—no place at all. The price is high. The reward is great . . ."

—Maya Angelou

All I Need Are Nice People

Before there was Facebook or TikTok, there were discussion forums. In case you never used one, you basically go on a website and there you'll find discussion forums related to various topics and interests. Each topic will have many "threads" and each thread will have sub-threads. Everyone posts questions, concerns, and wonders related to the thread topic and others respond.

My first memories of the internet (other than MSN Messenger) are of being obsessed with these discussion forums. My first ever was a poetry-related discussion forum. My second was related to Pakistani expatriates in the U.S., then infertility, and finally parenthood. If I had a problem, discussion forums were my answer. I loved these little sub-communities where all the people seemed to care about the same thing.

Nowadays, we have Facebook groups, and as you might already know, I manage a popular respectful parenting one, but I'm an active member of many others.

Communities are the bomb, as far as I'm concerned. There's nothing in the world quite like being in a place where everyone cares about the same thing. No matter what else we disagree on, we can agree on one major thing, and that's simply awesome.

So, on the surface of it, you can say my online life seems pretty fulfilling; I've always found "my people" and benefitted from these communities. But there's a dark side to this story that's embarrassing for me to tell, laden with shame.

That first forum I mentioned . . . the poetry one? I had to leave that in a total hairflip moment. The expatriate one, I was blocked out of by the admins. The infertility and baby one, I remained an inconspicuous "lurker" because any attempts at posting something original resulted in the kind of criticism and strife I couldn't deal with. In short, it would not be an exaggeration to say that almost every online community I've joined and actually "shown up" in, I've, eventually, either been kicked out or left in a huff and puff myself.

You see, if we never belonged in our family, we struggle to belong anywhere . . . even in online communities. And our ability to belong anywhere is seriously compromised. It becomes a vicious cycle of us trying to fill that hole of "where do I belong" with attempts at trying to fit in somewhere and failing and that hole just growing. And we try harder and become more paranoid and thus harder to fit in. It's an almost impossible cycle to break out of because even when no one is trying to kick us out, we have a nagging feeling of "not belonging" that makes us act in ways that does eventually get us kicked out.

SHAME THREATENS BELONGING

One of my brilliant workshop participants asked me—if every feeling has a purpose, then what's the purpose of shame? Shame is an evolutionary feeling, because if it didn't exist, we'd survive just fine. The reason it exists is to remind us that if we don't "shape up," we will lose our place in the tribe, and for the caveman, that meant certain death.

What happened my second semester at JMU (James Madison University) during my graduate program is a great example of this.

When I applied at JMU, I also applied at other schools (because, of course, I thought I wouldn't get accepted anywhere. I got accepted at all four schools). One of these schools' alumni told me I was crazy to apply at JMU. "Their interview process is insane . . . they make people cry! You don't want to go there!"

"They make people cry!" I thought to myself. My heart delighted at the prospect of this. I live for crying. I live for vulnerability. I decided right there that that's where I'd go if JMU accepted me.

That dude wasn't wrong. People *did* cry at the JMU interview. It was a group interview of six candidates and two faculty members. By the end of it, half the people were crying and the rest half, including myself, felt we'd been through the ringer. They required us to show up fully with no place to hide. I thought it was brilliant because now I can tell a good therapist apart from a bad one based on just this one thing: how willing someone is to see all the parts of themselves and not be afraid of them. I was delighted when I was accepted. I was in love with everything at JMU, the faculty, my cohort, the campus, the studies. Just everything. Here was a place I finally belonged.

Until I didn't.

Matt was our Counseling Process Professor. To this day, I'd say, he's the best professor I have ever had, and I learned more from him, in that one half-semester class, than I did combined in the first whole year. I say "half-semester" because he left midway. Or was made to leave. I don't know. All I know is that one day, on our cohort group chat, some people asked if we had seen the resignation email from Matt. "Resignation what?" I said and jumped over to my email. Sure enough, there it was . . . Something about how he doesn't think he's a good fit for us and he will be replaced. I was devastated! I immediately went back to our chat and typed, "Noooo . . . we have to stop this! He can't leave!" and another classmate wrote, "Actually, I'm glad he's leaving." A few others agreed with her and I was suddenly engulfed in a big ole smelly pool of shame, drudging up its usual vitriol of the "I don't belong" messages:

Am I missing something?
Have I done something wrong?
Does everyone hate me now?
I didn't know we're supposed to hate Matt!
Omg—I've done it again . . . they all hate me now!

Responding to this deluge of paranoid messages, I typed quickly, "Oh, I'm so sorry, I had no idea he'd done something wrong. I'm sorry if I hurt someone's feelings. Can someone please tell me what's going on?"

Immediately, I got a private message from one of my other classmates and he said, "Maryam, you know, you're entitled to have your own feelings about this. You don't have to agree with them."

Suddenly, the haze of shame lifted just a tiny bit and I thought . . . wait, he's right. I *am* allowed to have my own feelings about this. Matt is my favorite teacher and my experience of him is valid and relevant.

I told myself that as the other students explained what they felt he'd done wrong, I would, without invalidating their experience, say that I didn't agree with them or that whatever they felt was wrong warranted one of JMU's best teachers being kicked out. But I was too scared of losing my place in the cohort; I betrayed myself and just agreed with them. Virtually nodding and sending texts and emojis to affirm how some of my classmates felt about him, while deep inside, drowning in my cocktail of feelings of self-betrayal, shame, and grief.

At this point in my life, I had acquired enough skills to identify when I'm in a shame cycle. I recognized the behavioral symptoms of overexplaining, overthinking, self-betrayal, and people pleasing. I also recognized the physical symptoms in my body of shame being present: feeling trapped, scared, alone, and desperate. I knew I needed some help, so I reached out to my program supervisor who talked me down from the ledge and helped me see that I certainly wasn't alone in how I felt and that several other students were equally confused and unhappy with Matt leaving.

This, more than anything else, helped the shame dissipate. You see, the message shame always sends is, "You're so alone—nobody is where you are and nobody will ever be where you are." This is why Brené Brown's first book about shame is called *I Thought It Was Just Me (But It Isn't)*.[1]

My supervisor's empathy and compassion reminded me that I wasn't alone in how I felt, and how I felt and how I'd responded was understandable. I was then able to sit with all my feelings and practice some self-compassion, and I reminded myself that I've done nothing wrong in stating how I feel about Matt leaving and no one in my class is going to hate me for it forever. Just like I wouldn't hate someone forever for having an experience different from my own. *It is going to be okay*, I said to myself, *I haven't lost my belonging. I'm okay.*

And I was.

BELONGING DOESN'T ASK US TO BETRAY OURSELVES

When our supervisor addressed our whole cohort to talk through Matt's departure, she invited each of us to share how we felt. I listened compassionately to my classmate's experiences and validated their experience and then I bravely shared my own.

"I'm going to miss him. He's one of the best professors I've ever had, and I don't understand why he's not returning—it breaks my heart."

And guess what, my lovely classmates validated my experience too. They didn't hate me and they taught me a precious lesson: Belonging doesn't ask us to betray ourselves; in fact, it asks us to unapologetically *be* ourselves.

I can show up as myself, I can be who I am, and, if it's the right place, a place where I truly belong, then I'll be accepted and loved even when I'm disagreeing with almost everyone else. How many times in our families are we made to feel like something is wrong with us because we don't agree with our parents? Or "elders"? Or perhaps "the star sibling"? It's not a huge wonder why so many of us are ready to betray ourselves at the first hint of being an outlier. We'd rather sell our souls than lose our place. And despite doing everything in our power to win certain people over, we're always fighting a lost battle. The truth is that true belonging doesn't ask us to perform circus tricks to prove our worthiness; true belonging says, "I see you and accept you as you are—flaws and all."

THE EVIDENCE OF BELONGING

Recall my story about Bethany from The Librarian Without the Glasses; why did it take me so long to realize that she was "the one true best friend" I had been looking for? Because my trauma story wouldn't let me see what was in front of me. My trauma lens showed me a good person showing me kindness, not a loving friend showing me all the ingredients of love: care, affection, recognition, respect, commitment, trust, honest and open communication. But at this point I'd already been in therapy for a couple of years, and when you start loving yourself, a strange thing happens, and you meet people who insist on loving you, despite yourself.

And it's not so much that you meet them but that you take off those "trauma glasses" and can finally see people for who they really are. I decided that this one time, I'm not going to repeat my old patterns of looking for evidence that I'm not loved. I will only focus on the signs of love that I do see, and I will accept them. I will stop dismissing them as 'random acts of charitable kindness' and accept them as proof that I'm loved. Brené Brown, in *Braving the Wilderness: The Quest for True Belonging and the Courage to Stand Alone*, says,

> Stop walking through the world looking for confirmation that you don't belong. You will always find it because you've made that your mission. Stop scouring people's faces for evidence that you're not enough. You will always find it because you've made that your goal. True belonging and self-worth are not goods; we don't negotiate their value with the world.[2]

I decided that I would no longer walk the earth looking for proof that I wasn't worthy of love and belonging.

I promise you that once we accept our own worthiness or at least act like we do, we finally start belonging. To the end of my time in JMU, my entire cohort remained my wonderful friends, and to this day each of them has a place in my heart that will never be forgotten because they helped me conquer shame and learn how to belong.

I've also had the pleasure and joy of creating my own online community which has become a place of belonging for many. Our Facebook group, Respectful Parenting by Maryam Munir, is one of the biggest in Pakistan, with people from all over the world, and we are known for how we run the community: with empathy and compassion, and never, ever with shame. It doesn't matter if you're someone who hits your child, you're still welcomed with open arms, and we help you accept all the parts of yourself while you work on nurturing your authentic self in a place where you're loved with all parts of yourself.

Each of our courses also comes with a WhatsApp or Facebook group and, in the beginning, I used to get messages on the side from people expressing their fears of not belonging: "I feel like everyone else here is xyz but I'm not like that . . . . maybe this isn't the right place for me . . ." and I'd firmly tell them, absolutely they belong here—but I understand why they feel they don't. Over time, I decided to start each program with the quote from Brown I shared above.

COLLECTING THE EVIDENCE

If you're not sure where to start collecting evidence for your right to belong, start anywhere where you've experienced some acceptance and positive feedback. Put away your "trauma glasses" that insist that you're not "good enough" for this or that and just pay attention to the cold hard facts.

I remember distinctively that when I was considering starting my company, TPEP (The Parent Empowerment Project), I sat outside on my front doorstep and mentally did this exercise—a walkthrough of any evidence that supported the fact that I could start and run a company devoted to educating and empowering parents. This is a rough sketch of my evidence-collecting:

- I thought of my cousin Onabia, who often told me that I was wise and turned to me for advice and vulnerable sharing. I objectively considered her stance about me and knew immediately that whatever she thinks of me is legitimate. She's not someone who sugarcoats reality or is afraid to be honest. In fact, her direct but always kind truth telling has taught me a lot about staying authentic. No matter what my trauma lens, I knew I could trust her opinion of me. Turns out, I was absolutely correct. She's been a huge supporter for me in this journey and though our relationship went through some rocky patches, she's always shown up in our friendship with courage and honesty.

- Next up was my other cousin Tarbia who is easily one of the wisest, most "woke" people I have ever known in my life. I deeply respect her perspective on important issues and, despite myself, had to sit there on the stairs and admit that I enjoy Tarbia's love and respect as well.

- Since my evidence collection was for a career/work-related purpose, I decided to consider what some of my past professors, teachers, or colleagues had said about me. I had recently attended a training for becoming a certified Parent Educator and a seasoned workshop leader who was also there told me that I was a 'natural'.

- Since I was being impartial, I also considered my youngest brother-in-law's feedback on my writing. He was struggling with his university-level English class and asked me to write his papers for him. I knew he was the last person on Earth who was going to make up fake praise about me, and I remember him telling his parents that, if I really wanted, I could be a published author. (And yes, he got A's on all his papers and yes, I know that was an ethical grey area—anything for "fitting in," right?)

At this point I was a little surprised at how long this list was getting. If you had asked me the previous day how many people I knew who think I'm anything above average, I'd have said zero. Despite my surprise, I stuck to the task and went down the list like this for a lot of people in my life. I begrudgingly also started putting people on the list who, in my opinion, didn't really count because they were so biased.

Like my beloved *chachi* (paternal uncle's wife), Ruqaia. There's no doubt that she is incredibly biased, I reasoned. She's known me since I was twelve years old, and we've shared an incredible bond of unconditional love. She'd read my little short stories and ooh and aah at them. "You'll do amazing things one day, my love," she'd say with so much sincerity and kindness. Okay, I decided, she *is* biased, but I'll let her in.

My sister, Ayesha, is another such person whose unbridled love and admiration I've always taken for granted. However, I decided to be generous with myself and allow her often spoken kind remarks to feature on my evidence list. From this exercise, I learned a precious lesson: your trauma lens hides from you the very people who love you sincerely and you take their praise and appreciation for granted. They're the ones who actually see you for who you really are, years before you can see it yourself.

Since then, I've done many such evidence lists. I encourage you to do the same. I promise you that you'll be very surprised at what you'll discover. Doing this exercise and practicing your authenticity are the gateways to learning to belong to yourself and eventually everywhere else.

A Fire-Breathing Dragon

Many understand that labeling your child a negative label is harmful, but you'd be surprised at the harm that "good" or positive labels can cause.

What's most shocking are the stories from the "good guys" of the family.

The Golden Child.

The One Who Can Do No Wrong.

When I first met Asad, he took my breath away. Not in the sense you're thinking. He was my seventeen-year-old client whose sister wanted me to see him because he was having suicidal ideation. I was still working on my counseling degree and didn't consider myself the right person to be helping this sweet boy.

At first, I declined to see him and gave his sister suggestions for a few therapists. She told me he'd already been to two and not only did they not help, but he had gone deeper into his shell than ever before. Very reluctantly I agreed to see him once on the condition that he will also be taken to a psychiatrist so a licensed professional was aware of Asad's suicidal status.

The truth is that the way formal mental health training educates therapists and doctors on how to deal with children is incredibly outdated. A vast majority is still trained to teach parents about negative and positive reinforcements like rewards and taking away privileges. As Dr. Ross Greene says, "The reason reward and punishment strategies haven't helped is because they won't teach your child the skills he's lacking or solve the problems that are contributing to challenging episodes."[3] That is, rather than targeting the behavior on a surface level, we need to look beneath the tip of the iceberg and figure out what's really going on.

That was my task with Asad. Even though his suicide ideation and giving up on academics were alarming behaviors, what was significantly more important was figuring out what had led to these behaviors. Staring at this handsome young man on my screen, I couldn't help but feel out of my depth; what *had* caused this gentle young man to give up on life?

"Tell me what's happening, my dear. Sounds like you're tired of living . . . ," I tried to open lightly.

He smiled ever so slightly and said in a monotone voice, "It's not so much that I'm tired as I'm bored."

"Ah . . . I definitely wouldn't want to do more of something that bored me . . . say more."

"Well," he continued in the same flat tone, "I decided a long time ago that feelings are for average people and since I'm special, I won't be needing them, so I got rid of them. So, now, everything feels like nothing. Which is boring."

Feeling even more out of my depth, I worked hard to keep focused on his experience without letting my own fears get in the way, "Ahh . . . I see. That certainly makes sense. Now that you have no feelings left, why would you do anything . . ."

His flat expression flashed a hint of surprise and then it was gone. He simply nodded. Perhaps he hadn't had anyone consider his thoughts earnestly. Certainly, it was taking all the skills I'd ever acquired to not just freak out and keep going.

"Is it okay if I ask when you decided that feelings were for 'average people' and you must get rid of them?" I asked carefully.

He considered for a moment and then answered in the same flat tone, "Ever since I can remember . . . I've always been special. I'm not like other kids. Other kids throw tantrums and get angry and loud . . . I'm not like that . . . I don't do those things."

"I see," I used my "minor door opener" carefully (a term for using minimal words I learned in counseling school to encourage your client to share more).

It worked because he continued talking. "Emotions are basically beneath me. They're messy and ugly and really for weak people."

"You're right . . . emotions sure can be messy. So that's one thing that made you special. That you didn't have or express feelings like others. Was there anything else that made you special?"

"It's not that I was special," he clarified, "It's basically like I'm an outlier . . . an alien if you will. I'm just different."

"You mean, you don't fit in anywhere?"

"I can't, I'm an alien. I mean, not literally, but yes, I'm just not like other people."

"So, you mean you weren't like the rest of your siblings or cousins or classmates?"

He nodded, the loneliness and heaviness of his reality starkly visible in his vacant expression.

We ended our first session by going over a "safety plan" as I'd learned in my suicide training at JMU—a plan to make sure he will not hurt himself. Like a "good kid," he complied and made the plan with me and promised to honor it.

I was curious about his childhood and what had led him to believe that he was "too special" for a "basic" thing like emotions. I had taken permission from him to speak to his mom a little more about his childhood; he couldn't remember anything. His mom was a resilient, hardworking, and intelligent lady who bore the typical scars of a first-generation Pakistani immigrant. I asked her to tell me about Asad's childhood as best as she could.

"That's just it," she began. "He had the best childhood and the most love from all of us! He's the youngest of six siblings and from a young age, as little as four, he's just been the perfect kid. Have you heard of a child praying properly at age four? That's what he did! We were all so proud of him! He was so special! Always got perfect grades. Always behaved perfectly. All his life he's done everything himself and done it so well . . . I don't understand what happened suddenly! My poor Asad . . ."

I listened and thanked her for her time. My hunch had been correct. He naturally had a personality that was easier, and he got put into the role of "the perfect kid," "the golden child," so much so that he started to view anything in himself that was human or imperfect as a stain on his "perfect" image. Asad reminded me how perceptive children are and how well they respond to our mirroring. They become who we want them to become, who we say they are.

The truth is that one of the best gifts we can give our children is to allow them to be human, and elevate who they are rather than glorifying perfection and "perfect behavior." All children, all humans, when they're born are born with their own greatness and as we learned in the Validation chapter, parents can and should mirror that greatness back to them, flaws and all.

Creating an alternate image of our child, which is either too good or too bad, is damaging and as we learned in this case, downright life-threatening. I worked with Asad for the next year and he's easily one of the most delightful and intelligent people I've ever had the pleasure of working with. All I had to do was reflect it all back to him, but this time, while also embracing and celebrating the not-so-perfect parts of him. With fear, trepidation, and hope, I let him lead me into the darkest crevices of his heart and mind with compassion and acceptance. By taking me to these dark places, it's as if he was checking me, "Will you still think I'm worth helping and accepting when you see how 'bad' I can be?" Of course, my answer was always a resounding yes! Not so much by saying the word itself, but by continuing to show unwavering faith and genuine interest in him.

During one of our calls, I decided to use a Virtual Sand tray tool I had learned about in my Play Therapy elective class at JMU. Sand tray therapy is a tool certified Play Therapists use because children express themselves more effectively through play. This website allows us to use a virtual version of it with lots of characters and "props" on the left side of the screen and a "sand tray" on the right side. I asked Asad to make me a story in the sand tray and when he shared his screen, I saw a medieval family and a dragon "flying" on top of them. He then told me the story of the fire-breathing dragon who burnt his whole family with his fire.

"Wow! The dragon must've been very angry at his family," I observed.

"Yes . . . ," began Asad, his eyes no longer having that lost look of our initial meetings, "he thought he was angry . . . but he was actually sad. He didn't want to hurt his family but he didn't know what to do with the fire . . ."

"Ah, yes . . . it's not his fault all that fire is inside him . . . he's just really sad."

"Yes, sometimes the sadness makes him breathe fire, but he would never actually hurt his family . . ."

And with that, I saw his arrow move back to the figures on the left and recreate the burnt family with the dragon standing happily next to them, no longer breathing fire.

There is no doubt that his family's unbridled support, lack of judgment, and "allowing" his imperfections was the real key to his improvement and coming off the suicide watch. His wonderfully supportive sisters, brother, and mom rallied to hold him up while he healed and learned to love his imperfect self. He made his own decision to go back to school and finish high school quickly and apply for college, this time, knowing that "perfect grades" are not important. Ever so slowly, Asad is learning to be ordinary again so he can belong in his ordinary family of "not aliens."

Questions about Belonging

ARE YOU SAYING WE SHOULD NEVER PRAISE OUR KIDS?

Occasional praise on its own is fine, of course. Acknowledging our child's efforts or thanking them are also great options that should be part of any beautiful relationship. What's dangerous is using praise as a positive reinforcement gimmick as explained in the introduction: when we reserve positive feedback and connection for when the child is doing well and withdraw our good mood immediately when the child makes a mistake.

You can offer specific praise and appreciate the effort rather than the outcome.

"It was hard to fly that helicopter and you wanted to give up, but you kept trying."

Urdu: *"Ye helicopter urana mushkil hai aur ap ko thora tima laga laikin ap nai haar nahi maani."*

"You weren't sure how to write that essay but you figured it out, and now it's two pages long and even has lots of details."

Urdu: *"Ap ko samjah nahi aa rahi thee kai kaisay mazmoon likhna hai laikin phir ap nai thora damagh laraya aur ab do safay likh dalay.. wo bhi misaalon kai saath."*

"You used red and blue colors to make pretty round and round circles."

Urdu: *"Aap nai laal aur neelay gol gol pyaray sai daeeray banaye hain..."*

"You put on your clothes yourself! You're feeling so proud of yourself."

Urdu: *"Aap nai kapray khud pehnay hain . . . ap ko acha lag raha hai!"*

YOU SAID I SHOULDN'T GET INTO A BAD MOOD IF MY CHILD MAKES A MISTAKE, BUT HOW CAN I SHOW THEM WHAT THEY DID WAS WRONG?

We're human too and will obviously have some kind of a distressed response to a child making a mistake that affects us (milk being spilled, something being broken, fight with a sibling, the child violating a boundary), but there's a huge difference between a parent being mildly disturbed due to any of these things happening and having big reactions to them (that's when we go back to our triggers worksheet). Once we can manage our triggers, we can then respond compassionately despite the unpleasant feelings.

"Oh no . . . the milk spilled . . . Let's clean it up!"

"I'm so sad my table broke because you guys were climbing on it. I'm going to get it fixed, but let's come up with some rules for the new table . . ."

"Uh oh . . . looks like you forgot it's time to turn off the video games . . ."

"This time your grades are much lower than all the past years; would you like to find some solutions to raise them?"

A calm and connected response shows our child that they're still worthy of love when they're human. They don't need to be perfect to belong in our family.

ARE THERE ANY PHRASES I SHOULD TOTALLY AVOID SO MY CHILD DOESN'T FEEL LIKE I'M LABELING THEM OR PUTTING THEM IN A ROLE?

Here are some commonly used phrases you can avoid.

"Good girls don't do that!"

"Boys don't cry."

"I'll talk to you when you can calm down."

"Stop behaving like an idiot."

"Good children always . . ."

"You're becoming naughty/wild/stubborn."

BUT ISN'T IT NATURAL TO GIVE MORE ACKNOWLEDGMENT TO THE CHILD WHO'S BETTER BEHAVED AND GETS GOOD GRADES?

It's worth exploring why you're attaching positive attention to performance and behavior. As we've learned, behavior is simply an outcome of our ANS doing its best to protect us. Children don't deserve to be penalized for their "poor behavior." If anything, such behaviors should invite more affection and connection from us.

We put our kids in different roles based on various things, such as temperament, academic inclination, and sibling relationships because this is how we were raised. This conditioning sneaks up on us when we least expect it. For example, people often don't like sensitive children and label them as weak or oversensitive. However, all personality types are equally valuable and lovable. We cannot pick and choose, and if one child is more academic than the other, they should not be treated differently. There is a school of thought that schools are meant to help children do well, and those who are not good at school may be free thinkers or outside the box thinkers, traits which can help them succeed in life. Parents also tend to put children in roles based on their relationship with each other, such as the older child taking on more responsibility. When children don't feel heard or seen by their parents, they may become jealous of their siblings and take away things from them. Finally, it's important to remember that boys and girls should not be put in roles of men abusing women, even if they are young.

WHAT ARE SOME WAYS WE CAN RESTORE FEELINGS OF BELONGING FOR A CHILD AFTER WE HAVE PUT THEM IN A NEGATIVE ROLE?

Start by dropping all your expectations from the child, no matter what his age is. Even if he has O-level exams coming up, stop asking him to study. These nagging reminders only serve to remind the child that he's incapable and not worthy of connection and belonging. Losing these feelings of belonging are linked to addiction, self-harm, suicide ideation, and other destructive behaviors. Failing one year of school as the cost of repairing your relationship and healing your child's heart is absolutely a price worth paying. In my experience though, as soon as parents start doing repair work, they see their child start to thrive.

One such family I helped was shocked to see their teen taking responsibility for his studies, taking care of his chores, and helping out his family only after a few weeks of repair work. This is because children are hardwired for connection and belonging. Giving them back their rightful place in our families brings out the best in them.

WHAT ELSE CAN WE DO TO HELP CHILDREN KNOW THAT THEY BELONG?

Focus on their strengths and point them out using specific praise.

Thank them for their contributions to the family.

Ask their advice in everyday matters.

Give them spaces in the home that belong to them.

Listen to their concerns with validation and understanding.

Ask their help with chores and model graciousness when they struggle to do the chores.

Enjoy them.

NOTES

1. Brené Brown, *I Thought It Was Just Me (But It Isn't): Making the Journey from "What Will People Think?" to "I Am Enough"* (Penguin Publishing Group, 2008).
2. Brené Brown, *Braving the Wilderness: The Quest for True Belonging and the Courage to Stand Alone* (Random House Publishing, 2019), 158.
3. Ross Greene, *The Explosive Child: A New Approach for Understanding and Parenting Easily Frustrated, Chronically Inflexible Children* (Harper Collins Publishers, 2010).

CHAPTER 6

AUTONOMY IS YOUR POWER

Khudi Ko Kar Buland Itna Ke Har Taqdeer Se Pehle
Khuda Bande Se Khud Puche,
Bata Teri Raza Kya Hai

(Raise yourself so high that before every decree
God Himself, will ask you:
"What is it that you desire?")

—Dr. Illama Iqbal

Fountain Pens Are Better Than Fancy Computers

I hand my mother's x-ray referral to the skinny cleric behind the glass pane. He puts it down and reaches for a huge blue register. I say huge because not only is it at least a foot and a half long, it's also three to four inches thick. How does he even know where to open it?

But he does. He opens it to the half-filled page and reaches for a fountain pen to make an entry. He tries to copy down the details from the referral form but his pen won't write. It's out of ink. He twists open the back and tries to squeeze the last few drops of ink into the nib and tries writing again. It's a no go.

He then reaches out to his colleague, an older lady also busy scribbling in a similar register, and waves his pen.

She's not flustered at his interruption and hands him an ink bottle. No words are exchanged as he takes the bottle and refills the pen. He finally twists closed the bottom, affixes the lid on the back as well, and starts writing.

It's 2022 and this is one of the biggest hospitals in Rawalpindi, Pakistan. You'd think they use computers and keyboards. Not physical 2kg thick registers and old-fashioned fountain pens. But that's a military hospital for you.

Just a few days earlier I'd visited a private hospital whose staff probably wouldn't be caught dead with a register and ink bottle. And yet here I was, navigating a military hospital with all its usual scruffiness.

Why, you ask?

Autonomy. That's why.

When I went to the private hospital, the oncologist there reminded me no less than three times how superior his experience and opinion are. He started the conversation with a sentence that stripped me and my mom, the patient, of all our autonomy: "You might wish for one thing but it's of no consequence to me, I will tell you what to do and you should do it because I have thirty years of experience."

I'm sure that's not untrue. Certainly, the four-shelf display in his office that was adorned with his many plaques and accolades would also testify to his vast experience and expertise.

But it mattered little to me in that moment when he continued to dismiss all my concerns for my mother's treatment. When, instead of using his vast experience to address some of my concerns and alleviate the mind of a harried daughter whose already very sick mother had just been given a bleak cancer diagnosis, he instead chose to flash his accomplishments in my face.

In contrast, the uniformed doctor at the military hospital had kind eyes. She listened to my concerns and discussed them with me. Ironically, at the end I chose the same approach that the other doctor was suggesting, but now it made sense to me.

You see, we all have something no one can ever take away from us. And that's our free will.

When I say autonomy, what comes to your mind? Can you think of a few words or phrases here that pop into your head when you hear this word? Here are the words that came to my mind the first time I heard this word in the context of parenting:

Stubbornness
Not listening
Wanting what they want and only what they want
Demanding to be independent

I also ask people in a survey-like question what autonomy means and I get a host of answers varying from "no idea" or "can't verbalize" to the words/phrases I've stated above. Merriam-Webster defines autonomy as, "the quality or state of being self-governing" and "self-directing freedom and especially moral independence."[1]

It makes sense though why this seems like such a tricky concept when we think of this word in regards to parenting, mainly because it's the antithesis of what "good kids" are. As I discussed in the introduction, the world doesn't value children's individuality and personality. What we value in children, most of all, is compliance or even obedience. The latter is the word most commonly used in the subcontinent when it comes to children. It's the gold standard for being an *acha bacha* ("good child"). Lots of people seem to think that this word comes from Islam and kids are supposed to blindly obey their parents. I challenge you to find even one verse from the Quran or a quote/incident from hadith that supports this idea.

The same quality in children is lauded all over the world. Islam—a religion that values critical thinking, free will, and questioning everything—has nothing to do with this concept. It's a curious word, isn't it? If I asked you what's someone's most winning quality, you'd never say "they're very obedient/ compliant." If I asked you what are the qualities needed to succeed in life, you'd never say obedient/compliant. If I asked you what makes a wonderful friend? A good brother/sister? A good partner? Again, you will never use those two words.

Yet, when it comes to children. That's almost always our number one answer to what a "good child" is. Here are some variations of the answer to the question, "What is a good kid?"

- He listens
- He does as he's asked
- She doesn't talk back
- She never says no
- They always do as they're told

Notice the common pattern? A "good kid" is someone who has no will of their own and is ever ready to bend to the will of others. It's unclear who the others are but we can safely assume it must be all "elders." For example, what if she listens to her parents but not her grandparents, teachers, or aunts/uncles?

In other words, a good child is someone who listens to everyone except herself.

You might be thinking at this point, "But Maryam, don't elders know best? Isn't it good that she listens to everyone? This will make her a good child which will make her a good person. And we all need to be a good person to succeed in life."

Apart from the fact that we remember from the Introduction that elements of success include parents who allow their children to have a voice and that no body of research has ever found a correlation between compliance leading to someone making good choices in life, let's examine the idea that compliance to "elders" leads to becoming a "good person."

The premise of this idea seems to add up. Elders are "good people" who know right from wrong and so just doing as they say and following in their footsteps blindly will lead to every child also becoming a "good person."

Now examine all the "elders" in your life, and don't forget to include yourself. You're now supposedly one of the elders that children are supposed to blindly obey and follow to turn into a good adult. I hope that even a cursory glance within and around you will bring into light the reality that we are all incredibly flawed human beings. That often, the line between "right" and "wrong" is blurry in our behaviors. That we are often governed by our circumstances, our stories, our traumas, our emotions, and our often-erroneous beliefs.

We all secretly hope and pray that our children are nothing like us but in fact, a much more glorious, perfect, and flawless version of ourselves. Or more accurately, they're the person we wish we could have been if xyz hadn't happened to us or if we'd had more of this or that in our life.

Sometimes when parents are disappointed in their children's behaviors, they often even say to their kids, "I didn't have the resources I'm providing for you . . . how can you be so ungrateful and not take advantage of them?"

As if all that stood in our way of being a perfect human was resources.

Point being, we are *all* incredibly flawed humans, but children at least are devoid of the kind of corruption that only comes from being an adult. They are, in fact, the purest form of humanhood to walk the earth. Even the meanest "bully" in your kid's class is only acting out from learned behavior that can be easily reversed with connection and healthy, loving boundaries. It will take years and decades though, to cause positive change in even the most well-intentioned adult, mostly due to the hardwiring that's already in place.

Now, hopefully, I've convinced you that the secret to becoming a "good adult" is not being a "good/compliant kid." That the only real outcome for a compliant child is to become a compliant adult, otherwise known as a people pleaser.

So then what, you ask?

If our children don't listen to us and our (flawed) wisdom, then how will they become "good adults"?

The answer is "intrinsic motivation."

Fortunately, we all have a chip inside us that tells us when we're doing something wrong. It dutifully goes "beep beep" when our actions don't align with our values.

Values, you ask? What are those? Ah . . . those *are* something we can pass on to our child. Because unlike our flawed selves, values are the highest form of the aspirations we wish to live up to. If we could be perfect and flawless, we'd be living our values every single moment of our lives, but we're not, so we hold our values like guideposts, lighting up our way to our best life. I highly recommend that you download the values worksheet from Brené Brown's website[2] and listen to her podcast (linked on the same page) to help you figure out what your most important values are and how you can embody them.

But wait, you ask, what do values have to do with autonomy? Everything.

You see, the truth is that not only is it not helpful to be a compliant human (small or big), it's, in fact, downright dangerous.

Have you wondered how someone can convince another human to become a suicide bomber? How someone can convince someone else to commit heinous crimes in the name of gang loyalty? Think of the groupies that follow a bully around, validating their mean behavior or younger kids following older kids into dangerous situations, or workers staying late to work off the clock because their boss told them to, or the people who follow social trends, like unhealthy dieting or scams. There is no end to how we can fall into harmful behaviors patterns if our autonomy wasn't encouraged or built on sound values and the power of intrinsic motivation.

Not knowing or valuing our own autonomy means to not know who we are at the core and what's important to us. In fact, it's not even being aware of the fact that we have agency over our own lives. Lacking autonomy means to believe that we are at the mercy of others.

Unfortunately, this is something I get to see on a regular basis in my work. Women trapped in abusive relationships, waiting for some miracle to happen before they can escape or change their life's direction. Men, trapped in joint-family systems under the thumb of an empty-cup parent who won't "let them leave." Men and women trapped in joyless jobs under toxic bosses, thinking and feeling like they have no option but to suck it up.

On top of an upbringing where all autonomy was stripped, add the most misunderstood and oversimplified concept in our culture—patience. The main idea being, "If bad stuff is happening to you, step back, do nothing and you'll get truckloads of rewards on your *amalnama* ('book of deeds')."

Realistically what's happening is that the oppressor and oppressed are both enabling poor behaviors and depression; anxiety is rampant.

Let's pause here and go back to the "good kids," the ones that are lauded for being compliant/obedient and have no sense of autonomy. Either that, or as teens, they're in full rebellion mode. Whenever a parent begins, "My six-year-old is a perfect child. She listens to everything I say but . . ." I already know where the conversation is going.

A child who's been taught to value compliance over everything else has learned that her own ideas and thoughts are no good so they're best left unexpressed. She becomes timid, lacks confidence and joy in learning (because joyful learning is filled with trying out brilliantly original ideas), and most of all, she has stopped believing in her own abilities and waits for instructions—someone to tell her what to do and how to do it.

Conversely, I get a parent who says, "My sixteen-year-old used to be such a good child and now he's totally rebellious. I don't even recognize him. What has happened to my sweet boy? When will this teen phase end?"

Sadly, it will end. Every "good kid" lights up one last time during teenhood in a big blaze of self-assertion and self-expression, and then just as quickly and loudly as it came, the burst of light and sound fizzles out and you either get an adult who has learned that bad choices are better than others' choices for them or you get a compliant adult, who retreats quietly beneath the mask of "normalcy": a faded, jaded, and inauthentic version of his glorious self.

Hopefully, you've now started to appreciate the value of autonomy and are ready to take back your own agency and raise children who aren't afraid to exercise their God-given autonomy either.

Taking Our Power Back Is Scary Sh*t

It was early spring in 2021 and the lockdown of Covid-19 was a year old now. I sat on my mahogany farmhouse-style dining table cradling the phone on my shoulder as I sorted through our never-ending piles of laundry.

"The doctor said she has a year or so left before she's bedridden." Papa was telling me my mom's prognosis.

"Oh!" I said, "That's not much . . ."

"No, it's not but you'll visit us soon?" he asked.

"In the summer, I guess. The kids' school is still on," I said.

I could "see" him nodding on the other side. I know it was hard for him, but he understood. As a Pakistani father, he didn't expect much from his daughters. And I, as a daughter, wasn't supposed to hope that I could do more for my parents.

"It's ok, we'll see you soon. Summer isn't too far away," he said.

"Yes. Soon," I said.

After hanging up the phone with him, I sat there on the dining table, thinking about the future. I saw myself visiting Pakistan once a year. Popping into my sick mom's life like a guest and popping right out. These rushed trips to Pakistan mostly spent overcoming jet lag, my kids' stomachs settling, and perhaps some stolen moments spent with Mama. I then imagined myself, one day, getting there too late—and she's already bedridden and I'm bouncing between the regret of missing seeing her up and about mixed in with the guilt of wanting to take care of her but being held back by the limitations of another rushed trip.

Just then, I had the most remarkable thought of my life.

What if I move to Pakistan?

As much as this thought took my breath away, it also seemed to make the most sense. Regret is not my strong suit. I don't regret well. So just then my question became not whether moving to Pakistan was a good idea or not but what I would regret more five years from now—staying back or moving to Pakistan?

As much as I'd never loved living in the U.S., it was essentially the only adult life I'd ever known. I didn't really know how to adult in Pakistan. And from what everyone kept telling me these past eighteen years, it was pretty awful. So, on the one hand I knew that I'd have some deep regrets five years from now if I didn't move, and on the other hand I was also gripped by the debilitating fear of the unknown.

It wasn't even just the fear of the unknown but also the fear of "what will people say," the omnipresent fear of all.

She took her poor husband to Pakistan.

She's so selfish—didn't even think of her kids' future.

She has no idea what she's doing.

When she lives in Pakistan, she'll finally know how ungrateful she was.

She's not going to last a year there.

Bataain karna tou asaan hota hai, ab pta chalay ga.

I'm somewhat ashamed to say that all these fears won. I was disappointed in myself to know that when presented with the possible option of moving to Pakistan, I was scared. What if everyone had been right all along and I will absolutely hate it? Will my kids hate it? They won't adjust. My husband will hate me forever.

All these thoughts consumed me, and I gave myself some lame excuses about why it was better that I visit my mom alone every three months from the U.S., and why moving there wasn't the best idea. One day, though, my mom had a bad scare. Some of the test results indicated cancerous growth. All of a sudden, I realized that I'd made a decision from fear and not my heart. That I have to do the right thing here—what feels right to my heart and aligns with my values—and if I don't do this, I don't know about anyone else, but betraying my own heart would weigh heavy on me for the rest of my life. And so, I decided that moving to Pakistan was the only option.

Except my husband, as I've shared before, was never cool with this idea. So much so that all the beginning years when I went into depression from the loneliness and hardship of the move, he still never suggested moving back as a vague option even in the distant future. As far as he was concerned, he'd burnt the bridges. So you can imagine when I tried to tell him that I'd like to move back, he resisted with all his might. To give him credit, he resisted with kindness. He offered to sponsor my parents so that they could move to the U.S. and live with us. But that process takes years—years my mom didn't have. He then offered to apply for medical insurance for them and have them just stay with us for the majority of the year. I imagined trying to take care of my parents on top of everything else I was already drowning under. I knew that wouldn't work either.

It was time to practice autonomy. It was time to take back my power. I told him I was moving to Pakistan with the kids and he was welcome to stay back and keep the house, cars, everything. I will manage the expenses myself in Pakistan. There, it was done. I said it.

And I had never been so scared in my entire life.

At that moment I realized how much easier it is to let others steer your life and blame them for everything that goes wrong. And how much harder it is to take back the steering wheel and accept responsibility for your life.

Yes, I had a new business, and TPEP was doing relatively well, but was it enough to sustain me if my husband decided to stay back?

What if we moved there and everything was as bad as everyone said, and I had to move back?

What if something happens to the kids and I regret the move?

What if what if what if.

It would be an understatement to say that I was terrified.

And yet, it was also exhilarating. I had never done anything like it my entire life.

So far, my whole life had been orchestrated by others.

Dad said go to engineering school. Done.

Mom said get married to xyz. Done.

Husband said move to America. Done.

Society said keep living where husband is. Done.

For the first time in my life, I realized why I had unknowingly allowed others to dictate these choices for me. It had been so, *so* nice to be able to blame everyone for making me study what I didn't want. For making me get married when I didn't want to. For making me move to a country I didn't want to move to. For making me stay in a country I didn't want to stay in.

Who am I going to blame if this goes wrong? No one but myself.

It was the most petrifying realization ever.

So, if everything doesn't go well, I'd be *responsible*? I wouldn't be able to be a *victim*? I'd had no idea how much I'd been relishing not having responsibility for my own misery. Goodness, this was eye-opening stuff.

All of a sudden, I understood exactly why people stay in miserable situations. We would rather spend our entire lives blaming others and being miserable than accepting responsibility and relinquishing the role of the victim. Now, if anything bad happened, I'd have no one to blame but myself.

Why did this feel so significant? Why was I so scared to accept responsibility for my own life. And then I realized why.

The message we hear most of our lives is that we're not good enough.

See? You screwed up again.
See? I told you; you don't know how to do this.
See? You should've just listened to me.
See? Now it's all ruined.

In other words, I'm not enough and whatever I do will surely be wrong.

It's not so much that we are afraid of screwing things up, we are *certain* that we will screw things up. So much so that we'd rather let others screw things up for us because we will surely do a much worse job. But as it turns out, no one knows our own lives better than we do. No one is in a better position to make decisions about our life than we are. So, that was it then: I had to remind myself that I was, in fact, enough.

It sure didn't feel like I was, but I had to believe it. It was the bravest thing I'd ever be called to do, and I did it. And I don't mean brave because it was a big move across the world. Brave, because I followed my heart. I did what I had wanted to do since forever. I did what had been just a dream for so many years. I did what everyone told me I shouldn't do. I did what so many said I'd regret.

For once in my life, I didn't listen to anyone but myself.

And I was right.

These past almost two years of living in Pakistan have been the happiest years of my life. There are so many times when I'm outside going somewhere in the car, and I see the lush green Margalla Hills that I grew up with and they make me smile. Or I'm sitting on my lawn outside and I hear the familiar-to-my-nervous-system sounds of the motorcycles and cars outside and they make me smile. Or when I'm browsing my child-hood bookstore and the cashier recognizes me and it makes me smile. Just the randomest little things make me smile.

I'm home. After all these years, I'm home. And I couldn't be happier.

No one know us better than ourselves. The wisdom that comes from within us is the only wisdom we need to follow. But following that wisdom requires the kind of courage that will bring you to your knees. The question is not whether or not your dreams can come true; the question is, are you ready to take the responsibility of making them come true?

Giving Kids Their Power Back

Earlier this summer, we went to Egypt to see the pyramids. On our drive towards Cairo, I was explaining to the kids what we would be seeing. When I told them that that the biggest pyramid is made of more than two million very huge blocks, their eyes opened wide.

"Why would someone build such a big pyramid?"

This very basic question actually made me pause and reflect. Of course I knew why they were built, but conveying it to kids so that it made sense seemed a bit complicated. I decided to go with a simple explanation,

"I suppose they're just really big headstones. They mark the graves of important people from ancient Egypt."

"Wow, that's a really big headstone!" exclaimed Yahya.

"Yes it is, isn't it?"

"But why, Mama? Why did they need such a big headstone?" he asked.

Again, I had to pause and think. It did seem kind of over-the-top.

"I think it's because the pharaohs who built the pyramids for themselves believed that they were gods, and if you're god then your earthly body must be buried in a grand way—like under a huge pyramid that took years to built!"

"They believed they were god? That's so silly!" said the other twin, Muhammed.

"Well, I suppose if you were a pharaoh back then, it would have been kind of silly to believe that you're just human," I tried to explain.

And then my own remark caught me off-guard. I imagined what an act of courage it would have been for any of the pharaohs to actually say, "Hey, I don't think I'm god . . . I'm just a human responsible for the people I serve."

That's when I realized that it's easy to judge the pharaohs for believing that they were gods, but there's a pharaoh inside each of us—urging us to normalize abusing the power we hold over someone who is more vulnerable than us, like our children. The pharaoh inside us points to others and tries to remind us that people will laugh at us if we *don't* abuse our power. Isn't this why being a respectful parent is so difficult? Because people who don't understand it accuse us of being "too soft" on our kids and "letting" our kids "manipulate" us? If, like the pharaohs of Egypt, we give in to the pressure and use the power to control and dictate to our children while we insist on reverence and respect for ourselves, then we also become pharaohs for our kids. The best way to honor the power we've been blessed with is to make sure that we respect the power of those at lower tiers of power. We can do this for children by stepping back whenever possible.

One of my favorite bloggers, who fights for children's right to play and autonomy in learning, and on Facebook goes by the appropriate handle of The Occuplaytional Therapist, beautifully describes an incident where she discovered the magic of "doing nothing":

> While I played with my children recently, I had two shining examples of why sometimes it's better to say nothing at all. These are far from the only two, but they're the ones that stood out in this activity.
>
> My daughter was sticking foam stickers to a piece of construction paper. One of them wasn't lined up as neatly as she wanted it to be, so she started peeling it

up off the paper. The instinctual voice in my parent-brain said, "Don't peel the stickers off! If you peel stickers off construction paper, they tear up the paper and they lose their stickiness. It won't work."

Fortunately, I was able to catch myself a moment before I blurted out what my parent-brain was saying. Instead, I stayed quiet and watched.

Predictably, the first sticker my daughter peeled off took a huge chunk of construction paper with it..." ruining" the sticker, "ruining" the paper (from an adult point of view). My daughter looked at the back of the sticker curiously and considered it. She picked at the stuck construction paper for a while before abandoning the pursuit. Then she immediately peeled another sticker off the paper . . . this one much more carefully, and delicately.

It came right off the paper. It did not tear the page.

Pleased with herself, she stuck it back down in a new place. Then she continued at this pursuit . . . sticking stickers where she wanted, peeling them off, rearranging them. Some of them worked, some of them didn't. She developed some finger strength and fine motor skills. She developed a satisfying intrinsic awareness of the properties of stickers and paper, of the impermanence of this activity, of the tactile and tensile properties of the materials she was working with, of how much pressure it takes to rip paper and how much stickiness is on a sticker and how these things interact.

And I, in all my Adult Brilliance, had thought to "impart" a lesson about stickers and paper with my words. To a 2-year-old. Who would not have absorbed the words anyway. But through my silence, and her playing, she learned 10x better than I could have "taught."[3]

STAY QUIET/DO NOTHING

The best parents have lots of bite marks on their tongues. Kids are learning even when we don't overtly teach. Kids are slower than us. When we pause or stay quiet, they tend to notice their mistakes.

ALLOW FOR MISTAKES

It's impossible to learn anything new unless we're comfortable with mistakes. "Allowing" looks like saying, "Oops, no worries!" "You tried your best." "New things take time." "It happens." "That always happens to me too." Instead of lecturing your children when they make mistakes, teach them through modeling that making mistakes is part of learning. You can share aloud when you make mistakes: "This new recipe didn't turn out great, and I think I know what I did wrong, but I'm still proud of myself for trying something new!"

POINT OUT WHAT WENT RIGHT

When kids attempt something, it's often not done as well as we might have liked, but it's important to acknowledge the effort and focus on the positives. This gives children feedback about what they did correctly, and they can use that information as encouragement and guidance to accomplish harder tasks. For example, you can say,

"You built the tower quite tall before it fell."

"You were able to do most of your homework."

"Some of those spellings were hard—how did you learn them?"

"You were able to share some of your toys . . . how did you decide that?"

GIVE SPACE/TIME/GRACE

I remember when my son, one of my twins, was two years old. He would take, not kidding, a whole five minutes to zip up his jacket. If you're a parent, you know how agonizingly long those five minutes feel when you're standing there, waiting to go out. The urge to just take over is intense. I'm totally with you if you're thinking it would be so much faster if I could just do it. At such moments the only thing that motivated me to stay patient was the strong belief that this time is an investment in saving myself tons of time in the future. If I can use these fortuities to build his confidence in himself, he'll be doing care tasks for himself in no time. Cheeky, right? But it worked!

That delight and pride of zipping up his jacket himself allowed him to experience that awesome feeling that can only come from accomplishing a difficult task yourself, without help. Sure enough, at age six, he's completely independent in dressing himself and other basic hygiene tasks.

I'll also share here what not giving space/time/grace looks like to give you an idea of what not to do:

- "Let me do it!"

- "You're too little to do this."
- "You always mess this up."
- "See what happened now?"

An important note on giving space/time/grace: Sometimes we need to give them months or years. They'll be ready when they'll be ready. If we lose patience and start saying some of the above things, then we've essentially negated any space/time/ grace we *did* give them in the past.

HALF-HELP

Even if we're offering assistance, it can be limited instead of doing the whole thing for them. For example, loosening the lid of the bottle instead of opening it all the way, taking their hamper to the laundry room instead of doing the whole laundry, helping them divide the room mess into categories (trash, dirty clothes, dishes, etc.) rather than cleaning the room for them. This teaches them the profound lesson that they're worthy of help and we also have faith in their autonomy.

Examples:

- Child can't open the lid. We open the tight vacuum but then hand it right over for them to finish opening.
- Child can't put on his shoes. We help get the foot in and then let them finish up.
- Preteen can't decide what to wear. We narrow down her options and help her decide.
- Teen can't finish his homework. We give them some ideas for resources for help.

Why Angels Can't Learn

"Mama, do you know why angels can't learn?" then-seven-year-old Eisa asked me as he helped me tidy up our family room in our fabulous new rental in Centreville.

His question caught me off guard. Where did he get the idea that angels can't learn? And isn't that a bit of a broad statement? Like, learn anything? What's he talking about? I decided to keep an open mind.

"I have no idea, but I'm intrigued, Eisa," I said carefully.

"It's because they can't make mistakes, remember?" he said, a bit flustered that I didn't get it.

"Oh!" I was genuinely taken aback. He saw my surprised expression and continued explaining.

"You told me in Prophet Adam's birth story that Allah asked angels the names of things and they didn't know anything, but he knew the names of everything! Obviously, they can't learn because they're perfect and can't make mistakes, and if you can't make mistakes then you can't learn!"

I remember being a little blown away by the connections my wise son made. I had told him the story, of course, but I hadn't made those connections myself. The conclusions he reached are supported by research and studies. The ability to make mistakes is a gift, and the ability to learn from these mistakes is a miraculous outcome. I say miraculous because studies have shown that we don't even need to be aware of our mistakes to grow from them. This was obviously not how any of us grew up. Mistakes have always been viewed as barely tolerable, with warnings at best and unforgivable character flaws at worst.

MISTAKES MAKE OUR BRAINS GROW

According to Janet Metcalfe, in her scientific review entitled, *Learning from Errors*[4], the pioneer of behaviorism, psychologist B.F. Skinner, didn't even like his lab rats and pigeons to make mistakes, so he designed trials to train them to complete tasks correctly every time. He believed that if they made a mistake, it would become entrenched and that you would have to go back and fix it.

Metcalfe shares an interesting study in which researchers recorded Japanese and American classrooms during mathematics class. They noted that American teachers tended to focus a lot on memorizing the correct procedures and praising the correct answers. The Japanese teachers, on the other hand, focused more on the trial-and-error process of eliminating wrong answers and refrained from offering praise for correct answers.

American teachers tended to "lead" the class by taking on an authority role and pointing out the incorrect answers and veering the class towards the correct answer. The Japanese teachers allowed the students to solve the problems themselves first, instigating a slew of mistakes and wrong turns. Their discussions also focused a lot on the examination of these mistakes in a very neutral way by wondering about why a solution seemed plausible but didn't work out. The focus seems to be on the strenuous and error-filled task of solving a problem rather than getting the correct answers. The students accept that the process of learning is not paved with praises and ease.

Which country's children do you think are outscoring the other in math scores? If you guessed Japan, you're right. The researchers acknowledge that this disparity could be due to other reasons as well, but there are numerous other studies to showcase the power of normalizing mistakes, focusing on the effort and avoiding behaviorism-based praise (or positive reinforcement).

WHY IT'S HARD TO LET OUR KIDS MAKE MISTAKES

Most parents hesitate to allow their children autonomy over many things because they are afraid of the mistakes they will make.

I recall meeting Faiza at an international speaking event I was invited to in Lahore. She caught up with me after my presentation and said, "I just want to ask you one question, please! I'm so overwhelmed by it and don't know what to do!"

I love these interactions after my speaking events and asked her to settle down with me on a bench nearby.

"What's worrying you so much?" I asked her.

"Electronics! I'm so afraid of them! I mean afraid of everything that's on there these days! My daughter is ten and she's begging me to let her use the computer by herself, but I can't . . . what if she navigates to an inappropriate website? What if she gets addicted to video games? What if she starts chatting with random strangers on the internet!" With each sentence, Faiza seemed to get more and more dysregulated.

"You're really worried about this, aren't you? I totally understand. We didn't grow up with the internet, so it sure feels scary to let our children navigate it!"

"Yes! I keep a strict watch on her when she's using my iPad for school assignments; I check the history just in case. But it's not working anymore. I mean my daughter is so mad at me! She says all her friends are allowed to use the internet without someone hovering over them, but I can't do that!"

"Right, you're worried about her doing something unsafe on the internet . . ."

"Yes . . . but how will she learn to navigate it carefully?"

"How indeed . . . you're so worried about her making a mistake while using the internet that you're always there . . . making sure she never makes any mistake . . . and if she did . . . seems like you'd be very upset," I echoed her words.

I could see that something shifted for her when I repeated her words to her.

"She won't learn, will she . . . unless I let her make mistakes? Unless I let her use it on her own?"

I nodded gently.

"But it's so scary!" she protested.

"It is, isn't it? It's so scary letting our kids make mistakes when we could just protect them from life's every awful thing."

"But I guess we can't also just protect them from everything . . ."

"No, we can't . . . and even if we could, would it serve them to never have known the pain of making mistakes? The pain of getting hurt?"

"But it's so hard to see them hurt!" she repeated her protest again.

This time I just nodded and gave her a hug because I could see that she'd just been faced with one of life's hardest lessons as a parent: the biggest act of a selfless love is to actually let go, a little more with every passing year, and allow our children to experience life with all its highs and lows. Isn't it a wonderful thing that we're always here to cushion their falls? To offer connection and validation for those difficult times? Not "told you so" or "should've listened to me" or "how could you" or "what is wrong with you" but just "I'm here." Unconditional presence—it goes a long way in giving our children what they truly need from us instead of protecting them for every difficulty in life.

Opportunities for Giving Autonomy

CARE TASKS

One opportunity to give our children more autonomy is to slow down during care tasks, even when our children are babies. We can now give them more charge of their care tasks, and we know that they're ready for this when they start resisting the care tasks like running away when we're wanting to change their diaper.

It's easy to get frustrated at such times, but it's wonderful news that you've created safety and security in your relationship with your child and they're feeling comfortable enough to enter a new development stage where they come into their autonomy and free will. What better way to practice challenging authority when something doesn't sit well with you than with your caregivers?

Our wise guide Magda Gerber understood this very well and has very helpful advice that helped me survive those early years with my kids when running away from basic care tasks was my kids' favorite game! She says,

> Caregiving tasks become more challenging during the toddler stage. Children want to dress themselves and help in every aspect of their care, saying "me help" or "want." The solution is to allow and encourage your child to help as much as he can.

If he wants to help with diapering, ask him to lift his bottom or hold the lotion. An effective way to give choices to your child is to ask, "Do you want to walk to the changing table or do you want me to carry you?" or "Do you want to hold the clean diaper or the cream?"[5]

Of course, there will be times when we don't have the time or space to allow children to take charge of these tasks and that's when we will calmly use the simple choice boundary setting method for getting the job done.

As children get older, we want to continue to give them more and more autonomy over their care tasks even if these jobs are not done as well as we'd like. For example, brushing their hair, selecting their outfits, deciding whether or not to wear a jacket, what kind of haircut to have, etc. Remember, we keep our eyes on the prize, which is to raise children who feel confident, able, and independent even if they have haircuts, clothes, or styles that embarrass us.

MEAL TIMES

Let's face it, when we think of a "good mom," we see home-cooked meals, served piping hot and being put into the kids' mouths by the mom's loving hands. This is true for so many cultures across the board. In Urdu we even have a saying that roughly translates to, "This reminded me of my mom's hands' taste."

I remember listening to a random motivational speaker on TikTok who was saying that he's eaten at the world's best restaurant and he can verify that food can taste great even when it doesn't have your "mom's hands' taste". He was arguing that this is a trick society has used to keep moms stuck in the kitchen and not allowing them to have the kind of aspirations fathers are allowed to have.

I'm not sure if I agree with the conspiracy to keep moms in the kitchen, but I do ask moms if anyone ever asks them who watches the kids while they spend all day cooking in the kitchen versus the number of inquisitive and judgmental comments they get if they choose to spend that same time doing something for themselves instead.

The reason that I'm sharing this is because for so many mothers, what their kids eat, how much they eat, and when they eat is a rife source of shame for mothers. It's almost as if a mother's worth can be directly measured by the food she serves and how her kids eat. And we will not be able to raise healthy eaters who have a healthy relationship with food if we ourselves are steeped in shame around this subject.

So here it is: I hereby give you permission to not use how often you cook or how much your kids eat as metrics to measure how "good" a mother you are. You're a good mother, regardless of all that. Most kids, past the age of one, aren't particularly interested in food. They eat to live and don't live to eat until they're teens (and unless we're talking about sugary treats).

Ellyn Satter, whose book and resources we use to teach parents how to raise healthy eaters, says simply, "Kids eat when they're hungry."[6]

Satter uses a method called Division of Responsibility (DOR), which states that when it comes to meal times, both parents and children have their own responsibilities and everyone should only concern themselves with their own responsibility.[7] I'm sharing a modified version of her system here that has worked for our family in raising kids who eat happily at meal times, eat a large variety of foods, love many vegetables and fruits, enjoy candy and other sugary treats in reasonable amounts, and have thriving health. If this topic interests you, I encourage you to visit Satter's website and learn more from there.[8]

DOR as we've practiced in our family looks like this:

- Parents' responsibilities:
    - Have set timings for meals
    - Make available meals that are generally acceptable to the child
    - Have 2–3 various kinds of food groups at each meal (carbohydrates, protein, fat, etc.)
    - Enjoy their own food

- Children's responsibilities:
    - Eat whatever their body is desiring from any of the food groups provided
    - Pack up and put away any leftovers
    - Grow at their own pace
    - Enjoy their food

Most parents struggle with the idea that a child will make "good choices" when allowed so much autonomy over food. However, all we have to do is think back to when our child was an infant and knew exactly when to eat and when to stop. The reason that they've stopped eating and will only eat when "forced" or bribed or cajoled is because their autonomy has been taken away. Now mealtimes have become a battleground for autonomy, a struggle to get their power back. Satter writes,

If a struggle emerges about eating, a toddler will get so involved in the struggle and so upset that it overwhelms her need to eat.[9]

How many times has your child eaten and said, "See? I ate my food . . . now can I have that cookie?" How did the child come to believe that they're eating for their parents and not to survive? This is a sign that their autonomy has been compromised, but of course, we can always reverse things with a bit of patience.

- Things to remember:
  - If you have serious concerns about your child's weight/nutrition, seek out a pediatric endocrinologist and have your child be seen by them.
  - It's important for younger children to have a place designated for eating. Highchairs are alright, but the child should be allowed to get out when they indicate they're done.
  - Alternatively, they can also eat at a low table while sitting on the floor. This is what Gerber suggests.
  - As soon as children start eating, they are capable of feeding themselves. Being attuned to your child will allow you to give them the foods they can easily eat, like cucumber, avocado, egg, rice, etc.

- What's normal:
  - Kids throw food and make a huge mess when they're learning how to eat. I used a plastic mat under their chair and silicone bibs or nude mealtimes for easier clean up.
  - When you first switch to DOR, there might be a rough patch because it will take the child some

time to realize that they eat for sustenance and not to please you. Keep following DOR and trust the child. Refrain from old methods of cajoling and bribing. (This usually doesn't last for more than a couple of days. Keep a lookout for signs of malnutrition and dehydration and immediately seek medical help if these are present.)

- Young children's gag reflex is incredibly strong and nature's way of expelling anything that's too big to swallow. Stay close and attuned for those initial days of weaning. Gagging doesn't mean you're doing something wrong.

- Generally following the guideline that "food before one is just for fun" allowed me to relax and enjoy my children learning to feed themselves.

- Toddlers like to eat more frequently in small quantities. This is normal.

- Teens eat a lot. That's also normal.

- Young bodies are designed to burn sugar and carbohydrates like a furnace and scientists agree that children are attracted to sugary foods for good reasons. Dr. Julie Menella shares interesting results from a study that says when children are attracted to more sugary foods, they're seeking "pain relief."[10]

  Sue Coldwell, another researcher who has studied kids and sweets, says that this attraction to sugar automatically lessens in adolescence. Again, principles of autonomy would apply here. When this natural inclination is forcefully curbed during childhood, a child will learn to dismiss their body's signals and possibly continue their obsession with sugary treats well into adulthood.[11]

RESPECTFUL WEANING:

One obstacle I've observed in Pakistani homes is parents' reluctance to let go of milk bottles. If you're a parent who's struggled to accomplish this despite all your efforts, you have my full sympathy. I know that previous generations place a lot of importance on milk. I vaguely recall watching a documentary about how milk factories advertised diligently to make people believe that milk is some kind of special super food. In reality, kids aged 1+ don't need milk a whole lot; it's not formula or breastmilk and can be easily replaced with other sources of calcium and vitamin D.[12]

If you want to continue breastfeeding past age one, I don't see any reason to dissuade you unless it's interfering with your mental health. I nursed my son until age two but my daughter till age one because frankly, I was utterly exhausted and pregnant with twins. The only thing I do ask is to eliminate night feedings past age one. You'll also learn in the next section how bottles also interfere with children's sleep and are not good for oral health. That said, here are gentle weaning methods that worked for my kids and many of my clients' kids:

1. Prepare your child: Tell him one day that today is the last day of bottles/breastfeeding. For bottles you can say they'll be going away tomorrow. For breastfeeding you can say, "I love you and I'm done breastfeeding you now." (We tell them we love them so they don't perceive that as us pushing them away.) Explain the plan.

2. He can be an active part of collecting his bottles and trashing them so he knows they won't be coming back. For breastfeeding, they can have a goodbye ceremony with one last pat and bye bye.

3. When he asks for it, you acknowledge that he misses it and remind him that it's gone. "You really miss your bottle . . . I can imagine its hard . . . changes are hard!"

   "You miss breastfeeding/*doodo*! *Ap ko bohat Acha lagta tha! Mujhay bhee*! Shall we hug so we can both feel better?"

4. The day is usually easier but nights are harder. Especially the first night will be rough. You'll be ready for it. I remember I got my favorite snacks and a book and hunkered down for a "bad night." My son needed comfort almost all night and I was there for him, empathizing how hard it is. Validation is your best friend. Don't try to say a whole bunch of "But beta you know what we decided." Just focus on the feelings.

5. Stay strong and confident and remember that your doubts/fears/hesitation confuse kids.

   The second night will be 90% better! And by the third or fourth night, he won't even remember and you'll be bottle/breast-free forever!

Use the same method for getting rid of pacifiers. And get rid of *both* at the same time when you decide to get rid of one.

As you can see, allowing children autonomy around eating is imperative to their future health in various different ways. Here are some other salient points that have helped me raise healthy eaters:

1. Understanding and unpacking my own unhealthy relationship with food by learning how to become an intuitive eater.

2. Refusing to become a part of diet-culture that normalizes demonizing certain foods and turning them into "forbidden foods."

3. Making all sorts of foods available and trusting children to listen to their bodies about what's ok to eat and how much.

4. Not having our lives revolve around food and embracing various avenues of acquiring meals rather than spending a vast majority of the day in the kitchen.

Have you ever wondered or questioned the sanity of putting almost anything in your mouth and then having some kind of feeling about it? Either guilt or pride or self-loathing. I invite you to learn more about this subject and break free of "food shame"—the only way to raise children who will love their bodies, enjoy their food, and love being healthy.

"Honestly, unless you killed the chef or the farmer, there should be no guilt about your eating choices."

—Evelyn Tribole, *Intuitive Eating:*
A Revolutionary Anti-Diet Approach[13]

SLEEP

When it comes to respectful parenting circles, strangely enough, sleep is the single most controversial topic. There are people on various sides of this, each of whom seem to believe that their way is the right way. Recently I'm finding a lot of social media content that has good intentions done poorly. I'm vehemently on the side of anyone who wishes well for children, but I'm also equally vehemently opposed to using shame as a tool to "get'" people to make better choices.

In my part of the world—that is, Pakistan—children have slept with their parents since forever. Like my sweet mama would say half disapprovingly to me when I moved my kids to their own rooms, "I used to make you sleep hugged close to my chest all night . . . how can you separate your poor children?"

I'd laugh and say, "Yes, you hugged me close all night and used your *chappal* all day." *Chappal* in Urdu and *chancla* in Spanish have no equal in the English language as far as I'm concerned. One of my favorite "gentle parenting" social media personalities, Leslie Priscilla[14] from Latinax Parenting uses the tag line, "Ending Chancla Culture," and I absolutely love it.

You see, like I shared in the previous section about meal-times, "successful motherhood" is associated with a few things and having your children sleep next to you is one of them. As you've already guessed, where your children sleep doesn't define your worth as a mother. There's really no point in being obsessed with having your children sleep next to you if you're then going to be perpetually sleep-deprived and turn to your chappal or wine, for that matter, as a way to regulate yourself. In many Eastern cultures, the caricature of the mom running after her children with a chappal in her hand is so normalized and even humorized that we think nothing of it.

In my Western counterparts, I see a ton of memes about moms and wine as if again, it's totally normal and ok to numb yourself daily in order to raise kids.

If these images bring up shame for you, I want you to pause and check in with yourself, because it's definitely not ok for society to put impossible standards on motherhood and then shame mothers for resorting to various methods to self-regulate.

This is why I want to talk about alternatives to co-sleeping. Referring back to the trauma chapter and how brown bodies are holding on to trauma and its remnants, it's an incredibly privileged perspective to say, "Everyone should sleep next to their children and if they don't then they shouldn't have had children in the first place." I've observed that this kind of unbendable view is usually coming from white moms who have newly discovered co-sleeping as an option and alternative to the way that they might have been raised. A lot of "baby boomer" parents used Ferber's "extinction" method of "sleep training," leaving a baby to cry in their cot for hours unattended as a way to condition them to sleep on their own. It makes sense for these white moms to be cycle breakers in their own way and embrace what they believe is a more wholesome Eastern practice of co-sleeping.

I wish that co-sleeping was as "exotic" or "wholesome" as some white attachment parenting moms have made it out to be. In reality, most people in my country never had an option of not co-sleeping. Either because of lack of resources or judgment from the in-laws. I know plenty of brown mothers and grandmothers who toss and turn all night, trying to sleep between several of their children. Only to wake up in the morning and be solely responsible for those same children and a slew of in-laws, waiting to be served by their daughter-in-law.

So, you can be certain that when one of my clients is sitting before me, her DNA carrying the exhaustion of her mother and grandmother before her, her shoulders carrying the burden of serving her family and in-laws, and she asks me for a solution to her children's sleep problems, I'm not going to start telling her about the merits of co-sleeping.

Every family is going to have different needs and different physical and biological resources when it comes to where their children sleep, and no family is morally superior based on the location of their children's beds/cots. Every mother has a right to rest and reasonable amounts of sleep, and if this is achieved better by not co-sleeping, then that's best for that family. Babies/children sleep just fine in their own cot/room as well, and that doesn't mean they aren't being parented.

Dr. Nadine, the amazing Ted Talk speaker and pediatrician who also worked with BIPOC mothers says, "Researchers have found that infants of depressed moms have a harder time regulating their sleep; they sleep an average of ninety-seven fewer minutes a night than infants of nondepressed moms and have more nighttime awakenings." This means that if a mom's mental health is not ok, her infant's sleep is affected regardless of whether they co-sleep or not. She continues,

> During sleep, levels of cortisol, adrenaline, and noradrenaline drop. As a result, lack of sleep is associated with increased levels of stress hormones and increased stress reactivity. . . . [T]hese stress hormones kick off the party, triggering brain, hormone, immune, and epigenetic responses to stress. The downstream effects are impaired cognitive function, memory, and mood regulation. Sleep deprivation doesn't just make you groggy and cranky; it also makes you sick.[15]

Note the point she makes about epigenetics: we can't assume that every mother's body is capable of showing up as a parent in the nighttime the same way, any more than they're capable of showing up in the day time. If my mother had me sleep with her all night and it affected the quality of her sleep, but then during the day, she had to be in the kitchen all day, serving her family and in-laws, she will inadvertently fall into a cycle of stress that someone in her line of genetics has to actively break.

Ideally, the only thing that's important is that children are tended to whenever they need us, as best as we possibly can individually. But we have got to understand that everyone's best is going to be different. Someone might be able to do this from across the bed, others from across the room, others from across the house, and for some, their child, despite being loved fiercely during the day, might not get attention every time they wake up. This last parent isn't any less worthy of being a parent than the rest.

Is it ideal? No. Is this the legacy of trauma? Yes. Does shaming someone heal trauma? No.

NURTURING HEALTHY SLEEP HABITS

There's a reason why this section is in the Autonomy part of the book. Children were sleeping before they entered this world. They know how to sleep. Shocking, I know, but true. Now, if it makes you happy to rock your child to sleep, nurse them to sleep, or swing them so hard that your arms hurt (true story from a client), absolutely do so and skip this section. If I was reading this book now, I'd skip this section because I'm at a place in my life where I have enough support and opportunities for self-care that I enjoy lying down with my kids until they sleep, and I also love when they come to my bed at night for extra cuddles.

However, this was not always the case. As I've shared previously, there was a time in my life when I was the default parent of four children, aged four and under, with zero help or support from anywhere in a foreign country, all by myself. No family. No friends. No money for childcare. At this time, learning how to nurture my children's natural abilities to fall and stay asleep probably saved all our lives.

Like I said earlier, children are born knowing how to sleep, and we have to facilitate them. Gerber makes a really good point that parents and children equally dread the word "sleep" because it conjures scary images for both; parents being upset that the child won't sleep and the child upset that their parent is so unhappy with them. To reverse these negative associations, Gerber encourages parents to think of children's sleep time as a "time for rest."[16] Don't you think that's a lovely shift? It's a matter of showing children that their body needs rest, just like we learned in the last section to show them their body needs food.

Ages Newborn–4 Months: Feed them, burp them, and as they start to get sleepy, get ready to put them down awake. "Sleepy but awake" are your key words. Always keep feeding *separate* from sleeping. Follow the eat-play-sleep routine. This prevents nursing and bottle-feeding from becoming crutches.

Place of sleep: Small portable cot next to your bed.

Step 1: As always, attunement is of the utmost importance. Gerber says, "Watch for the soft signs of tiredness in your baby before she starts rubbing her eyes, like slowing down or poor coordination. This is when you can start preparing for bed. Tell your child that bedtime is coming, 'It will be time for bed in about ten minutes,' so she can start preparing for it."[17]

This dialogue is the child's first cue for sleep.

Step 2: Turn on white noise. The womb was a loud place and white noise mimics that loudness. It needs to be as loud as a running vacuum cleaner. That is also sleep cue number two.

Step 3: Confidently walk away and rest yourself, if that's an option for you.

Once they fall asleep, don't rush to them if you hear a cry or two. They should settle down themselves in a few seconds. It's like how we wake up to adjust our pillow, etc. Naps at this age need to be at least 1–2 hours long without a break. If they proper start crying and it's been less than an hour, then check their diaper or give more milk, preferably without picking up. They should settle back down. Always talk to them when leaving them. Tell them it's time for rest. Let the white noise stay on if sleep is not finished.

Reminders: Babies this age need to eat every 2–3 hours. Don't let them sleep longer than 3 hours during the day and longer than 4 hours during the night. Wake them up to eat and then follow the same routine. Middle of the night feedings don't need to follow the eat play sleep routine. They can sleep right after.

4 Months+ (more like closer to 6 months): This is when 'object permanence' happens, meaning they remember you were around when they fell asleep and are not now, so they'll start to protest a little. Use a calm voice to reassure them as you leave them, "You don't want me to leave but it's rest time. I will be back soon. Nighty night!" (I say this even at nap time, just a short phrase they associate with bedtime.)

Place of sleep: small cot next to your bed

Follow the same steps as above.

6 Months+: If you're starting at this age and the child is already 6 months+ but less than 18 months, you will have 2–3 days of them expressing their feelings about this change. Accept this as a healthy form of expression. Change is hard for little children. You will acknowledge their feelings and co-regulate as best as you can. You'll go back as often as you need to, to do what's called a "gentle reset." That is, give them the pacifier if they've lost it during crying, reassure them that you're there, offer hugs and cuddles, but the key is to remain confident in their ability to sleep. You might recall from the sections on brain science that our children are hardwired to sense our emotions and respond to them. If they can sense that we're uncertain and afraid, it will be difficult for them.

18 Months–2+ Years: At this stage, I found this book by Kim West to be very helpful: *The Sleep Lady's Good Night, Sleep Tight: Gentle Proven Solutions to Help Your Child Sleep Well and Wake Up Happy.*[18] The idea is that at these ages, kids can get out of the bed and walk away, so we should be ready to bring them back as often as needed. She also suggests sleeping right next to their bed on the floor the first night and gradually, over the next few days, move farther and farther away. I tried this for the first time with my eldest when he was two years old, and it worked really well. The first night was relatively easier because I was right next to him on the floor and even held his hand on and off as he requested. The fourth day when my bedding moved to just outside his door, that was the hardest because he'd leave his bed several times and I'd gently carry him back. This happened perhaps 10–12 times, which was less than what I expected.

What's important here, again, are our co-regulation skills. We have to remain warm, loving, and accepting while being firm with what we're trying to accomplish so the child knows they're loved and this is a boundary.

> *Step 1:* Prepare them first for what will happen. Tell them how it will happen. "If you walk out of bed, I will walk/carry you right back." Make sure they have water and white noise, and that the bathroom is done. That way when they want this or that, you just nod gently and walk them back. Minimal engagement is key. "I won't be able to talk to you after it's bedtime. I will help you back to your room and that's all. Is there anything I can get you now?"

> *Step 2:* Do a nice calming bedtime routine. PJs, favorite book, surah, quick massage (my kids *love* this part), "Good night, shabba Khair," and then walk away.

> *Step 3:* They'll walk right out, but you're ready for this! Now prepare yourself to take them back 100 times that first night if necessary. I promise it takes only 2–3 nights.

Helpful Tips: My eldest is scared of nightmares so when we did this, there was a lot of "but Mama, I'm so scared!" and I made an exception to the minimal engagement rule and offered more reassurances and hugs. Always in a calm and confident tone. "Yes, you're scared. I understand. Would you like a hug or kiss or both?" After receiving one or both, he'd fall asleep.

The first night this happened, I was astounded. I honestly didn't think it would "work." But now that I understand better how most of children's fears are relative to their parents' reactions about those fears, it makes a lot of sense. My son, now ten, still has occasional nightmares—and he knows that he's always welcome in our bed, as do his other siblings.

Just yesterday my husband said to our six-year-old, "Will you come to our bed for snuggles tonight?" and he responded matter-of-factly, "Only if something is wrong."

Turns out you can raise perfectly well-adjusted and secure children even if you don't co-sleep.

RELATIONSHIPS

In our small townhome neighborhood in Clifton, Virginia, a bunch of families in the cul-de-sac had struck up intimate friendships and consequently their kids got to experience something that's an unavailable treat to most urban kids today—the ups and downs of neighborhood friendships. Me and my kids would often observe them when we were out for our walks or trips to the playground. One day Eisa decided that he'd like to also play with them, and I could see that it was going to be hard for him to fit into this clique, but it was not my place to stop him or give him dire warnings.

One day he came home very upset because those boys "chased him away" on their little motorbikes while he was on his bicycle. At first, he mostly just cried, and I held him and told him I understood it was hard, and then he wanted to talk more about it. When he shared his experience of being chased and feeling scared, my nervous system also started to slide down the ladder, but I was able to use my emotional regulation skills to stay present. My mama bear instinct was to right away go outside and lecture these boys or tell their parents what they'd done. But the wiser parts of me knew that that would actually create more problems for my son if I did that—and I'd also be taking away his autonomy to manage challenging situations. I always checked with him if he wanted me to intervene and we discussed the pros and cons of that, and he decided he didn't want me to intervene, but he asked me to stay close and I did.

One time, a boy even slapped him, and it took every fiber of my being not to call the police. Maybe many of you reading this would insist that I should have, but here's the thing. That boy who hit my son was also seven years old, and I had already seen his mother shaming him in front of everyone for other things. As much as I was hurt for my son, I didn't see how getting him into trouble would improve things. I did decide after that, though, that I would stay outside as well and keep an eye on these kids, making sure I could intervene if anyone was about to get physical.

When someone physically harms our child, we are deeply triggered to lash back immediately. It's a trigger that seems to bring back all our own pains of childhood when someone hurt us and we were alone and unprotected. Our trauma response is to jump in with all guns blazing and annihilate whoever has hurt our child. We seem to forget all about child development, nervous system states, and the fact that the person who has caused harm is also a child. We immediately start throwing around words like "bully," "thug," and other unkind labels.

Don't get me wrong, I'm not saying that we should let other children hit our kids and certainly we need to proceed with responsibility and accountability (see next section) and make sure the event doesn't repeat itself, but here's a simple rule: responding to violence with violence keeps people stuck in defensive states of the nervous system. It creates a world where fear and power rule while harmony and compassion are eliminated. We all say we want a better world for our children, but we tend to forget this as soon as someone lays a finger on our child, then we absolutely want revenge and believe violence is the answer.

If you're a parent, I can promise you one thing, at one point or another you'll be at the receiving end of this sentiment of revenge, and you will wish and hope that the other parent takes a more compassionate approach and seeks to solve the underlying issues rather than come at you and your child with blazing guns going pow pow pow!

Here's the thing, as parents we all wish that our kids could get through their whole entire lives without having someone hurt them. Or without someone being harsh, unkind, or judgmental towards them, but as wise adults we know that that's not realistic or helpful.

Life is going to be filled with challenges and we want to raise our children with what scientists call a resilient brain. This is the kind of brain that faces adversity in life with aplomb and finesse; it doesn't cower before trials and tribulations but overcomes them and comes out the other end, stronger than ever. It's what Pakistanis call being "tough." Except, no, we don't raise "tough" children by being tough with them, we do so by not "bubble-wrapping" them and instead providing support, assistance, and understanding through hard times.

I do believe that parents have such a strong reaction to anyone hurting their child (physically and emotionally) because they perceive it as something deeply damaging or what we call toxic stress (as explained in the trauma section). But they don't realize that the reason others' hurt caused them so much hurt as children was because they felt so alone, because their own parents refused to offer validation, understanding, or support. On the contrary, when these events happen in our life that scientists call tolerable stress or positive stress, they're opportunities for building resilience.

Unfortunately, some parents seem to think nothing of hurting their own children through daily interactions of invalidation, shaming, and punishing but will have a huge reaction to another kid hitting their kid. The first is an example of toxic stress, the second is an example of positive stress. The former requires serious interventions to come, the latter can actually be a source of building resilience.

We can do this by being an active listener and not a rescuer, by letting children talk about their experience without jumping in with our own feelings (just "hmm" or "ahh I see" are enough). When they're ready, we can pose thoughtful questions aimed to get them to think critically about the situation ("Do you think Sadia really means she will *never* play with you?" "Have *you* ever said that to a friend? What did you mean when you said it?" "So, if Sadia keeps saying words you don't like, what's your plan for that?") are all they need.

If we make ourselves responsible for either protecting or manually rescuing our child from every unpleasant experience and interaction, we would be seriously hampering their ability to learn resilience, to foster self-esteem, to learn about healthy boundaries and the value of compassion.

Back to my son's situation with the neighborhood kids, it was hard to watch and hard not to intervene. It was hard not to grab him and bring him inside and keep him safe. But I think we've all been there where our parents, in their love and kindness, tried to "save" us from those kinds of "friends," and all it did was push us further towards those people.

I had to respect his journey while also being a responsible adult and keeping an eye on the situation. It was more inconvenient than telling on that little boy and required me to be outside more often than I'd like, but over time things did settle and my son came out learning some important lessons. I noticed in his next altercations with friends, he was less bothered, more confident that he'd make it through, and over time his social skills have improved vastly to also include boundaries and empathy.

POINTS TO REMEMBER:

1. It's healthy and normal for children to have heated altercations and even to hit each other sometimes. These incidents don't make someone a bully and someone a victim.

2. If we are concerned about physical harm, we should stay close so we can prevent the hitting and mediate between children (see mediation skills in sibling rivalry section of the Connection chapter).

3. Instead of using the label of "bullying," we can say "bullying behavior" and the focus should be on resolving the issue rather than punishing "the bully."

4. When the relationship issues are with an adult and the adult is causing toxic stress to the child, then it's our job as caretakers to protect that child from that person.

Yes, even if it's their own parent. We can recognize the signs of someone getting triggered and ask them to remove themselves from the situation or remove ourselves and the child. If acting in this manner is also a threat to your own safety, you know it's time to be the cycle breaker.

5. For other adult relationships where the stress being caused is tolerable, be your child's safe space by offering validation, thoughtful questions, and empathy. In my experience, most children will avoid such adults themselves.

ELECTRONICS

If you have kids, chances are you've wished electronics didn't exist. Like we learned from Faiza's story above, they can awaken our most primal fears about our children. I have also fantasized about moving to a long-forgotten village in Pakistan and raising my kids there and shielding them from the "evils" of electronics.

To the soundtrack of *What a Wonderful World*, I imagine my kids frolicking in the village fields, wind in their hair, possibly butt-naked. No phone, video game, or YouTuber in sight.

Sigh. Just the fantasy fills me with peace and zen . . .

Until I realize I'd be in that village with them. Also, minus my own electronics. And then my fantasy comes to a screeching halt to the sound of the record getting stuck in the player. But I love my work! And I need electronics for it!

The truth is. We can fantasize all we want, but electronics are here to stay, and we can either learn how to navigate them with our kids or be forever fearful of them. And I share this with the disclaimer that I mostly feel like I have no idea if what I'm doing is right or not and what will be the outcomes exactly. Also, so far we don't have long-term researches about what is a "safe" amount of electronics use. But the following list is the closest I have been able to get in navigating this very new arena of parenting.

1. No electronics before age 2. This is non-negotiable. I'm sorry! But I promise to help you help your child develop amazing play skills so that they simply won't need electronics even until age 3.

2. Ages 3+ can have parent-regulated TV/laptop only. No personal devices please.

3. Once kids start playing videogames, really watch your connection closely with them. Use videogames as a way to connect with them. Be sure to enter their world. This is exciting for them. Show interest.

4. The world is ever changing. Our parents probably thought we were weird for wanting our alone time with our books and friends and stuff. I spent most of my teenager years holed up in my room with Judith McKnaught novels and Backstreet Boys songs (very much over them now). I'm fairly certain neither of my parents ever had their own rooms! I turned out fine though. It didn't destroy me.

5. We can have a nice attitude about their electronic use. We can smile at them after they stopped watching/playing. Ask them how it was. Use positive language about this part of their life since clearly it's dear to them.

6. We also have to talk about safely navigating media with our kids. They *are* going to come across weird

stuff on the internet. They need a plan for what to do when that happens.

I gave my kids the analogy, "Would you go anywhere without me? The internet is the same. It's a big world with all sorts of people and things. If you see someone or something that scares you or disturbs you, please come to me right away."

Amaze.org is an amazing resource for watching some videos about media awareness with kids.

7. Try not to overthink. I think all of us did come across some disturbing content during our lives and, well, we're all still here to talk about it. Having said that, make sure that everything has parental locks and codes. It's our job to set up our kids for success and not put them in unnecessary "tests."

8. Life is too beautiful for any child to be addicted to electronics. If that's the case, something is not ok. Investigate. Don't attack the behavior. Don't judge and penalize the child. Measure the connection and belonging scale. Is their real-life cup so empty that they need to constantly escape to videogames to fill it? Yes, they're fun and sometimes they overdo it, but no, it shouldn't be a constant thing. That's 100% an indicator that all is not well.

9. We need to regulate ourselves too. This is such an area of "work to do" for me!

10. Once again, the takeaway is to lead with trust, not fear!

HOMEWORK AND ACADEMICS

Teacher Tom owns and runs a popular play-based preschool in Seattle, Washington. His blog and work are an inspiring resource for me to share with parents. Whenever we talk about this model of education, parents have two concerns:

1. But if they don't "study properly," they won't fit into "regular" schools.
2. There are no play-based schools in Pakistan.

To answer the first question, one day I reached out to Teacher Tom and asked him how the kids in his school do when they later go to a "proper" school after being in his program. This is what he said,

> The children from our school do very well in kindergarten. The local K teacher told me that she always knows which kids went to our school because they know how to take care of themselves and take care of others. [K in America is equal to Prep-3 for age 6 kids in Pakistan][19]

He also asked me to share this post of his titled, "What The Research Tells Us to Do" from his blog. It contains links to the research in favor of no forced academics before age seven. Here's an excerpt from his post,

> In Finland, they do not try to teach kindergarteners to read because the *evidence* tells us that formal literacy instruction should not start until at least the age of seven and that children who are compelled into it too early often suffer emotionally and academically in the long run.[20]

I think the fear is that if my child doesn't learn now, then they'll have missed a window and will be "behind" their peers. It's helpful to remember that this is not how brain development works. Children are on the fitrah; they do things when their brain is ready and being forced to do something ahead of readiness worsens their learning and causes damage to the learning relationship. Again, you'll need to examine your own biases, beliefs, and insecurities to really be able to support your child the way they need. That's what being a cycle breaker is about.

As for concern number two, this is the mantra we live by for academics, "Be the change you wish in the world." This means if we can't homeschool or deschool, we advocate for our children. Leading with appreciation and respect, we can communicate with teachers that we are not worried about our child being "left behind," and even though we will continue to support them academically at their pace, that sometimes the homework won't be done or done completely, and the child shouldn't be shamed or penalized for this.

Almost all teachers became teachers to support and love children. They're not the enemy. Whenever I've asked for extra support and understanding from teachers, they've been very helpful and patient. A lot of parents in fact put more pressure on teachers if they think their children are not doing as good as xyz, so teachers are more than happy to learn that you're not going to be pressuring them.

THINGS TO REMEMBER:

When kids don't study as well as we'd like, we do some of the following:

- Tie rewards and privileges to studying
- Take away privileges or punish/shame kids
- Give them lectures about the importance of studies
- Give examples of how *we* studied no matter what
- Hire a more expensive tutor
- Sign them up for *more* classes so they can "catch up"
- If all else fails, we resort to hitting our kids or yelling at them—thus ensuring their brains jump into stress/survival mode and reject anything worth learning anyway.

All of these solutions don't work or only work momentarily because we're not addressing the root problem. It's like trying to paint a dying flower instead of paying attention to what's happening to the roots, so literally, it's a "root problem."

But before I get to that, I want to talk about why we try those solutions in the first place. We try them because society has led us to make some basic assumptions about kids and studies. Here they are (please let me know if you disagree and haven't been led to these beliefs):

- Kids are often just "lazy" about studies and don't really like learning.
- Schools are amazing centers of learning and have it all figured out how and what kids should learn.
- All kids learn the same way . . . by reading books and writing down things. Anyone who doesn't want to do this has something wrong with them.
- All kids of the same age should learn the same things. If they can't, then they're "behind."
- School is the only way kids should learn because it's the best place to have that social interaction that all kids need.

- If a kid isn't doing homework or completing class-work, he's failing and needs more rigorous studying or tutors.
- Going to school and doing almost everything it asks us to do is the only way to succeed in life.
- Success in life comes from high academic achievements.
- Success means having a job in the more high-paying sectors of the job market (like being a doctor, lawyer, engineer, etc.).

Honestly, I could go on forever. But I listed these assumptions because at the end of the day, they're the reason we smack that kid or make her feel like a complete failure. They all contribute to the quality of our relationship, and you know from the chapter on trauma that a sound relationship with parents equals a healthy brain that can learn and grow. And that is the root problem. When our relationship suffers with our kids, they get demotivated and lose the joy of learning. Their brains literally start turning off.

Here are some ways to support our children with academics:

WAIT FOR READINESS

That is, if your child isn't yet doing what other kids their age are doing, wait: give them more time. They'll get there.

TRUST

That is, know that all children were born to learn, and they are avid learners and were learning *a lot* before we put them in school. Schools are a man-made system and far from perfect. Tons of experts are working on education reform because research tells us that schools rob children of their creativity and innovation.

HELP

Children of *all* ages need help and not punishment and judgment. "I notice you're struggling to do your work. How can I help?"

SUPPORT

I can't tell you how many kids I've talked to who have broken relationships with their parents, and they say they want to make their parents proud, and they want to study except that they're sick and tired of having their entire worth being placed on how much they want to study.

Kids are always doing the best they can. Always.

PLAY: INDEPENDENT PLAY AND RISKY PLAY

This usually comes as a huge surprise when I tell people that children of every age are hardwired for independent play.

In *Your Self-Confident Baby,* Gerber says,

> From the beginning, your baby can learn to play or explore on her own in a safe environment. You can set up a gated play area in her room or another place of your choice . . .
>
> Tell her you are going to let her play in her play area for a while and that you will be in the next room, listening. If she cries, you have learned to read the cries and can respond appropriately so she doesn't feel abandoned.[21]

This is where your awesome skills of co-regulation and confident boundary setting will come in handy. As we learned in chapter two in the section about child-led play, we can't dictate kids' play. Even if they hand us a ball, we still don't take the initiative of throwing it. We merely state what we observe, "You handed me a ball. Its round and a bit hard. What should we do with it?" Let them tell us.

FOSTERING INDEPENDENT PLAY SKILLS

If you feel guilty leaving your child alone to play, Gerber has very helpful advice for you:

> There is benefit in not only playing alone, but in simply being alone. Solitude is healthy at times. A child can learn to do this very early and is happy when left in this type of environment, although it takes time to build her aptitude for being on her own. Remain within hearing distance. If your child protests, she will find comfort in hearing your voice from the next room, which reassures her of your availability. Say, "I hear you. I'm in the bedroom. I'll come to see you in a few minutes."

The reason so many children struggle to be independent players is that their parents have been entertaining them so much that they're quite exhausted from it. They're there but never really there when playing with their children. As Gerber says, "The key to her playing happily alone is being fully with her when you're with her."[22] However, if you practice child-led play skills discussed in chapter two, then you can be confident that your child is very capable of learning how to play on her own.

At first, they'll no doubt ask us to do this or that. We can validate their desire and stay firm on not providing the heavy assistance they're asking.

Gerber advises,

Start leaving her for a few minutes at a time and then for longer and longer periods. She should always be placed on her back until she can get into other positions on her own. Even a young baby can be left to play alone. However, supervision is always necessary by intermittent checking-in on the parent or carer's part. The younger the child, the more frequent check-ins are necessary.[23]

We can become part of their play by observing them and gently saying what they're doing when they make eye contact with us, "You were observing the light . . . you liked how bright it is." Resist making loud sounds in their faces. Remind yourself that you're not there to entertain them, only to enjoy their play.

PLAY SPACES BY AGE

0–7 Months: Recall the brain science from the chapter on boundaries—too many synapses means that babies' brains are much slower than ours. They thrive on a relatively simple, quiet, calm, and predictable environment. Once they're fed and changed, they're ready to play. They can have a play pen or another small, enclosed area for playing. Children this young also don't have a wide vision and not seeing an enclosure is actually scary for them, like it is for us when we're near a cliff. Enclosed spaces encourage feelings of safety and autonomy in kids' play. You must have noticed how young kids often like to build forts and tents as well, naturally honoring that innate need for enclosed safety.

8–18 Months: Once babies become mobile, things get a bit trickier. But if we did our job right until now, they recognize and understand the concept of boundaries and will happily play within a confined space for up to an hour. Try your best to keep all electronics away from them until age two. I say this because not exposing them to electronics will actually make your life easier in the long run.

18 Months+: The play space can now be extended to include a whole room. It's important to keep it child-friendly and allow for minimal opportunities for saying no to them. This is, no doubt, a difficult stage for parents as children's curiosity is at its peak and their mobility is also efficient and swift. Keep unsafe areas of the house like the kitchen and bathroom gated. If you've followed safe boundary setting methods, you'll see that, for the most part, your toddler understands what is and isn't ok to touch. She'll also be noticeably more regulated and cooperative.

Preteens and Teens: These ages usually don't have an issue playing alone but it's important to keep connecting with them over their play. Lots of parents tell me they're exhausted hearing their children talk about video games. As the mother of two preteens, I understand completely. Just know that you're allowed to say, "I love hearing about what you did in Roblox today but I'm wondering if we can talk about something else now." This boundary will allow you to engage more fully with them on other occasions of Roblox wins. It's important to keep the lines communication open during these years so they'll keep sharing the big stuff with us as they get older.

"RISKY PLAY"

I had started to follow Resources for Infant Educarers (RIE) when my daughter was a toddler. RIE is a big proponent of allowing children to take measured risk while staying close if need be. The Pikler triangle is a popular climbing structure among schools and families who follow the Montessori system or Magda Gerber's parenting wisdom. We could never really afford that expensive contraption, but I did buy a cheap plastic slide for my kids and any other climbing toys we could fit inside our tiny townhome in Clifton, Virginia. I also somehow managed to frequently take my older two kids (at the time, my only kids) to our neighborhood park. It's one of the most fascinating things in the world to watch a little child who can barely walk climb stairs and other structures so nimbly.

I can still recall the judgmental looks I received from many parents in the park because I was "letting" my daughter do "dangerous" things. In reality, I was always close enough to catch her should something go awry, but at the same time I wanted her to engage in "risky play," which is proven to increase children's spatial awareness, coordination, and agility. Sure enough, at age eight, my daughter has excellent climbing skills, beautiful flexibility, and coordination, and she rarely gets hurt because her body-awareness is excellent. Ironically enough, the only time she's needed stitches in her forehead due to a deeper than usual gash was because she tripped at a playground, something that can happen to anyone.

CHORES

In the boundaries section we already talked about how expecting our children to do chores can't be a boundary situation (even though of course, you can have your own boundaries around housework). Any chore involves several steps and is an advanced executive functioning skill, so just ordering children to clean up or do dishes or put laundry away isn't going to work anyway. We would have to help them along, perhaps for many years and with good spirits, to teach them these tasks. Sometimes, the biggest thing that prevents us from doing so is once again, our own triggers.

When we moved into our spacious new house after living in a tiny townhouse for many years, I was absolutely thrilled. All of a sudden we had so much space that I got lost in visions of an impeccably decorated and spotless house! I forgot that I still had the same four kids who were coming with me to the new house.

At first we made some collaborative rules about how to keep the new house tidy, how to contain the toys, etc., but we know that no amount of collaboration helps when a child is not developmentally ready for something. However, in my dreams of my impeccable new home, I'd conveniently forgotten that. Every time I'd see clutter, I'd go sliding down the ladder into fight or flight. I'd get mean and unkind to my kids and they in turn, would run scurrying away. Even in that moment of being so triggered, a part of me felt proud to have raised kids who knew to run in the opposite direction when someone is shaming them. How many of us stay rooted to our spot and allow people to belittle us?

Anyway, back to the "messy situation." Those days I was attending an online course with Tara Brach, who's one of my favorite mindfulness teachers and author. During the course, she said something that was a real hallelujah moment for me.

She said, "When we see ourselves as victims, we become abusers of ourselves."

That was it! I realized every time I saw the mess after I had cleaned up, I feel like a "martyr" for having to clean it up again. We know—everyone knows—that kids are messy, and you just get their help and everyone cleans up together and it's ok! But to feel like a poor martyr is not helpful and makes zero sense from the kids' perspective and clearly was not helpful for me either.

I also realized that my kids actually love cleaning with me and helping me, but when I act scary, they run away, and then no one wants to help me. Did you see how that worked? Feeling like a victim made me slide down the ladder and become "scary" for my kids, who then, understandably, didn't want to help and I ended up hurting the very cause I wanted help with.

Point being, if we've built a sense of belonging for our children and nurture our connection with them, they'll be more than happy to help with house chores and anything else. I'm continuously surprised at how incredibly cooperative and helpful my young children are. Without coercion, bribes, or threats, they love helping out. Of course, sometimes they don't, just like sometimes we all don't feel like lifting a finger. In those times, instead of feeling like a victim, I model graciousness and show them that it's alright to be human and rest.

The Final Word

> "They keep coming up new all the time—things to perplex you, you know. You settle one question and there's another right after. There are so many things to be thought over and decided when you're beginning to grow up. It keeps me busy all the time thinking them over and deciding what's right. It's a serious thing to grow up, isn't it, Marilla?"
>
> —Lucy Maud Montgomery, *Anne of Green Gables*

IT'S EASIER TO FAIL IN PAKISTAN

> "You are not a small star, you are a reflection of the entire cosmos. Can you hear the big bang in your heart? Eighty times a minute God knocks on the doors of your chest, to remind you that He has never left, and that He is closer to you than the jugular vein in your neck (Quran 50:16)."
>
> —A. Helwa, *Secrets of Divine Love: A Spiritual Journey into the Heart of Islam*[24]

YOU ARE NOT YOUR TRAUMA

In the beginning of this book I shared the story of hurting my son. That moment was a pivotal one in both our lives, mine and my son's. That was the moment I decided that my trauma wasn't going to define me, even though I didn't necessarily think those words, I felt them. As I shared before, that day I went to my local library and parked myself in the parenting books' section. I didn't know what I was looking for, but I knew that I never wanted to hurt my son again.

The more I read, the more I became fascinated with learning how to parent with mindfulness. In all honesty, most of the

301

books I read were not helpful because this is back when gentle/ respectful parenting was not really a thing. Most books were filled with "tricks" on how to get your kids to comply, but since they didn't involve physical harm, I gave their advice a try. Eventually I came across Janet Lansbury's blog and book called *No Bad Kids*. She and RIE (Resources for Infant Educarers) were my first real introduction to RP.

I've since read and met many amazing authors and activists of RP, but I'll be infinitely grateful to Lansbury for making this information so accessible back when it was not at all mainstream. Everything I was learning about RP was slowly changing my life and my relationship with my kids. I tried my best not to be obnoxious about it, but I couldn't keep from sharing my enthusiasm about it with Bethany, who soon enough encouraged me to do a workshop on the topic.

I couldn't deny that I had fantasized about it, but of course, my brain was resistant to this path because it's so much easier never to try something difficult than to try and fail at it. This is the logic of our inner critic whose main purpose is to keep us "safe." We don't want to do things that challenge us because we are afraid of the unknown and having a history of trauma always equates unknown to bad. It never occurs to our inner critic that the unknown could actually be the best thing that ever happened to us. Or that the good stuff will almost definitely follow the "bad stuff."

Of course, I dutifully listened to my inner critic any time Bethany told me I needed to do a workshop. One time I was planning a trip to Pakistan and when she asked me once again when I'd do a workshop, I said, "I'll do it in Pakistan."

And she, in her absolutely matter-of-fact tone said, "Is it because it's easier to fail in Pakistan?"

We often reminisce about this memory because it's the one sentence that changed my life and Bethany doesn't recall even saying it. It changed my life because I realized that that's exactly what I thought. It was as if I already believed that my workshop would be a failure and since I don't live in Pakistan, no one will ever have to know that I failed. Once I recognized that this is why I was stalling, I also realized that it didn't make any sense. Failure is not limited by geographical locations and, also, if I did fail, I could always try again. This was a relatively new way for me to think but I had already started therapy and medication to treat my depression and was no doubt starting to feel more hopeful about the future. This is also when I did my "evidence" activity I shared in the chapter about belonging (section entitled "All I Need Are Nice People").

START SOMEWHERE

Once I made this decision, it felt very natural, as if of course I was going to do a workshop. Even though I had no history of teaching or really any idea how to do a workshop. But that day onward, I also learned one of life's most remarkable lessons: once you take even one step on the path that has been waiting for you, you see all the doors opening for you as if by magic. I used to think it was miraculous that those doors just "happened" to find me, but I know now that those doors were open because I had stepped on to my path. And there is nothing unique about me or my path. This is life's greatest secret, we each have a path we are meant to walk, and when we find it, it opens before us like the Red Sea parting for Moses.

And it doesn't feel any less of a miracle than it felt for Moses, I can assure you of that. Only one couple came to my first workshop but that day I knew that there would be many more of these. Almost five years later, even my most expensive workshops have no less than fifty people. We have to waitlist participants whose disappointment at not being able to get in is heartwarming.

Alex Hormozi is a business coach and influencer who allegedly helps people become multi-millionaires. He famously says, "Outwork your self doubt."[25] In other words, we will have lots of self-doubts when starting out, but all we really have to do is start somewhere and do whatever we do enough times, despite the setbacks, that it's clear that there is no need to doubt ourselves.

The day I decided that I would do the workshop, I had plenty of doubts, but right away, just doing the work started to eliminate many of the doubts. I had asked my cousin Zoshia, who's a brilliant photographer, to come take pictures of my first workshop. She was super supportive and did an amazing job with the pictures (pro tip: pictures speak louder than words; I highly recommend hiring a professional photographer to document whatever you intend on doing). More importantly, though, Zoshia had to sit through my entire workshop and her genuine feedback and admiration right away told me I was on the right path. I had also asked my friend Shamyla, who is a licensed social worker and therapist in Maryland, to also accompany me and help me out. She also confirmed what I felt, that the one couple who came was extremely impressed and inspired.

I had started to outwork my self-doubts.

HOW DO I FIND MY PATH?

As we begin to unpack our traumas, we inevitably feel a cocktail of difficult emotions; grief, loss, remorse, anger, and sadness. We might say, "I didn't deserve that!" and you'd be right, you didn't. You might also say, "My children don't deserve this . . . they deserve a parent who's mentally healthy."

We wonder what our life might have been like if we didn't have to deal with the repercussions of trauma. Would we be more productive and efficient if we weren't bogged down by depression and anxiety? Would we be more effortlessly kind and gentle if we weren't shackled by perfectionism and self-loathing? Wouldn't our children be so much better off if they had parents who never got triggered and caused them harm?

If you are having these thoughts now, I invite you to sit with them and allow for the grief of what could have been. I want you to mourn the life you wish you and your children had. It's alright to feel whatever comes up for you because it's very human to compare and wish for something we believe to be better.

These are all valid thoughts and feelings. The sense of grief of what could have been is intense. Susan Cain, author of *Bittersweet: How Sorrow and Longing Make Us Whole*, calls this feeling "longing," and what she says about this feeling opened my eyes to a new way of looking at this particular emotion. We normally think of longing as something we want but can't get or we must accept that we will never get it— much like our trauma-free childhood—and Cain says,

> But longing is momentum in disguise: It's active, not
> passive; touched with the creative, the tender, and the

divine. We long for something, or someone. We reach for it, move toward it.[26]

I have certainly shed many tears mourning the loss of a life I imagine I could've had if I didn't have to deal with the aftermath of trauma. But I can also see now, how my longing for that perfect childhood has not only given me momentum to become a cycle breaker but it has carved my life's path for me. It has enabled me to have a purpose-driven life that allows me to experience fulfillment and joy.

This is what Simon Sinek calls "finding your why." He's a motivational speaker whose life's work is to help people discover what they were meant to do on this earth. One technique he suggests to do this is to tell ten of your life's stories to a close friend and let them reflect back to you what they're hearing and saying.[27] I use this technique in my Mentors' program with the participants, and it's magical to witness as they uncover their "why" and we find over and over that it's tied to the story of their greatest pain.

Someone who has struggled to succeed in a male-dominated industry wants to create a company that empowers women in that particular industry.

Someone who had to pinch pennies just to get an education wants to open a school for kids who can't afford education.

Someone who always felt weird and different wants to help the transgender community.

Someone who longed to save their sick parent's life and couldn't wants to build a hospital that offers free treatment to qualifying patients.

What is most remarkable about our trauma story is that once we become the narrator of it, we can write the ending.

Now that I have allowed space for my grief and longing, I have started to feel the stirrings of something else as well. As time goes on, I'm noticing that I feel more and more of the "something else." I hesitate to use the word "gratitude" for the something else because the last thing I'd want is to force toxic positivity on you by saying a fancier version of, "Whatever doesn't kill you makes you stronger" (which is not always true).

I don't think anyone needs horrible things to happen to them to become stronger. In fact, all the research on children raised with love shows us that such children are resilient and strong. There's no doubt that having a "tough" childhood, doesn't in fact, make you tough—as shown by the ACES research, it makes you susceptible to various physical and mental health issues as well as reducing your overall mortality.[28]

So if gratitude is not the right word, what is? I like the term "radical acceptance" that Tara Brach and other Buddhists use. In Islam we have a very similar term called "Qadr Allah"—a belief that whatever happens was meant to happen—which to me, is different from "it happened for a reason." To me, these concepts simply mean that what has happened has unfolded the way it was supposed to and there is no other way that it could have unfolded. Sort of how a puzzle piece must be shaped a certain way to fit into the slot meant for it, and even a slight alteration of the nooks and crannies of the piece would result in a skewed looking final product. This is how this life on Earth is. Pain is an inextricable part of it, and whatever arises from pain can't arise from anything else.

As Cain writes, "The tragedy of life is linked inescapably with its splendor; you could tear civilization down and rebuild it from scratch, and the same dualities would rise again."[29]

When Old Is Not Gold

I grew up in what I think is the most beautiful part of Islamabad, the capital of Pakistan. The P.A.F (Pakistan Air Force) complex in E-9 is an impeccably planned neighborhood nestled in the Margalla Hills. Not only does it practically sit in the lap of the luscious hills, but it also has its own hospital, school, shopping center, and various other amenities. I spent a vast majority of my childhood wandering the paved roads and manicured landscape of this beloved neighborhood. When I was little and my dad was a younger officer, we lived in an apartment building, or a "flat," as we call them. I walked to school and back home hundreds of times over the many years that we lived in that flat. I think even now if you blindfolded me and asked me to walk home from that school, I'd have no trouble getting straight back to that beloved old place.

By the time I was a teenager, my father was promoted, and we got an independent house that was much closer to my school than our previous flat. Again, I'd often walk home with my friends, laughing and talking as we made our way to our respective homes. One day though, I had a big fight with my friends. It left me heartbroken and in tears. I grabbed my backpack and ran out of the school alone. I made my way back home, wiping off tears the whole time and feeling sorry for myself. However, when I finally arrived "home," I realized I'd walked right past our new house and had arrived at our old flat. The path that I had walked a hundred times in younger childhood was the one that prevailed when my thinking brain was offline.

WHY WE OFTEN TAKE THE OLD BUMPIER ROAD

It can be so frustrating when we're trying to learn something new and practice it but our old path keeps showing up. This feels very distressing and almost as if we will never be able to form new neural pathways, but I promise you that's not the case.

It's very natural for our brain to go to old roads when we are stressed out. No matter how much we've learned something new, the weight of the stress obliterates the new pathways. We return to the well-traveled road even if it's inconvenient and unhelpful. This phenomenon is called heuristics and scientists explain that our brain does this to conserve energy and work. It is a way to problem-solve an immediate issue that relies on one's prior knowledge and past experiences. It involves almost zero thinking or contemplation.

In fact, in many cases, the brain's ability to take "mental shortcuts" is actually very helpful. It's because of heuristics that we are able to chat while driving, dress ourselves without thinking much, move away from a rustling bush to stay safe etc. It wouldn't have been realistic or efficient if our brain had to figure everything out from scratch every time it needs to do something. Imagine how inconvenient it would be if you had to learn how to drive each time you wanted to go somewhere. So, on the one hand it's incredibly useful for the brain to have this ability to operate from past knowledge and take shortcuts. On the other hand, it can really suck when you're trying to learn something new and relying on heuristics is unhelpful and counterproductive. This means that when learning something new, our brain has to go the extra mile (pun intended) and *not* take a shortcut and expend extra energy to create a new synapse. It's almost like updating your GPS device or app when a shorter/faster/smoother highway becomes available.

Here are a few things we can do to help our brain through this "upgrading" process that is inconvenient but necessary for our growth.

UPGRADING OUR BRAIN'S GPS

NORMALIZE AND CELEBRATE MISTAKES

Now that you understand why our brain often takes old roads, I hope you can learn to accept these errors as a normal function of learning something new. This is a sign that your brain is upgrading. Also recall the first story in the history of mankind and how the angels are perfect but someone who makes mistakes but also learns from them is not inferior to perfection! There is no learning without consistently screwing up, and instead of viewing these screw-ups as failures, we can remind ourselves that they're opportunities for growth. I taught my twins this idea of how their brain grows whenever they make mistakes, so they'd make a mistake (like spilling something) and clap and say, "My brain just grew!" So go ahead, celebrate your mistakes because they're the reason you're improving and learning.

PRACTICE SELF-COMPASSION

A lot of people feel confused when they're asked to have compassion for themselves. This is mainly because their experiences of someone showing *them* compassion are few and far between, but also because they think we're asking them to *feel* compassion, rather than just practice it. Feelings are an outcome of actions or experiences—we can't conjure them up from nowhere. That's why I ask you to *practice* self-compassion which means, *do* something compassionate so that you can *experience* compassion. Example, you just yelled at your child despite reading this whole book. Immediately your inner critic will say, "Look at what you've done now. This is horrible!" and that's when you notice this inner dialogue and talk back to yourself, "You know what, I'm learning and in this process I will make many mistakes. This doesn't mean everything is back to zero." Then you take a deep breath, apologize to your child, and move on. Now you have acted in a compassionate manner towards yourself and you will soon start to feel the self-compassion.

Whenever I say this, parents always ask me if their child will take their repeated apologies seriously or if they're simply learning that you can do whatever you want, apologize and repeat. I tell them they have a point. Are they, in fact, not changing anything and simply apologizing? Over time, we should be becoming a better parent and if we're not then it means we're stuck and something needs to change. I will discuss this scenario later.

CULTIVATE JOY AND REST IN YOUR LIFE

As you learned above, creating new synapses and not relying on heuristics is a lot of work for your brain. I call this emotional labor because, just like any other form of labor, this kind also needs rest and fuel. The biggest fuel for emotional labor and really, life, is joy. It breaks my heart that we not only don't know how to be joyous as a nation but we overtly shun joy.

"Don't laugh too much or else you'll be crying later!"

"Don't brag about your accomplishments, you sound so arrogant!"

"Don't mention your blessings because you'll evil eye them!"

Religious Content

As a Muslim I totally believe in jinxing our blessings or *buri nazar* but I also believe in *dua* ("prayer"). Recite your morning and evening protection *duas* regularly but for the love of God, literally . . . allow yourself to experience joy. It's the best form of gratitude. Share your good news, be proud of yourself, and laugh. Add alhamdulilah every time because, of course, we believe all good things are from Allah, but also relax, enjoy, be happy. It's ok, really.

Also, rest is not something you earn after you've been "productive" every second of every day that you had available. Rest is a basic need for all humans, and since all humans are different, their needs for rest will also be different. Only your body decides when it needs rest and you must allow for rest. If you're resting physically but your mind is rebuking you the whole time or holding a to-do list over you, that's not really rest. Be gentle with your body and you will notice that when you listen to it and honor it, it will help you get through your to-do list much faster. If you don't allow your body the rest it deserves and pleads for, you'll pay the price with costly medical procedures. I don't want to be doom and gloom about this, but this is a heavily studied concept with a whole branch of science called psychoneuroimmunology (PNI) devoted to it. I invite you to learn more about it if the topic interests you, but for this book's purposes, it's important to understand that our physical health is closely linked to our mental health. Unless you're a robot, your worth doesn't depend on your productivity (though I understand that this is easier said than done).

UNDERSTAND MOM GUILT

If you're a mom, when you first start taking care of yourself, you'll constantly be hit with what feels like enormous amounts of guilt. This is what I mentioned earlier in the boundaries chapter as well: conditioned guilt. Mothers are historically seen as self-sacrificing, self-obliterating creatures who give up anything and everything in service of others. Notice that I didn't say "in service of children" because "others" are an important part of this picture, but that's another book. Suffice it to say here that the function of guilt is to nudge us to ask ourselves if we're doing something wrong, and I can assure you that there's nothing wrong about taking care of yourself. The guilt you experience is your female DNA feeling horrified that you're daring to do what women were never permitted to do before (and still aren't mostly); that is, give themselves the same kindness they give everyone else.

KNOW THAT 'HOW TO BALANCE' IS A LIE

People often ask me how I do so much. Four kids, running this fast-growing business, volunteer work, being there for my parents, and working on new projects. How do I do it all? There's really no trick here for me. I just prioritize. Everything has its own place and depending upon the situation, different things get different priorities. If anyone says they're doing it all, they're not telling you the mental health cost they're paying for "doing it all," and they might be alright with that. Like I said, prioritize what's important to you and leave the rest.

GET THE HELP YOU DESERVE

You are not an island. You were never meant to do this alone. This was the single most difficult thing for me living in America: how isolating it was to be a parent there. I can guarantee you that at some point, you will feel stuck in your respectful parenting journey, as if you can't possibly continue on this path. That's when you'll know you need some kind of additional help. Let's examine the different kinds of helps people need on this journey:

1. **Hired Help:** When I was having my twins, I scoured the internet for advice because I was absolutely freaking out. One advice that stuck with me and I've gone to over and over is: if there's a problem you can throw money at, do it. I admit that we don't have a lot of savings or assets, but being able to pay for help whenever it felt important has literally saved my life. Even if you live abroad, you can find some kind of paid help within a reasonable budget. In fact, you'd be surprised at how possible it is to find reliable help if you commit yourself to looking for it and being willing to invest in your mental health. In my experience, the real issue here doesn't seem to be that families don't have the actual money to spend on help, it's that mothers don't feel they deserve to be the beneficiaries of this financial expenditure. I've had many fathers ask me to convince their wives to let them hire help and do less

themselves. Even if someone doesn't have such a supportive husband, I'd encourage mothers to ask for this expenditure when the going gets tough.

2. **Ask family/friends for help without shame:** Many times we don't even ask people for help because it feels like a vulnerable process. In my workshops, I ask participants what they think is superior: asking for help or giving help. A vast majority say they think giving help is better but the question is, if everyone wants to offer help and no one wants to ask for help, then who are you going to help? When I lived in America, quite a few of my friends actually did offer help and I used to feel uncomfortable accepting it and thought they were just being nice. Eventually I reached a point where I realized they wouldn't keep offering me help if they couldn't give it so I started accepting their help and I can't tell you how much it improved the quality of my life. My friends were clearly very happy to help me, and my heartfelt gratitude was all they wanted in return. Now that I'm in Pakistan and have so much help, I'm thrilled to offer help to my friends and family.

3. **A tribe of like-minded people:** Practicing RP and working on your own healing can both feel like very isolating experiences. You get a lot of judgment from almost everyone around you because everything you're doing seems so unconventional. It's vital to have some kind of support on this journey. You can start a Facebook group of your local parents who are practicing RP or you can attend one of our online workshops. Each course comes with a built-in community of parents just like yourself who're starting out on

this journey. During the course we communicate on Whatsapp or a designated Facebook group. It always makes me delighted when past participants come and tell me they found their best friend during our course!

4. **Formal learning:** A big part of my work is to nurture communities where parents feel heard and seen, where you can learn in a judgment-free zone. This book is a great start for your healing and cycle-breaking journey but books have their limitations. Whether you take our course or any other RP and/or healing course, I highly recommend that you learn in a community setting. I promise you that it's a life changing experience to formally learn these concepts with others in the same boat as you.

5. **Psychotherapy:** I dream of the day when mental health help in the form of therapy and/or medication is as normalized as treatment for other health concerns. If you're really struggling to apply the concepts in this book and you evaluate your growth over the past six months and it's really not significant in any way, then working on your healing with a trauma-informed therapist can be incredibly helpful. Sometimes it can take a few tries to find a good therapist but I encourage you not to give up. If someone needed cancer treatment, they wouldn't give up just because their doctor didn't seem to understand them.

Yes, it can get a little expensive, which is why I encourage people to take our healing course, Anokhay Mentors, because it can speed up your growth and learning. In my experience, participants who are ready for the journey report that the three-month course helped them more than a year of therapy.

6. **Medication:** I put this in the last because even though it's 2023, sadly most of our culture's attitude towards using mood stabilizing medication leaves a lot to be desired. The truth is that you can do everything in the world to make yourself better and yet there are things only modern medicine can accomplish. Taking medication for anxiety, depression, or any other mental health concern is not a moral failing on your part. It doesn't mean you are now officially a failure. If it weren't for the medication my doctor prescribed me, I don't think I'd be where I am. Can you wean yourself off eventually? Sure. Just like some type-2 diabetics can wean themselves off insulin pens and medication. It requires a total lifestyle change and hard work, but it's definitely possible.

I hope this chapter has helped clarify some things for you and given you more hope for the future. It bears mentioning that as a first-generation cycle breaker, some things are going to be hard for you. Instead of trying to escape these difficult truths, let's embrace them. Say this with me,

"I'm a cycle-breaker parent. Respectful cycle-breaker parents are *not* like generational respectful parents. We screw up more. We fall back into old patterns sometimes. We hate ourselves some days. We are too hard on our kids and ourselves other days.

But our kids are getting front row seats to what struggle looks like. And what hard work on yourself looks like. That this hard work is necessary so we don't hurt others. They are learning how to recover from one's mistakes. They're learning that to err is human and not a reason to devalue someone. They're learning that being imperfect is more than ok when we're aware of our areas of work.

More than anything else, our kids are learning that someone loved them so much that they decided to unlearn almost everything they'd known and experienced about parenting. They might not know this now but one day they will and they'll be awed and so proud of us!"

You got this!

The Future Is Glimmery

It's bedtime and as she often does at this time, Husna says she feels hungry. A lot of children do this, I know because I get this question asked many times by frustrated parents. Why does my child feel hungry or thirsty exactly at bedtime?! A lot of parents believe it's a delaying tactic, and maybe it is, but it's also true that children find eating to be boring and are only interested in it when something even more boring is looming ahead—sleep. Regardless of why, it makes sense that parents feel frustrated whenever this comes up because we're tired and just want our children to sleep so we can also rest.

This is also a time that Husna's nervous system doesn't feel particularly safe because in the past, I have gotten triggered at her requests to eat something. Perhaps the trigger comes from my own desire to eat something at bedtime being dismissed or just the general compliance that was expected of me at bedtime. *"How dare she even make a sound, any sound, at bedtime?"* my implicit memories seem to say. I'm ashamed to say that I have responded poorly many times to her seemingly harmless request. Over time we have worked at it and found solutions so she doesn't say this exactly when it's time for her to close her eyes.

However, sometimes, such as tonight, I missed the routine of making sure she'd already had the opportunity to eat so that it doesn't come up. Of course, she hasn't forgotten.

"I'm hungry," she says for the second time.

I feel those old big feelings start to rumble inside me. I'm not as triggered as I might have been once but I'm definitely sounding frustrated. It's been a long day.

"Well, that's too bad because now it's time for bed," I say in a combative tone. I can feel myself sliding down the autonomic ladder into the red zone. Of course, that means I've pulled her down there with me. She shakes her head no, ready for the fight.

"I'm hungry," she says again, locking her eyes with mine. Unafraid. Almost challenging me. *Do what you can.* Or at least, that's how my mind interprets her unwavering gaze. Ah, the trauma story kicks in whenever we're stressed, doesn't it?

"Ok fine! Go and eat something if you want, but I'm done with you! I'm not going to put you to sleep!" I threaten meanly, and to my utter shock, she actually gets up and leaves.

My trauma story blows up . . . weaving a storm of messages from my inner child.

How dare she? Do I have no respect in this house? Ok fine, let her come back and sleep alone tonight!

I remember what my new therapist has taught me, to allow my inner child to step into these moments and acknowledge her concerns verbally: "Yes you didn't get to voice your needs when you were Husna's age, I hear your needs now. I'm here to take care of us. We are safe now," and with these words whispered to myself, I sense the shift in my body. I'm back in the green zone and I notice that my thoughts are also more positive and focused on the present.

"Wow look at this little girl honoring her truth!"

"You've done it, Maryam. You've broken the cycle and your daughter is not afraid of you."

"She'd rather do what she wants/needs to do than care about your threats. You're not treating her well and she's not entertaining you. Good for her!"

Which voice wins, do you think?

It's been a few years of practicing RP now, and more and more often it's the latter voice that wins. I also stayed calm as Husna made her way out of the room. In my mind's eye, I saw my old reactions. I saw myself screaming at her and shaming her. But in the present moment, there was only the gentle whirring of the split A/C on the wall.

By the time she returned to the room, I was breathing evenly and feeling calmer. She looked at me questioningly, as if to ask, "Are you still mad at me?" and I went and lay down next to her and hugged her. I apologized for being mean and told her I was so proud of her for listening to her body over my mean voice.

"Did you know, Husna . . . someone who listens to their own heart and body instead of someone who is stronger than them but also being mean, is super brave!"

She smiles and hugs me back.

Us cycle breakers are a confusing bunch for our kids, no doubt. One moment we act like we will destroy everything in our wake and the next moment, we're a puddle of apologies. Sometimes this back and forth feels like we're going around in circles, but as internet memes will tell you, healing is not linear. We *are* going around in circles, but the circles are like a spiral staircase. Once we begin this journey, we are ever so slowly making our way up the staircase even though the circular motion is sometimes dizzying and makes us want to give up. All of that is normal. And sure, our kids will grow up and need to continue the cycle-breaking process. Perhaps they will complain to us about how we did things but that's not a problem. No parent is ever perfect. What truly matters is how we respond to our kids bringing something to our attention.

"You're saying I hurt your feelings when I did xyz; I want to know more about how you felt and what I can do to help you heal from that." That's all it takes. Openness and willingness to work on difficult things instead of blaming, shaming or hiding.

PAUSING: THE HOLY GRAIL OF RP

When I describe such incidents as the above to my clients or workshop participants, they're incredibly awed and enviously say, "How did you not react? I would have grabbed my daughter and flung her back on the bed!" or "I'd have totally lost it at that time!" Of course, I totally get where this question is coming from because I was there once too.

If you recall the chapter on triggers, I used the metaphor of triggers being a "button" that's pressed. What presses that button is called a stimulus. When we're starting out on our journey, there is no gap between the stimulus and the response. Imagine two bookends with no books in between. That's where most of us begin. Certainly, that's where I began, as you know from my story in the very beginning of this book. Over time though, practicing everything you've learned in this book, you start to create a gap between the stimulus and the response and in that gap or pause lies your freedom. The freedom to make a different choice. As someone who began with a zero ability for pause, I can promise you that your "bookends" will start to diverge with more and more room for choices in between.

One of the most glorious things in the world is being in a situation, watching your old self react and noticing in the present moment that you haven't reacted at all. This is called a "glimmer" and what some experts call the opposite of a trigger. I have so many "glimmers" daily that their combined light fills my heart with pride and joy at the work I've been able to do and I know that you can do it too.

THE 'P' WORD NO ONE LIKES

Some people have said to me occasionally that to be able to practice RP is a privilege. Most people who have said this to me don't use these words, but they say some version of:

"RP is not possible in a joint family system."

"RP is not possible when your husband is not on board."

"RP is not possible if you're struggling to put *roti* on your table."

I totally, completely, wholeheartedly understand the pain these statements are coming out of. They are not at all a parent trying to "make excuses." In fact, I hear them as a parent expressing their grief at not being able to give their children what they know they deserve. And my heart really goes out to all such parents. There is no doubt that being in any of the above situations does, in fact, spike your stress levels and since RP is emotional labor and self-care is a non-negotiable component of it, the challenge becomes even harder.

I absolutely acknowledge that since my husband is not abusive, I don't live in a joint-family system, and I don't have to worry about putting food on my table, I'm able to commit to the self-care and emotional labor needed for RP.

The only thing I'd say is, at the end of the day, all children deserve to be treated with respect and respect should not be a privilege for children, it's their right. And it's upon us to provide them that right. Yes, this means we will have to make many changes in our life to be able to do what we need to do, but religious and secular experts alike will assure you, when you set your mind to something and decide that you will do it, you will find ways from where you never expected.

"And, when you want something, all the universe conspires in helping you to achieve it."

—Paulo Coehlo[30]

Religious Content

"And whosoever fears Allah and keeps his duty to Him, He will make a way for him to get out (from every difficulty). And He will provide for him from sources he never could imagine." (Quran 65:2)

BUT FIRST, ALL HELL WILL BREAK LOOSE

Whether it's parents who first start on their RP journey or it's my clients who start on their own healing journey, I hear one thing over and over.

"Maryam . . . I thought things would get better but all hell has broken loose!"

They will tell me how their previously somewhat "stable" child is now loud, emotional, and "overly sensitive." Women will come and tell me, "My husband says, 'You've become so angry since you started therapy. What kind of treatment is this?'"

To me, all of this is as simple as basic physics laws:

- Every action has an equal and opposite reaction. (Newton's third law of physics)
- Any pressure change is transmitted without loss. (Pascal's law)

Whether it's a child or ourselves, if someone has been conditioned to not react or their reactions are not allowed any room, no matter how much stress and pressure is exerted upon them, it makes sense that when they're finally given that room, we will see an excess release of reactions and energies.

Someone whose parents never learn to parent with respect will grow up to become an adult who has "unexplained" explosions, anger, and reactions or conversely the perpetual effort to compress those emotions will result in major depression—literally "depressing" everything that's accumulated inside in an effort of preservation.

Which means, when we first start creating space for our kids and our own authentic feelings and experiences, things do seem to "get worse" but that's a normal and healthy sign of moving towards authenticity and recovery. Marshall B. Rosenberg, author of *Non-violent Communication,* calls it the "obnoxious phase."[31] With some time and patience, this phase passes and we do in fact see and experience more peace and command over our emotions, as do our children.

BUT THEN YOU'LL UNLOCK A NEW DIMENSION

I do want to add that sometimes, going through this process of healing and recovery exposes parts of our life that we can never unsee again. Previously we were caught up in our trauma stories and unable to see that we are worthy of true love and respect, but once we begin to accept this, we can no longer tolerate certain people or circumstances that are a clear abomination to our self-respect.

One of my brave workshop participants shared how he and his wife were constant targets of everyone's vitriol because he was the youngest in his family. He had never realized prior to being married that everyone seemed to treat him as some sort of a punching bag. Once his wife started getting the same treatment, he put his foot down and announced that they'll be moving out. Complete and utter chaos ensued.

His mom claimed that his wife had cast a spell on him. His brothers accused him of being "hen-pecked." His father threatened to disown him. He admitted to me that he was scared beyond belief, but he knew for sure that he wanted to be a cycle breaker which would be impossible living in that home. After moving out, he continued to meet with his family and even found himself more emotionally available to meet their needs. The initial chaos created an eventual calm in his life that he had never known before in his life.

As you can see from this chapter, the path to becoming the kind of person and parent you want to be is paved with the kind of pain you might never have experienced before, but there is something special about this pain. It's unlike any other pain you've experienced before in your life because it morphs into the kind of peace, compassion, and beauty you've also never experienced before. To do all this work and allow for the suffering is basically like unlocking a new dimension of your life—one filled with light and joy.

> "Then a woman said,
> Speak to us of Joy and Sorrow.
> And he answered:
> Your joy is your sorrow unmasked."
>
> —Kahlil Gibran[32]

AND THEN YOU'LL LIVE HAPPILY EVER AFTER (MOSTLY)

It's Eid of 2023 and all my siblings are in my home. All of us are playing Bingo together after having a yummy feast. All our children are playing with us too. My mom no longer has the mental faculties to play with us, but she's enjoying our laughter and beaming from ear to ear. My dad is unwell with Covid, but he's also near us in the next room. When my younger brother wins, there are good-natured groans of disappointment that soon dissolve into applause for my brother. He's smiling widely, proud of his win but then his expression shifts a little bit, becoming graver as he says, "Thank you, Maryam . . . thank you for giving us the best Eid ever. Since you've moved here, all our lives are so much better."

I don't know if you guessed this but I wouldn't say that such professions of love are the norm in my family. These words spoken so sincerely fill my heart with gratitude and love.

"It's my pleasure, of course. I'm so grateful for all of you," I manage to say. Everyone moves in to hug me and I realize how much I meant what I just said. I really, truly am grateful for these relationships that needed a little watering and nurturing, and now they're unrecognizable beyond belief in how beautiful they've become.

That's how healing works. You're casting a pebble that will have ripple effects across your whole family and generations to come. "She's the one," they will say. "The one who broke the cycle."

NOTES

1. *Merriam-Webster.com Dictionary*, s.v. "autonomy," accessed 10 Jul. 2023, https://www.merriam-webster.com/dictionary/autonomy.

2. Brené Brown and Barrett Guillen, "Living Into Our Values," *Unlocking Us*, 26 Jan. 2022, podcast, https://brenebrown.com/podcast/living-into-our-values.

3. The Occuplaytional Therapist, Facebook, August 25, 2022, https://www.facebook.com/occuplaytional/posts/pfbid02oupmJa4qpQC9eBtBjddQp1vxrbtDB5HRAkG9YVyY15esPqgfR2CJnaNiy7a544zBl.

4. Janet Metcalfe, *Learning from Errors,* January 2017, https://doi.org/10.1146/annurev-psych-010416-044022.

5. Magda Gerber, *Your Self-Confident Baby: How to Encourage Your Child's Natural Abilities—From the Very Start* (Wiley, 1997).

6. Ellyn Satter Institute, https://www.ellynsatterinstitute.org/.

7. Ibid.

8. Ibid.

9. Ellyn Satter, *Child of Mine: Feeding with Love and Good Sense* (Bull Publishing Company, 2012), 393.

10. M. Yanina Pepino and Julie A. Mennella, "Sucrose-Induced Analgesia is related to Sweet Preferences in Children but not Adults," *Pain,* 15 Dec. 2005, 119(1-3): 210–218, https://www.ncbi.nlm.nih.gov/pmc/articles/PMC1364537/pdf/nihms7936.pdf.

11. Gretchen Cuda Kroen, "Kids' Sugar Cravings Might Be Biological," *The Salt,* 26 Sept. 2011, https://www.npr.org/sections/thesalt/2011/09/26/140753048/kids-sugar-cravings-might-be-biological.

12. Tia Ghose, "Do Kids Really Need to Drink Milk," *Live Science,* 25 Jan. 2015, https://www.livescience.com/49551-should-kids-drink-milk.html?fbclid

=IwAR1FYlPAAMn1-M8oLypVKxz0nyy-H6Y2FO7JZepwHTrncc1fM97
4s9np810.

13. Evelyn Tribole and Else Resch, *Intuitive Eating: A Revolutionary Anti-Diet Approach,* 4th Edition (St. Martin's Publishing Group, 2020).

14. Latinx Parenting, *Facebook,* https://www.facebook.com/latinxparenting.

15. Nadine Burke Harris, *The Deepest Well: Healing the Long-Term Effects of Childhood Trauma and Adversity* (Mariner Books, 2018), 102.

16. Magda Gerber, *Your Self-Confident Baby: How to Encourage Your Child's Natural Abilities—From the Very Start* (Wiley, 1997).

17. Ibid.

18. Kim West, *The Sleep Lady's Good Night, Sleep Tight: Gentle Proven Solutions to Help Your Child Sleep Well and Wake Up Happy* (Hachette Books, 2009).

19. Teacher Tom (blogger and pre-school teacher), Comment exchange on blog post with author, 9 December 2019.

20. Teacher Tom, "What The Research Tells Us To Do," *Teacher Tom: Teaching and Learning from Preschoolers,* blog post, 13 Dec. 2018, https://teachertomsblog. blogspot.com/2019/12/what-research-tells-us-to-do.html?fbclid=IwAR34Hi BjHZQS1QIvytq3zFqCK_b1d0FC87YzWcn8UKOnXQ9oR2jS9KYQUB8.

21. Magda Gerber, *Your Self-Confident Baby: How to Encourage Your Child's Natural Abilities—From the Very Start* (Wiley, 1997).

22. Ibid.

23. Ibid.

24. A. Helwa, *Secrets of Divine Love: A Spiritual Journey Into the Heart of Islam* (Naulit Incorporated, 2021).

25. Alex Hormozi (@AlexHormozi), "Outwork your self doubt," Twitter, Sept. 18, 2022, 4:20 p.m., https://twitter.com/AlexHormozi/status/1571625128 806715392.

26. Susan Cain, *Bittersweet: How Sorrow and Longing Make Us Whole* (Crown, 2022).

27. Simon Sinek, *Start with Why: How Great Leaders Inspire Everyone to Take Action* (Penguin Publishing Group, 2009).

28. Felitti VJ, Anda RF, Nordenberg D, Williamson DF, Spitz AM, Edwards V, Koss MP, Marks JS. "Relationship of childhood abuse and household dysfunction to many of the leading causes of death in adults. The Adverse Childhood Experiences (ACE) Study." *Am J Prev Med.* 1998 May;14(4):245–58. doi: 10.1016/s0749-3797(98)00017-8. PMID: 9635069.

29. Susan Cain, *Bittersweet: How Sorrow and Longing Make Us Whole* (Crown, 2022).

30. Paolo Coehlo, *The Alchemist* (HarperOne Publishing, 1988).

31. Marshall B. Rosenberg, *Nonviolent Communication: A Language of Compassion* (PuddleDancer Press, 1999).

32. Kahlil Gibran, *The Prophet* (Knopf Doubleday Publishing Group, 1923).

ACKNOWLEDGMENTS

My first and humblest *shukr* (thank You) is to Allah Az wa Jal for blessing me with not just the gift and joy of writing, but also giving me something worthwhile to write about. I've always found His promise to be true; when we turn towards Him with hope and effort, He comes running towards us with miracles.

One of those miracles was coming across Azul Terronez's Ted Talk while working on my teacher training program. This book would probably never have materialized if it weren't for Azul. His encouragement, support, and faith in my work has made it all happen. I will be forever grateful for his gentle nudges and wise practical advice throughout the process. I'm also very thankful to Mandala Tree Press's entire team for walking me through all the stages of the publishing process, and being so patient with me. All of you helped make my childhood dream of becoming a published author come true!

I'm also grateful to my own team at TPEP for their never-ending support and encouragement—mainly conveyed in the form of excited shrieks at every juncture in this book's process. Without all of you, TPEP wouldn't exist and I wouldn't have gotten this far. Thank you, Sana T. Malik, for being my first ever "partner in crime," Saman Saeed for being my first ever employee and agreeing to work for me when I didn't even know what I was doing, Garima Bisht for adding Hindi poetry to our lives, Nabila Haris for bringing order to the chaos, Afra Khurram for being our official therapist and sounding board, and Sehrish Syed for taking every technical task off my hands! You're all one amazing group of women!

Thank you also to all the TPEP volunteers who put in so much heart and soul into becoming part of this noble work of helping parents. Thank you especially to my beta readers who read several drafts in record time with incredibly helpful and thorough feedback. Thank you Hafsa Khalid, Remi Sainillabdeen, and Rabia Batool. Your detailed comments, thoughts, and encouragement were priceless!

I'm so grateful for the work of authors and change-makers that I've quoted in this book. Each and every one of them has changed my life and work in profound ways. As have my actual teachers and professors from James Madison University and Liberty University. They've taught me what unconditional positive regard looks like in practice. I can't say enough good things about the field of counseling and what a gift it is to the world to devote your life to sharing the burdens of others. My own therapists/coaches, Racquel Semeraro, Bill Redmiles, and Dr. Melissa Reilly have been my beacons of light in my healing journey. Without their warm and gentle guidance, I'd be nowhere.

Of course, a big thank you to my family for letting me sequester myself in my office (and sometimes other places) so I can hyper focus on my writing—the only way I can ever get work done! My husband, Umar, continues to do the hard work of breaking more stereotypes of Pakistani men by taking my dreams seriously, and for that I'm incredibly grateful to him.

Not a day goes by when I'm not grateful for my sister Ayesha, who's been my biggest fan ever since I can remember. Her joyful spirit that also oozes love and kindness is what all families should be made of. It makes me infinitely happy that my siblings and their families have all become my partners in our healing journey. Thank you, Zeeshan, Waqas, Murtaza, Asma, and Sana for doing this work for my bonus kids; Hamna (the OG princess), Fatima, Zynah, and Ali.

I'm grateful to my dad for letting me read whatever "junk" I wanted as a teenager, because it's those books that sustained me as a reader. Thank you for taking me on several weekly thirty-minute drives to the British Council Library in Melody Market and letting me buy any number of books from the trusty old book shops in Jinnah Super. You taught me that books matter and readers are plain superior to other beings. Thank you also to my mama, who was utterly confused and even mildly petrified by my love of reading and writing but indulged me fondly nevertheless. She would've been very *very* proud of me had she been able to see this book.

If every author had an origin story like super heroes do, mine would include my *chachi*, Ruqaiya (Raquel) Amin. In a world full of skeptical grownups who told me girls shouldn't write and writers don't get jobs, she treated my writings as works of art. She oohed and aahed over every poem and childishly stapled together "storybook" I showed her. She kept some of these as precious relics. Her unconditional love for me and her presence in my secret world where I was a writer, probably saved me in ways she will never fully know. Thank you *chachi*, you're a gift to this world.

When I speak of family, I have to mention the special family I created during my years in America that helped me survive and, many times, thrive in what felt like the hardest time of my life. Bethany Hunter Rasheed, thank you for your courage to be fiercely and unapologetically yourself so I could stop being afraid to be myself. Andrea Jayne, thank you for validating my pain for me when no one else would. Elizabeth McKnight, thank you for becoming my savior on days when I had no one. Shamyla Tareen, thank you for showing up just to see me and the kids. Sundus and Bilal, thank you for being my baby siblings when I didn't have any. You're all beloved beyond words.

I don't think I could've survived America without my Minto cousins, Tarbia, Onabia, and Zoshia. Thank you for letting me infiltrate your sister squad by practically letting me be the fourth sister. You were the first women in my life who showed me that women can also be strong, independent, and real. The lessons you've taught me about womanhood have allowed me to become who I always wanted to be.

I also feel truckloads and bucketloads thankful to my clients, friends and family who've allowed me to share their stories in this book despite the terrifying feelings that come with becoming a part of published work. In the telling of these stories, there was so much learning and growth for me as well. Thank you!

I feel immense gratitude for all the parents who've followed my work for so many years and transformed their lives through my writings, coaching, and workshops. These cycle-breaker parents gave me the courage to keep going and doing this work back when very few people even knew the words "gentle/respectful parenting." Every parent who's a part of our circle has left their mark on me. I wouldn't be where I am without your willingness to do this work.

I have to put in a special note of gratitude for our clients and workshop participants who are Pakistani women living in Pakistan. *Ap Pakistani maon ko nahi badal sakti*, the world told me, but you have proven them wrong. What you carry on your backs while you do this work of becoming a cycle breaker is astounding. Your courage and struggles, all at once break my heart and fill me with awe. You deserve so much more love and support. Thank you for letting TPEP be a part of your brave journey.

No book of mine written in my second language, English, would be complete without thanking all my English teachers throughout my childhood who allowed me to deviate from the norm and write my own poem summaries and essays. Especially my principal Group Captain Niazi (retd.) from when I was in sixth grade. The image of him holding up my essay in front of the whole class as an example of "excellent writing" has stuck in my mind like a beautiful melody that lingers even years after you first heard it. Every child deserves teachers like mine who wholeheartedly focus on their strengths.

Finally, no words can ever be enough to thank my amazing kids. Eisa, your gentle soul is a balm to everyone who comes in contact with you. Husna, your delightful and creative spirit is the light in our days. Yahya, your humor and tenderness are an irresistible combination. And Muhammed (Aami), your wisdom and thoughtfulness are a joy to behold.

The four of you are the reason this book exists. You've inspired me to help this world become a better place for all children, including my own inner child. It's life's highest honor for me to be your mama.

Love,
Maryam

APPENDIX A

(Give yourself a 1 for every YES answer)

ANSWER ALL THESE AS PRIOR TO YOUR 18TH BIRTHDAY:

1. Did a parent or other adult in the household often or very often . . . Swear at you, insult you, put you down, or humiliate you? Or act in a way that made you afraid that you might be physically hurt?

    O Yes   O No

2. Did a parent or other adult in the household often or very often . . . Push, grab, slap, or throw something at you? Or ever hit you so hard that you had marks or were injured?

    O Yes   O No

3. Did an adult or person at least five years older than you ever . . . Touch or fondle you or have you touch their body in a sexual way? Or attempt or actually have oral or anal intercourse with you?

    O Yes   O No

4. Did you often or very often feel that . . . No one in your family loved you or thought you were important or special? Or your family didn't look out for each other, feel close to each other, or support each other?

   O Yes   O No

5. Did you often or very often feel that . . . You didn't have enough to eat, had to wear dirty clothes, and had no one to protect you? Or your parents were too drunk or high to take care of you or take you to the doctor if you needed it?

   O Yes   O No

6. Was a biological parent ever lost to you through divorce, abandonment, or other reason?

   O Yes   O No

7. Was your mother or stepmother: Often or very often pushed, grabbed, slapped, or had something thrown at her? Or sometimes, often, or very often kicked, bitten, hit with a fist, or hit with something hard? Or ever repeatedly hit over at least a few minutes or threatened with a gun or knife?

   O Yes   O No

ANSWER ALL THESE AS AFTER YOUR 18TH BIRTHDAY:

8. Did you live with anyone who was a problem drinker or alcoholic or who used street drugs?

   O Yes   O No

9. Was a household member depressed or mentally ill? Or did a household member attempt suicide?

   O Yes   O No

10. Did a household member go to prison?

   O Yes   O No

YOUR TOTAL SCORE _____

APPENDIX B

What is the incident that has triggered me?	What exactly am I feeling right now?	What is the story I'm telling myself right now?	What's the trauma story here?	What are the facts of the situation?	Does my "story" have evidence in the present?	If not, what's a healthier way of looking at this situation that allows me to be in control?

APPENDIX C

FEELINGS WHEEL

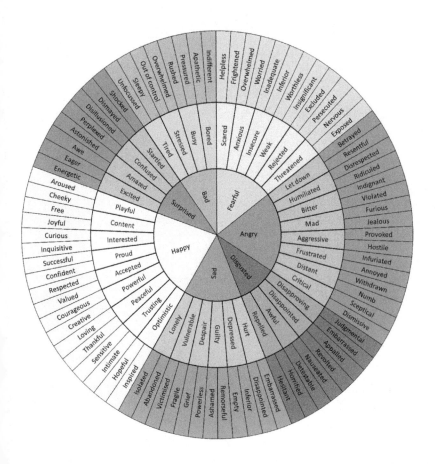

Used with permission from Geoffrey Roberts, https://imgur.com/tCWChf6

ABOUT THE AUTHOR

Maryam Munir is a Pakistani-American author, Parent Coach, and CEO/founder of The Parent Empowerment Project (TPEP), a visionary initiative dedicated to equipping parents worldwide with trauma-informed and evidence-based parenting practices. Through workshops, courses, and consults, Maryam and her team members have been empowering parents for more than five years to become cycle breakers. Maryam is currently pursuing a master's degree in Human Services Counseling with trauma focus from Liberty University in Virginia, USA. She recently relocated from the U.S. to Pakistan to spend more time with her mom who has Alzheimer's. She now lives in Islamabad with her husband and four kids.

I would appreciate your feedback on what chapters helped you most and what you would like to see in future books.

If you enjoyed this book and found it helpful, please leave a **review** on Amazon.

Visit me at

WWW.TEEPEP.COM

where you can sign up for email updates.

THANK YOU!

Made in the USA
Middletown, DE
25 August 2024

59139281R00205